bombshell in the Barrio

How educators exploded a "cheating scandal" and defeated the FBI, DOJ, the Texas Education Agency and El Paso's oligarchy

parrhesiapress.com

ISBN 9 798654016867 9000

Cover design by: Glenda J. Tanner
Library of Congress Control Number:
2018675309
Printed in the United States of America

Acknowledgments

No one knows better than the defendants that their win in this case was nothing less than miraculous. In the current federal US justice system, the odds are always stacked against the defendants no matter how innocent they are. Innocent until proven guilty does not apply. When the Department of Justice concocts a case, they are basically assured of a win. Instead of asking "What if a defendant wins?" the more realistic question is "How much time will be served?"

The defendants prayed. Their friends and families prayed. Rosaries and Novenas were dedicated for the benefit of the innocent defendants. Prayer groups were formed and meditations were practiced. God intervened. Whereas it is true that the defendants along with their attorneys worked diligently on this case, God provided Divine Intervention. First and foremost, we give thanks to God. Or in the words of Richard Rohr, we recognize the presence of the Universal Christ.

The spouses of the defendants suffered through the ordeal as well. Despite the extreme trials and tribulations of those who were tried, all marriages thrived. The husbands and wives of the accused stood strongly during the bad times talked about in their wedding vows. They comforted, cheered, stayed up nights, and defended the integrity of those they love. They dried tears, calmed fears, and understood deep and intense anger. Although they were not the ones on trial, they faced trials of their own.

Along with the spouses were many friends, family members, students and colleagues who never doubted the innocence and integrity of those on trial. Their prayers, texts, letters and phone calls helped the defendants through the toughest times. Truman Wills, one of the most respected educators that Austin High School has ever had, postponed a necessary orthopedic surgery in order to be available to testify for the defendants during their trial. Danna Sadler, secretary of Austin High, refused to be manipulated by the unjust tactics of the FBI/DOJ. It is not far-fetched or overly-dramatic to claim that this undying support saved lives.

Many friends became family not just through spiritual support, but financial as well. Solid attorneys are essential in a case like this and they are not cheap. Tanner would not have had the attorneys who fought for him had it not been for an old college roommate and friend—fitting the definition of brother—who financed his defense. He would further like to thank his brother, Marty, for his loving support and practical guidance to a new career.

Along with the incredible support and prayers of the parents, siblings and their families, Mark and Ida Tegmeyer give special thanks to their brother-in-law, John Falzone, Mark's sister Susan and brother Matthew for providing financial assistance, employment and room and board in that horrific year leading up to the trial and the years of struggle that followed. They would also like to acknowledge the counsel and support of their longtime friends, Jon and Tricia Law as well as Gabriella and Jesus Acosta and their families. Their comfort and concern were a selfless gift of sanity when everything else seemed to indicate they were losing their own.

There is no way to properly thank all those who aided the defendants during the most trying time in their lives. Hopefully, their desire to express their gratitude fully will suffice.

Contents

This is a book about defying the odds.

It is about being a .2 percenter.
It is about turning the tables when 99.8 percent of cases in the Western
District of Texas in 2017 ended in conviction.

This is a story about underdogs.

It is an extraordinary example of winning with a losing hand.

It is a detailed account that exposes serious questions about the methods
and motivations of the FBI, the Texas Education Agency, the oligarchy of
El Paso and the El Paso media.

This is a real-life David and Goliath story.

It is an attempt to set things right, if that can ever really happen.

Prologue: The setting

Known as the Sun City for its 297 days of sun annually, El Paso, TX sits at the border of Texas, New Mexico and Mexico. It is a geographical, historical and political triad that combines Hispanic tradition, Native American spirituality and American resourcefulness.

In its own rugged way, El Paso, a part of the Chihuahuan desert, is a countryside of harsh beauty. Here, bright yellow wildflowers dot the Franklin mountains. Looking across from the Mexican border, viewers can see the "land of promise," or downtown El Paso, TX. A border wall constructed of concrete and steel separates the US and Mexico. *photos from istockphoto.com*

Geography

Geographically, El Paso is the largest inland metropolis that borders two countries in North America. With a population of about 2.7 million between the cities of El Paso and Juarez, Mexico. The latter is the larger of the two cities, comprising almost two million of the total.[1]

When looking down on the landscape from an airplane, viewers cannot clearly see the border between the two cities and two countries and they have to squint to find a trace of the once mighty Rio Grande.

That river of legend no longer exists, due to human manipulation of its water–used for irrigation, recreation and the daily needs of a population that has grown exponentially in the past century. No longer a channel of swift, flowing water, the Rio Grande (called Rio Bravo in Mexico) is often a great place for dirt biking.

In this stark desert setting, beauty, adventure and danger present themselves in the form of mountain hiking trails, flowering yellow and purple weeds, and the rattlesnake as it leaves its twisted trails in the dust, its rattle softly vibrating into the vast negative space. Cacti and tumbleweeds punctuate the landscape.

Descriptions of El Paso claim that it is a semi-arid climate in the Chihuahua desert. That translates into about nine inches of rain a year with summer temperatures that can reach in excess of 110 degrees and winter nights that can get into the teens, all at an elevation that ranges from 3,700 to 7,100 feet.[2] Natural inhabitants of the area include the aforementioned rattlesnakes, along with prairie dogs, coyotes, deer, mountain lions, huge cockroaches and scorpions. And even with very little water, the attacking mosquitos are legendary.

Economy

On the ground, dramatic differences define the two sister cities that lie adjacent to opposite sides of the border. El Paso, considered one of the poorest large cities in the US,[3] looks like the Land of Oz when viewed from the Mexican side.

In Juarez, the poverty is undeniable: scenes of third world scarcity are complete with young children and limbless men begging and selling chícles (gum) on the pedestrian bridge between the two worlds. Although both cities have a majority Hispanic population, El Paso's tends to be American middle class, while Juarez's is more likely to fit the stereotype of a desperately poor Latin American country.

Paradoxically, Juarez is considered one of the most dangerous cities in the world, while El Paso is deemed one of the safest cities in the US.[4] This disparity explains why so many from Juarez desire to enter El Paso on a daily basis, whereas few El Pasoans travel to Mexico through Juarez. This contemporary rule of thumb has been a result of the drug cartels that have run Juarez for over 30 years and have turned the Mexican border city into a killing field, while ensuring that El Paso is safer than it has ever been.

Similarities and differences

Although the combined population of El Paso and Juarez is large by most standards, the area is isolated. El Paso's closest major city is Albuquerque, which is nearly five hours driving time to the north. San Antonio is the closest major city in Texas, and it is almost 600 miles southeast. Interestingly, the Sun City is closer to San Diego than it is to Houston. As a rule, El Pasoans do not have a Texas accent, and when they go on vacation, they usually head to California rather than any place in Texas. As for Juarez, its closest major city is Chihuahua City, a four-hour drive to the south. The distance from Juarez to Mexico City is 1,120 miles, closer than the 1700 miles from El Paso to Olympia, WA.

Despite their obvious differences, El Paso and Juarez influence each other greatly. For many in this area, the border is a nuisance that creates obstacles between family members, friends, business and romance. The spirituality is decidedly Roman Catholic.

—

Even Protestant churches are influenced by Rome, as the Virgen de Guadalupe is the bonding component of those with a Mexican heritage. Almost 45% of the El Paso population identifies as Catholic, while Juarez boasts an 85% affiliation.[5]

The outward sign of this religiosity is the statue of Cristo Rey ensconced atop the mountain of the same name. It is reminiscent of Christ the Redeemer in Rio de Janeiro, Brazil. Legend dictates that the statue sits at the point where two countries (US and Mexico) and three states (Texas, New Mexico, and Chihuahua) meet. The truth is much less interesting: the statue, white and stoic, stands entirely in Sunland Park, NM.

History

It is a phenomenon that the city even exists. There are few natural resources and it is hardly a vacation destination. However, the settlement developed because it was a stopping point for the Spanish conquistadors as they traveled the Camino Real from Mexico City to Santa Fe over 400 years ago. It was named El Paso because it was the natural pass to the north (El Paso del Norte) from what is now modern Mexico to the United States. Specifically, the pass is a natural flat land area between two mountain ranges: the El Paso Franklin mountain range at the end of the Rockies and Mexico's Sierra de Juárez.

Historically, this natural resting spot attracted settlers who brought with them businesses, prostitution, saloons and lodging. In time, more settlers came in and established routine places of work, schools, churches and hospitals.

But Fort Bliss, a military post, was the industry that transformed El Paso into a permanent settlement. Its genesis was in 1849 as a military base for the Mexican War. By 1861, it was a base for the Confederacy.[6] This Confederate history still has remnants today in the form of street and building names. Ironically, most of the population is unaware of the significance of such buildings and schools named for Sul Ross, Jeb Stuart and Robert E. Lee, all Confederate generals. Because the El Paso area is not a part of the American South, the history of the Civil War escapes the average El Pasoan.

Ft. Bliss continues to have an immense impact on the area. Today, it is one of the largest Army posts in the nation and a city unto itself. 7 Fort Bliss is the largest employer for El Paso County and will remain so for the distant future because of its advantageous land area that is perfect for military air combat training. From this perspective, the area has its place in history, particularly regarding nuclear weaponry with the Trinity site at White Sands Missile Range.

Military personnel stationed at Ft. Bliss often have a complicated relationship with the El Paso area. On one hand, Ft. Bliss residents can embrace the area complete with its Hispanic culture and cuisine. Many will learn Spanish and may even settle in the area by literally marrying into the culture. However, others experience a culture shock that is akin to living in a foreign country.

Culture & politics

To someone who is acclimated to "middle America," whereby the population is primarily white non-Hispanic (or at least diverse), and where the common language is English, El Paso can seem like an alien country.

The common language really is English *y español*. English is the language of commerce, education, and the law, but Spanish is the language of casual conversation. For those dominant in one language or another, Spanglish, an inherent blending of the two mother tongues, becomes a common dialect. The homogenous 85% Hispanic majority can elicit a cultural shock. To put it in perspective, El Paso is more Hispanic than Minneapolis is Anglo. Thus, El Paso is not as diverse as one would imagine.

Yet, diversity is present. Religiously, El Paso is decidedly Catholic accented by other Christian denominations, but it is also beautifully enhanced by Judaism, Hinduism, and Islam. In addition, various cultures have made El Paso a home including a vibrant Korean community known for their popular businesses in downtown El Paso. In all, El Paso's culture is rich. Anyone who might experience a cultural shock will soon acclimate and embrace this one-of-a-kind environment.

Politically, El Paso offers more anomalies. Within the border of Texas, comprised of an enormous US military base and high rates of Christian religiosity, it might be expected that Republicans would fare well.

However, the opposite is true. El Paso is solidly Democratic. If there is one thing to count on, it is that if El Paso decided every presidential election, we would never have had Presidents Nixon, Reagan, Bush I, Bush II or Trump.

The irony is that El Pasoans' personal lives are rather conservative in that most attend church, tend to be pro-life, like their guns, and are suspicious of the federal government. El Pasoans would probably vote like

Floridian Cubans if the immigration laws for those coming from Mexico resembled that of those emigrating from Cuba.

The function of the local government contributes to its anomalies. In a city that is dominated by Hispanic culture, it is disturbingly noticeable that most of the city's government and high-profile businesses (banks, energy companies, newspaper), and military are run by white males, even to this day. Since 1873, El Paso has had 50 mayors of which only four have been Hispanic (and only one woman during that history).8 Although there are wealthy Hispanics in the area, the substantial wealth of "old money" belongs to the prominent Anglo families that have lived in this desert nation for generations.

This concentration of wealth and power resembles the political structure of the country it borders. On one hand, the democratic process of the US is used to elect officials to public office. The election process looks like most elections across the US. But those who are elected and those who are served resemble an oligarchy, much like Mexico and various areas in Latin America.

If you are part of the oligarchical realm, then life seems fair and just. If you are not a part of that inner circle, then you learn how to operate within the system and ignore the realities of the power structure. Or you open your eyes to the innate corruption of this type of system and realize—painfully—that corruption is the status quo and fighting it can cost you your livelihood, dignity and reputation.

Chapter 1: There was no cheating in the "cheating scandal"

Let's get straight to the point. There was no cheating in the El Paso Independent School District "cheating scandal." The last five people standing, a troupe of committed educators, have waited nearly a decade to present the facts, and the only way to do so publicly is to publish this book. Under the uncompromising directive of the federal government, they were not allowed to speak to each other, much less share their story with the public. Make no mistake: the government muted their voices, trampled their reputations, and tried to break them financially and psychologically. But they held on, survived impossible odds, and now they speak the truth.

"A lie repeated a thousand times becomes the truth."

Although its author is unknown, this truism has itself been falsely attributed to many, including Joseph Goebbels, Hitler's right-hand man. Our perceptions of the world are replete with examples of "truths," which simply aren't correct.

"Edelweiss" is not, and never has been, the national anthem of Austria, despite the popularity of The Sound of Music. Buddha was not obese. Mary Magdalene was not a prostitute. Marie Antoinette did not say, "Let them eat cake." George Washington did not have wooden teeth. But try and correct these misconceptions, and you will find yourself in arguments with all sorts of people. The same is true when claiming that there was no EPISD cheating scandal.

The narrative of the EPISD cheating scandal was repeated, both in print and over the airwaves, so many times that it became the undisputed truth in El Paso. It began like this: a prominent El Paso politician, Eliot Shapleigh, made the allegation for reasons explored later in this book. He happened to have the ear of the editor at the *El Paso Times*. His story was accepted and promoted as the truth, so the printing presses went to work, and that narrative reverberated out to television news stations. In its genesis, it was the "alleged" cheating scandal that eventually morphed into the cheating scandal.

Despite the constant repetition, there was no smoking gun, never any concrete evidence. But the idea of cheating is sexy, and it's easy enough to understand in its most basic form, so the lie caught on and spread like wildfire. The phrase was repeated ad nauseam: nearly 700 articles published by The *El Paso Times* ran in conjunction with four local TV stations reporting their version of the story continuously for nearly a decade. Those who tried to clarify or correct the misconceptions were accused of being a part of the cheating conspiracy, and their voices were snuffed out.

On the one occasion when the case saw the courtroom lights, the total lack of objectivity on the part of the media and the judicial system became clear. During jury selection on June 12, 2017, the jury pool was asked, "How many of you have heard of the EPISD cheating scandal?" Thirty-five out of 37 potential jurors raised their hands. The pool was then asked a second question, "How many of you have heard or read any thing from the point of view of the defendants?" Not one hand went up. And yet, the judge saw no need for a change of venue.

"Never doubt that a small group of thoughtful, committed citizens can change the world; indeed, it's the only thing that ever has."

This quote from Margaret Mead, a highly regarded US anthropologist, is a powerful phrase that has been illustrated throughout history, both for good and for evil. The thought behind the phrase has inspired such extremes as the founding of religious orders to the formation of the Third Reich.

The oligarchs and the educators

In this account, the focus is on two groups whose objectives were sorely at odds. The first group, the oligarchs, was comprised of a shrewd, exclusive set of individuals.

This ruling class of El Paso set the contrived story in motion, and they had a definite purpose in mind. Their objectives were to change El Paso politics, power and property lines, all while lining their pockets.

If you follow the money trail, and there always is one, you will see that they intended to funnel tax money earmarked for EPISD into projects that would benefit them personally, all the while dismantling the school district.

The second group, the educators, was a small cadre of administrators and teachers who lived typical middle-class lives. True to their calling, they wanted to elevate the lives of their students, provide a quality education and make a difference for marginalized students in EPISD.

For the first year or so, the educators were completely unaware that the battle had begun. As they tended to educational concerns and discipline, budgets and testing, they didn't notice the noose that was being tightened around their necks.

It was initially puzzling. While central and south El Paso schools were performing poorly in academics, political leaders were silent, and the media never called the educational system to task. But things changed when these public schools began to improve. Instead of being positive, the media and politicians voiced skepticism of the success and eventually began to allege corruption. Dr. John Tanner, principal of Austin High School at the time, was confused about this negativity, but he admits, he was naive.

"I didn't understand and it did make me wonder what was going on," Tanner said. "But I had work to do, and at the time, I had the philosophy that all would come out in the wash. All we had to do was make the school better and all would be fine."

Except it wasn't. Improving schools threatened the oligarchs' plans to obtain El Paso property, since failing schools would be closed, reorganized or forfeited to a charter school system and leave the property available for the taking. Thus, the cheating scandal was born. It was an answer requiring power and connections, and the oligarchs had these in spades.

As if taking a page from psychology, the oligarchs exemplified Freud's concept of projection, a defense mechanism wherein the accusers implicated innocent individuals in the very crimes they themselves were committing.

In short, and to use language that the federal government frequently threw around, this was the group that actually "schemed" and "conspired," not the educators they scapegoated.

After ten years, this "cheating scandal" fizzled into oblivion, except this much-ado-about-nothing affair cost taxpayers an extremely conservative estimate of around $11 million including costs incurred by the FBI, DOJ, USDE, TEA and EPISD, just to name a few. Though the government's appetite for vengeance was voracious, implicating over 50 educators in this concocted cheating scandal, the takedown was small. Only two people were convicted, and that was without a trial.

The first individual indicted in the case, EPISD Superintendent Lorenzo Garcia, chose to take a plea deal in summer 2012. Rumors swirled around him and his alleged indiscretions in equal measure regarding the scandal that made a daily appearance in the news. In the end, to save himself from an unrelated charge involving money and a mistress, he chose to plead guilty.

Although Garcia may not have understood it at the time, his plea became the catalyst that gave the government the leverage to proceed. In the end, Garcia served less than two years in prison.

Two years later, in November 2014, a second individual, high school director Myrna Gamboa, took a plea deal. Debra Kanof, lead prosecutor in the case, called it the "Blue Light Special." Likely, Gamboa took the deal for two reasons: she had a small son at home and she had been terrorized by the federal government.

Understandably scared and anxious, but going against her own attorney's advice, Gamboa decided to plead guilty before the government had charged her of a crime. She has served her five-year probation sentence, but a felony charge remains on her record.

In summer 2016, two more educators, Maria Flores and Vanessa Foreman, made plea deals as well. Flores, forced to retire in 2013, was the primary caretaker for her terminally ill grandchildren. Foreman, a single mother, was running out of money. They gave in to the government's pressure. Former EPISD associate superintendent Damon Murphy rounded out the fifth plea in January 2017.

So there you have it: out of 10 defendants, five plea-bargained and five hung on for their lives. It is the latter group, the educators, who would go on to turn the last three plea-bargains on their heads. Inexplicably, in the summer of 2019, the government offered these three a chance to revoke their pleas. It was an unheard-of twist of events, indeed.

This should be made clear: No convictions were handed down by a jury. Not one. The government's modus operandi was to wear down the defendants. It wanted the defendants to fall on their own swords, but those swords were forged with fear, financial instability, mental anguish and ruined careers.

Those who were convicted and those who made plea deals were so very human; they were afraid and broken. They feared the government's crushing power and retribution, and most pled, hoping that the government would leave them alone. Proverbially, they agreed to give their lunch money to the bully in exchange for not being terrorized even more severely. But the bully, by its very nature, does not stop.

The government banks on human frailty. Most defendants cannot hold out after years of being intimidated. At least in this case, the government judged wrongly, as the five Educators who refused to plea were an unusual group: John Tanner and Mark Tegmeyer were committed to Catholic social teaching, Nancy Love and Diane Thomas were devoted to their careers and their students, and James Anderson, an honest assistant superintendent, whose integrity is matched by his stubbornness, wanted to run the district in accordance with the law, frequently calling the Texas Education Agency when he had questions.

All these characteristics played key roles in their refusal to fall. They were not in their careers for money, fame or power. Lying about each other simply went against their morals and was never a consideration at all. Lying about oneself wasn't an option, either.

Though they were not allowed to communicate with each other, individually, each made the decision that he or she would rather serve time than lie. Threatened with long federal prison sentences, they were certainly scared, but they weren't weak.

In refusing to make plea deals and admit to something they did not do simply to save themselves, the educators endured federal indictment, public humiliation, and a court trial whose prosecuting attorneys committed outrageous and egregious prosecutorial misconduct. That misconduct resulted in a mistrial on June 23, 2017, after three weeks of testimony. The case ended before the defense had a chance to present their side.

If standard procedures for justice were followed, the judge would have dismissed the entire case. But there was nothing standard about this case. Because of the years invested, the public spectacle, and the expectations of the oligarchy that rules the city of El Paso, the judge determined that the case would continue. Never mind that the prosecution withheld well over 50 boxes and boxes of exculpatory evidence. Never mind that the lead attorney, Debra Kanof, was removed from the case by her boss, John Bash, the US Attorney for the Western District of Texas. Never mind that she was to go before the Texas Bar Association and eventually be censured for her misconduct. No, it was life as usual in the El Paso courts, and the case would go on.

The government offers the revocation of plea deals

It all reached a tipping point in summer 2018 as the charges began to completely unravel. Eventually, Diane Thomas, one of the five educators was completely cleared when the only charge against her was dropped with prejudice.

Two others, Mark Tegmeyer and Nancy Love were offered pre-trial diversion with no admission of guilt. (Pre-trial diversion results in the charges being dismissed and the defendants having no record of conviction.) The two remaining defendants, John Tanner and James

Anderson, refused to plea by admitting guilt of any kind and things seemed to be at a standstill.

By early April 2019, these final two defendants had made peace with the idea that it could take several more years just to get back to a trial. But they were wrong. On April 18 of that year, unexpectedly, the government offered them a package deal: pre-trial diversion with no admission of guilt and the dismissal of their charges.

But there was a caveat: both had to accept. If one said no, the two of them would remain in limbo, a place of stress and uncertainty they knew all too well. This state of limbo kept them from working in their fields of expertise, and in several instances, working at all, because they couldn't pass background checks. Heck, they couldn't even drive for Uber. So much for innocent until proven guilty.

After a case of public humiliation like this one, generally defendants have a choice. Moving and starting a new life is an option. Hanging one's head and hoping that, in time, people will forget is another. After lives and careers have been derailed, getting back on track isn't easy. But for the people who would not fall to the federal government's threats, who would not allow a lie about themselves or others to cross their lips, there is only one choice. Speak out.

Now that the nightmare is over, they are finally free to present the facts that contradict the oligarchical narrative. And so it goes....

Chapter 2: Shapleigh targets Tanner

It was late morning, June 25, 2010, but already hot outside. Crowds of people parked and walked toward Texas State Senator Eliot Shapleigh's office. Shapleigh had announced that he was holding a press conference to show that Austin High School had cheated on its Texas Assessment of Knowledge and Skills (TAKS) exams. Students were required to take exams for the core subjects at the freshman, sophomore and junior level and the junior exit exams were a requirement for graduation.

Shapleigh was a charismatic individual who had strong support in the El Paso area. He won elections and re-elections with ease. Physically, he is striking. He stands at 6' 2" with a medium body build and a full head of gray hair. His words seemingly express power to the people as he touts the cultural struggle of Hispanics in west Texas. His ability to transition from English to Spanish garners praise from his constituents and even his detractors; when he speaks, he is believable.

The day before, the principal of Austin High School, John Tanner, had come across a flier that announced the press conference. The flier advertised that Austin teachers and community members would be there to corroborate Shapleigh's story.

Yet neither Shapleigh nor anyone else had bothered to talk to him about any such issues. Confused and angry, Tanner followed the crowd. "Who is Shapleigh to judge what is happening at my school? He has no background in education," Tanner thought to himself. "I don't have time for this. I have a job to do. I don't need criticism; I need help to keep Austin moving forward."

In August 2008, Tanner began his stint as Austin's principal when the school was in severe academic trouble. This was during the difficult days of No Child Left Behind (NCLB), the education legislation instituted by the George W. Bush administration that was intended to increase the academic prowess of students in US schools.

Austin High School had not fared well during this period and by the time Tanner became principal, Austin was in Stage 5 of Adequate Yearly Progress (AYP), the worst stage under the federal rating system. If Austin didn't improve drastically, the state of Texas—more realistically, The Texas Education Agency (TEA)—would mandate a process that would result in ultimately closing Austin or making it a charter school.

In order to remain open and get out of trouble, Austin High had to show two consecutive years of significant academic growth. Long story short, the Austin High faculty, students, administration and community worked hard and saved the school. One would assume after such a momentous event, there would be inquiries as to how they did it. Maybe even some congratulations or a small party.

But instead, the improvements were met with disbelief. Austin had long been the "whipping boy" of El Paso schools and any news of its improvement was met with condescending skepticism. This accusation of cheating simply followed the national trend of poor schools, which had showed such improvement.

Shapleigh, in the days leading up to the press conference, had already alleged that another school had cheated. Now it appeared he was going to include Austin in his attack.

Tanner was surprised at his allegation. This was a politician Tanner had supported; Tanner believed that Shapleigh was a friend to education. Deep down, Tanner believed a resolution would be reached. Deep down, he was wrong.

Tanner went to the press conference and stood in the back of the room. Shapleigh began the process by introducing the panel that he claimed was from Austin. He lied. Not one person on the panel was from Austin High School. Not one. Not one had ever worked at Austin. Shapleigh proceeded to claim that Austin cheated on the state exams by hiding over 200 students on the days of testing. Tanner's blood was boiling. Nothing could be further from the truth.

State testing guidelines were so strict that there was no way to hide students. In fact, Austin High personnel even went to the homes of students who were absent on the day of testing. When found, Austin administrators drove those students to school so they could test. Raising his hand to be recognized by the senator, Tanner waited, but Shapleigh would not acknowledge him.

Shaking his head 'no' at almost every allegation, Tanner caught the attention of one of Shapleigh's assistants who told him that he was being disruptive and would have to leave if he didn't settle down. "But he is lying!" Tanner said.

Finally, Shapleigh acknowledged Tanner and said, "I assume you must be a concerned parent, but I am now only taking questions from the press."

"No sir," Tanner responded. "I am John Tanner and I am the principal of Austin High School. I am here to answer any and all allegations you are making about the school."

Despite Shapleigh's allegations about Austin High School, he didn't know the principal. They had never met. Shapleigh had never visited the campus, nor did he ever ask Tanner questions about the school's data. When Tanner responded, the media outlets quickly turned around and focused their attention on him. He was escorted by one of Shapleigh's aides to the foyer of Shapleigh's office building. The media followed. Tanner was asked to explain the data that Shapleigh provided. Tanner complied.

"Basically, the senator has highlighted a problem that has existed at Austin for decades; namely, a large dropout issue. But cheating? No way," Tanner told the press.

Then Shapleigh entered the foyer and a television news station reporter put a microphone to his mouth and asked, "Have you ever had a conversation with John Tanner?"

Shapleigh responded, "Who's that?"
"The principal of Austin High School." The reporter pointed his finger at Tanner.

Shapleigh responded, "Austin High School. My father went there…."

After the conference, Tanner continued to speak with many of the reporters. He even guided some of them through the TEA website in order to show the errors in what Shapleigh was claiming. Most were satisfied.

"There's nothing here. I told him his evidence needed to be solid. This has been a waste of time," an Associated Press reported said.

Nonetheless, the *El Paso Times* reported the story with a title that read, "Austin High Pulled Scam."[1] Within the body of the article, Tanner was mentioned, but the reporter did not include the information that Shapleigh's panel of Austin employees was a sham. In fact, no one from his panel spoke to any allegation regarding Austin. They were just decoration.

For the record, no organization or authority (including TEA, the Texas State Board of Education, the Department of Education, or FBI) has ever found any validity to the allegations the senator made that day toward Austin High School.

The lesson Tanner eventually learned from this event was not learned that day. Underestimating Shapleigh's power and pettiness, it took years for Tanner to understand what he had done. He had unwittingly humiliated a very powerful politician who valued his reputation, his authority and his wallet more than the truth.

"Shapleigh wanted to let me know that I had overstepped the boundaries. He was determined to let me know that he controlled the news sources; he wanted me to know the extent of his power and influence in El Paso," Tanner said. "And he wasn't going to let me interfere with his income."

Given the fallout that happened to Tanner after this press conference, the former principal says he has thought hard about whether or not he would make the same decision again. "With great hesitation, I must say yes. Shapleigh had targeted Austin and his plan for the school district was already in motion," Tanner said. "It didn't matter who was principal at Austin High. That person was going to be targeted, no matter what."

That day, under the hot sun and the cold gaze of the cameras, Tanner established that he was going to defend Austin High School. He just didn't know that his time was limited.

Congratulating senior and 2013 valedictorian Ivan Baker, along with Baker's parents, Principal John Tanner presents confirmation of Baker's UTEP (University of Texas, El Paso) Promise Scholarship. In addition to earning the local scholarship, Baker was accepted into Emory and the University of Texas at Austin, and he chose the latter, earning a civil engineering degree. The four are standing in front of the school mascot, Elroy the Panther, who was named after legendary English teacher Elroy Bode. *photo courtesy of Austin Publications*

Chapter 3: The ambitious senator and *Equipo* Bowie

Eliot Shapleigh, a fifth generation El Pasoan, was born on November 11, 1952. Naturally competitive, Shapleigh saw his career grow alongside the far west Texas city. El Paso's population was not quite 200,000 at that time, a fraction of its current population of 800,000. Like many desert cities of the southwest, it started to expand post WWII. Shapleigh's family saw El Paso's Westside grow from its infancy to its reputation as the wealthy side of town, and that is where they resided.

After graduating from Coronado High School in 1970, Shapleigh attended Rice University in Houston, graduating in 1974. Before attending law school at the University of Texas, he joined the Peace Corps and served in Sierra Leone.[1] By 1981, he graduated law school and eventually returned to El Paso. By all accounts, Shapleigh was ambitious and focused, and he seemed to have a heart for public service.

In 1983, Shapleigh established his own law firm and earned a reputation for his desire to improve the El Paso area, which ultimately catapulted him into a career in politics. In 1996, Shapleigh won a senate seat in the Texas legislature and continued to serve until the end of his term in January 2011.[2]

While serving as a Texas senator, Shapleigh inserted himself into the arena of public education. As a prominent member of the Senate Education Committee, he published manuals on statistics in Texas, using data to make educational determinations for students' academic progress.

As one of the creators of the Texas Accountability System, he passed Senate Bill 286 giving flexibility and revenue for schools with students who faced historical challenges. This same bill allowed for the establishment of initiatives such as accelerated instruction, the very same initiatives Shapleigh and the FBI later claimed were at the heart of the alleged EPISD cheating scheme.

During his time as a senator, Shapleigh also became close with TEA deputy commissioner, Adam Jones, who held the office from 2003 to 2012.

In addition to a seemingly strong friendship, the duo worked on school accountability. A little more than a year after Shapleigh left the senate, Jones resigned from TEA and began working for the Weaver Group, the largest private auditing firm in the US. As Shapleigh was trying to establish malfeasance in EPISD, Jones and the Weaver Group became an important link in the chain toward manufacturing the scandal.

In the latter half of his Senate term in 2009, Shapleigh's relationship with EPISD became strained, but that wasn't always the case. In fact, he enjoyed a good reputation with all the school districts in the El Paso area as he was known as a friend of education. Often, he would offer public kudos to various districts for their outstanding achievements in educating El Paso's students; but oddly enough, he did not do this with EPISD. He rarely mentioned EPISD at all in his public statements even though EPISD struggled to meet the same levels of academic progress as the other El Paso districts.

During his tenure as senator, Shapleigh enjoyed great privileges within the area's nine districts. He came and went as he pleased in central and district offices and had apparently established that he could speak to any school superintendent without having an appointment. Further, his clout allowed him to make decisions for EPISD without consulting the superintendent or school board. One example of this was his diligent work to implement an organization of his own making called *Equipo* Bowie.

Equipo Bowie: Team Bowie

Equipo Bowie was Shapleigh's creation for the stated purpose of improving academics and future employment opportunities for students at one of the most economically disadvantaged schools in the United States. In Shapleigh's effort to forge an agreement with EPISD and *Equipo*, he planned a conference in May 2009 to be held at the namesake school of the project, Bowie High School.

A featured speaker for this event was Dr. Colby Stover, a research statistician known for his expertise in using demographic data for educational purposes.[3]

After the event, Shapleigh blindsided Dr. Lorenzo Garcia, the EPISD superintendent, by informing him that the district needed to pay for Dr. Stover's appearance at the event. This demand violated protocols and mandates established for public entities when disbursing payments to vendors for the district. More succinctly, the demand violated Texas state law.

But in order to maintain peace with Shapleigh, Garcia complied by having EPISD staff rectify the situation. The key point here is that Shapleigh is the one who organized this event and Shapleigh himself was destined to be a benefactor of the implementation of *Equipo* Bowie. He did not consult anyone in the district about hiring a speaker at the district's expense. Nonetheless, he placed the burden of payment for a speaker on taxpayer money earmarked for public education.

Equipo is a Spanish word that means "team"; thus, the term translates to Team Bowie. As one of the oldest schools in the district, its inception dating back to 1927, Bowie is an urban high school located near downtown El Paso in a neighborhood called Segundo Barrio, or Second Ward, that borders its sister city, Juarez, in Mexico.

From its founding, Bowie has been the school for new and first-generation immigrants from Mexico. Graduates are proud of their heritage as it provides stories of struggle and triumph that align with the American Dream.

When No Child Left Behind (NCLB) was implemented by the George W. Bush administration in 2002, Bowie became one of its earliest victims. Whether or not it was the intention of NCLB, draconian measures were mandated for schools that consistently did not meet the standards set. By the time Shapleigh's *Equipo* Bowie was being implemented in 2008, Bowie was just about to enter Stage 5 of sanctions outlined by NCLB. Ultimately, this meant that Bowie had two years to make significant improvement or face the consequences.

Purportedly, *Equipo* Bowie was Shapleigh's brainchild for the alleged purpose of saving the school. As Shapleigh laid it out, *Equipo* Bowie was to examine all the data of students in the south El Paso area with the stated aim of improving education; however, there was no explanation pertaining as to how this data would be used.

The rhetoric presented was convincing to the general public, whereby Shapleigh utilized verbiage that promoted a can-do attitude with a strong work ethic. But behind the hype and the positive messaging was the wording of the *Equipo* document and the signatures that were on it.[4] The wording suggested a concerned community that addressed the needs at Bowie with special attention to its academic struggles. The methodology, however, replicated the responsibilities that were inherent of the school district.

In hindsight, one must ask why Shapleigh saw a need for *Equipo* as it proposed to address what was essentially the district's responsibility. There was no need nor precedent to create a completely different entity that had the ability to usurp the decision-making power from a superintendent and an elected board that was legally charged with improving the school. As a senator, why did he want to create this separate organization rather than assist a district that was already showing significant signs of improvement?

Instead, *Equipo* was a committee ready to take over a school that was possibly going to turn into a charter, school according to the mandates of NCLB if it did not meet all the required standards.

Many of those who signed the ratifying document were prominent business and civic leaders of El Paso who did not have any expertise or training in the field of education.[5] This included Beto O'Rourke and Veronica Escobar.[6] O'Rourke was a city council member at the time and Escobar was a county commissioner before she became a county judge. O'Rourke went on to become a US representative before his unsuccessful campaigns for the US Senate and for the US Presidency. Escobar replaced O'Rourke in Congress.

This group of "concerned" individuals was allegedly invested in the best interests of the Bowie community. However, they purposely established themselves as a separate organization from the school district by stressing collaboration instead of partnership. Never mentioned in public discussions about Bowie's future was the impact on the community if Bowie were to become a charter school.

Additionally, *Equipo* did not explain to the public that a charter school was not considered a neighborhood school where students are assigned based on their address. In other words, if Bowie became a charter school, the former attendance zone would no longer apply. The students in that attendance zone were not guaranteed a spot in any future charter school should they apply. They would have to be reassigned to another EPISD school.

Furthermore, removing a public school from students can render a neighborhood as blighted and neighborhoods designated as blighted are often subjected to eminent domain laws when real estate developers want to gentrify an area of a city.[7] El Paso's south side was targeted for redevelopment and some of the signatures on the *Equipo* Bowie document were prominent investors in the redevelopment.

Equipo Bowie violates FERPA

While Shapleigh was establishing *Equipo* as its own entity, he was also requiring EPISD to provide all access to vital data of every student in the Bowie attendance zone. That included grades, test results, family information, addresses, parent information, social security numbers, student identification numbers and military status. Shapleigh needed Garcia's full cooperation with his plan.

But legally, Garcia couldn't comply. Shapleigh was asking Garcia to violate the Family Educational Rights and Privacy Act (FERPA). With Garcia's refusal to give Shapleigh legally protected information, an amiable working relationship became tense. Unknowingly, Garcia was jeopardizing the long-range plans Shapleigh had not just for Bowie, but for major portions of EPISD.

In a video entitled "*Equipo* Bowie MOU (Memorandum of Understanding)," dated Sept. 23, 2008, Shapleigh said, "I predict that we will learn through this process lessons that we can use at Austin, Irvin, Andress, and some of the other schools that may not be doing as well as hoped."[8] In this statement, he foreshadowed his plan to take charge of the district. First Bowie, then the rest. He did this without consultation with any of the educators or elected officials who were given the responsibility for improving any of those schools.

In sum, *Equipo* Bowie was to become the de facto school board for Bowie High School that would usurp any decisions made for it by the citizen-elected EPISD school board. Shapleigh would be its leader, not the EPISD superintendent, Lorenzo Garcia.

If successful, Equipo Bowie would set the precedent for the takeover of other EPISD schools. As per the agreement, *Equipo* would be allowed to hire third party consultants to collect and evaluate data for Bowie. Most likely, EPISD would pay for the consultants, not *Equipo*. Yet, *Equipo* could apply for grants and other funding separate from EPISD and it would be *Equipo* executive members who would administer any grants awarded without any input from EPISD board members or the superintendent's cabinet.

Administrator fees, in the form of stipends, are implicit in this type of arrangement. Those fees are typically earmarked for the chair of an entity and, of course, Shapleigh was the chair. In addition to being the intended recipient of these funds, Shapleigh would also make decisions regarding how any revenue awarded from grants was to be spent, with accountability only from the *Equipo* board.

Because Bowie was in danger of closing, *Equipo* Bowie was prepared and eager to handle the consequences of such an event. This would have given Shapleigh and *Equipo* control of its financial future and all the opportunities associated with it. Hence, Shapleigh and the oligarchs had everything to gain from a Bowie fail.

But Lorenzo Garcia stood in the way.

———

Chapter 4: The superintendent

The EPISD school board had the task of hiring a new superintendent. No longer could board members ignore the state of the district's schools and their goal was to find someone who could put EPISD on track to academic success. Their choice was Dr. Lorenzo Garcia, who was hired as the superintendent in spring 2006.

Garcia possessed an impressive resumé. Coming to EPISD from the Dallas Independent School District where he served as an associate superintendent, Garcia previously proved his credentials while he served as a high school principal in the Houston area. His success at Spring Woods High School resulted in Garcia being recognized as Principal of the Year for the state of Texas in 2003.[1]

Like many successful school administrators, Garcia had his supporters and his detractors. His supporters followed him wherever he went, and his detractors threw parties after he was gone. When coming to El Paso, Garcia's acolytes followed and many of them were placed in high profile and well-paying positions in EPISD.

Garcia is Hispanic and that was about the only characteristic that he had in common with the average El Pasoan. He was an outsider who did not understand the El Paso nation. Although he came from a migrant farming family whose dominant language was Spanish, Garcia told stories of pulling himself up by his bootstraps and taking the opportunities offered in the US and Texas to propel himself into a position of power and prestige.

That should have been a selling point, but Garcia was perceived as arrogant. Some believed that he viewed El Paso as a stepping-stone for his career, and he definitely underestimated the spirit of its citizens. He spoke with an authentic east Texas accent and refused to speak Spanish either publicly or privately. Perhaps that practice was appreciated away from the border, but in El Paso, it was an insult.

Nonetheless, Garcia was competent in the area of K-12 public education in Texas. He had proven himself in the classroom and as an administrator, both on a campus and at a district level. In addition, he had earned a doctorate in educational leadership from the University of Houston where he was also honored as one of its outstanding exes.[2] Outside of El Paso, Garcia had clout.

But in the El Paso district, Garcia was not admired; instead, he was feared. He took over a district that was mired in neglect, citing weak excuses for failure. He remedied this situation with rash judgments and quick terminations. Some of his decisions were good, some not. Regardless, his actions were often the hot topic for district personnel. For the most part, his school administrators followed his demands and the schools, overall, were performing better under his leadership.

When he entered EPISD, the district had 22 failing schools. By the end of his second year, fewer than 10 were still in trouble. However, two of those schools were in the serious stages of sanctions and were facing closure if academics did not improve significantly. Bowie was one of those schools. Austin High School was the other.

At first, Shapleigh and Garcia were friendly, with a mutual goal of improving Bowie. But when Shapleigh made demands on Garcia about *Equipo* Bowie, Garcia could not and would not comply. Legally, Garcia, was right to deny Shapleigh's demands. Shapleigh wanted access to all the student data of EPISD. Purportedly, this was for the benefit of the students whereby *Equipo* could provide opportunities that were designed for each student's needs. However, having data is having power. That data had the ability to produce income in the form of federal, state and private grants.

As a sitting state senator, Shapleigh should have understood the conflict of interest by trying to run a Texas public school. Second, Garcia was the one hired to improve Bowie and that was part of his job description. Even if Garcia wanted to, he didn't have the authority to give this responsibility to an outside entity. Finally, and most importantly, Garcia was prohibited by federal law, the Family Educational Rights and Privacy Act (FERPA), from giving the Shapleigh-created *Equipo* Bowie the vital statistics of the district's students to the senator and his constituents.

To appease Shapleigh, Garcia offered an alternative contract for *Equipo* Bowie. Garcia was willing to provide district reports to the organization, but Shapleigh rebuffed Garcia's compromise.

In a letter sent from his assistant, David Edmondson, to Garcia's chief of staff, Tomas Gabaldon, on September 18, 2008, Shapleigh stated that access to the data was "simply non-negotiable for us."[3]

By upholding the law and parameters of his job, Garcia garnered a powerful enemy in Shapleigh, one that the superintendent underestimated. However, the senator was not the only enemy Garcia had gained in the process.

Chapter 5: The city has plans

When you have seen Paris, it is hard to go back to the farm. If you are coming from the farm, El Paso can seem to have it all: restaurants, a mid-major university, sports, a downtown area, and a small, but impressive art museum. But when you have seen Paris, it is hard to return to the desert desolation of the Sun City. Merited or not, common complaints include a lack of arts, a low level of education, an undeveloped infrastructure, few tourist attractions, and an unappealing downtown area. Every now and then, concerned citizens see enormous potential in El Paso and want to develop it into a first-class metropolitan area. But in the end, plans stagnate and those ambitious souls conclude what natives knew all along: if you want a big city life with big city amenities, you're just going to have to move.

The Paso Del Norte Group

A new group in El Paso formed in the early 2000s. It was first known as the El Paso Leadership Council, but then changed its name in 2004 to the Paso Del Norte Group (PDNG). It is also informally known as El Paso's Illuminati or Oligarchy, due to its secretive nature that includes anonymity for its current members. Very few actual members are known, and most seem to have ties to El Paso's old white families of money.[1]

Of the known members, mogul Bill Sanders is most notable. Sanders, a native El Pasoan, earned his vast fortune in real estate (estimated by some to be in the billions) while residing in Chicago. Considered to be the driving force of the PDNG, he also happens to be the father-in-law of former US congressman and former Democratic presidential hopeful Beto O'Rourke. Beto married Sander's daughter Amy in 1998. Interestingly, both Beto and Amy have been cited as members of the PDNG at one time or another.[2]

The PDNG is best known for developing a plan to revitalize downtown El Paso. Normally this would not be problematic, but in this case the plan was created in secret and the only individuals allowed to give input were members of the PDNG.

Even more alarming, those making the plans did not live in the area where the plan was to take effect. There was no consultation with the residents. Additionally, the difference in income between the planners and those who lived in the redevelopment zone was substantial. Billionaires and millionaires created a plan that would displace the poorest residents of El Paso without any input from those who would be impacted most. In short, the revitalization plan included eminent domain to ensure the larger land-grabbing real estate plan of the PDNG.

The plan

When the oligarchs' plan was revealed to the public, it was met with enthusiasm, especially to the El Pasoans who wanted a more vibrant city. The plan included positive objectives, including the destruction of an eyesore, the old American Smelting and Refining Company (ASARCO) smoke tower. ASARCO, a copper smelter no longer in use, left its mark on the city in the form of a red and white 828 ft. tall smoke tower. At the time of its use from 1888-1999, ecologically, it was a disaster and it caused significant air pollution for both El Paso and Juarez.[3]

The plan also included a redevelopment design for the downtown area, which was mostly known for a failing infrastructure and a retail market that attracted Juarez residents to street side vendors. Like many downtown areas in the country, El Paso's began its death in the 1960s due to urban sprawl, an interstate highway system that eliminated neighborhoods and pathways near the downtown area, along with the introduction of the shopping mall.

What once was a thriving city center had turned into a place of government business and banking. There was no nightlife and it was virtually a ghost town on weekends. The new plan included an area for nightlife, a revitalized arts district, renovated hotels, condominiums, a minor league baseball stadium and a new sports arena.[4]

Many residents saw this as a pipe dream, but a good dream. However, there were opponents. With no regard for the residents who would be displaced under eminent domain, opponents saw injustice.

Even the presentation of the plan raised controversy. The plan's developers depicted the Sun City as a stereotypical "Old El Paso." There was a picture of an elderly Hispanic man in a Stetson hat walking on a downtown street with a caption underneath that read, "Dirty, Lazy, Uneducated." The "New El Paso" revealed headshots of Matthew McConaughey and Penelope Cruz with the caption, "Educated. Bilingual. 30-40."

The criticism directed to the developers included the plan's secrecy and the fact that it was created by the rich, white elite of El Paso without any input from a typical El Paso resident, much less anyone from the neighborhoods being affected.[5]

Other concerns raised regarded how this project was to be funded. While it is true that El Paso does have some wealth that comes from a few families, the city is known for its overall poverty. A CBS news report on February 18, 2018 ranked El Paso as the 8th poorest major city in the nation.[6] This accounts for El Paso's ratio of renters to owners being one of the highest in the nation. This may explain why El Paso's property tax rate is the highest in Texas while Texas has the 3rd highest property tax rates in the country with an average of 1.86%. El Paso is sitting at approximately 3%.[7] Even with high tax rates, a city this poor could not generate the revenue to fund the El Paso redevelopment plan.

However, the PDNG saw potential in the revitalization and they teamed with elected leaders of El Paso to implement their plan. In particular, the PDNG aligned with four individuals who labeled themselves as "The Progressives."

First, there was Veronica Escobar who was a county commissioner and judge. Second, there was Susie Byrd, a city council member with many ties to El Paso's elite including Eliot Shapleigh. The third and fourth in this group were aforementioned Robert "Beto" O'Rourke and Steve Ortega, also city council members. Beto's ties to the PDNG were more direct: his father-in-law made the direct connection.

The Progressives used their leadership power to enact the redevelopment of downtown. In many ways, it was their job to make El Paso a better place. It was also their job to come up with the methodology used to make the plan a reality. Seemingly, they did have a plan.

The Progressives first sought the support of the community, following up with other ideas to enrich the quality of life within the city. They were able to garner this support through a press that was willing to buy into the PDNG and The Progressives' vision. That wheel was greased with the friendship between Byrd and the editor of the *El Paso Times*, Bob Moore. Byrd was always free with her claim that she and Moore were best friends.

The issue wasn't so much to get El Pasoans to support the plan. It was getting El Pasoans to believe the plan could come to fruition. At least two generations of El Pasoans had no memory of downtown being a vibrant area. In fact, it was quite the opposite. It was hard to imagine a new downtown area that had clean streets, good restaurants, and a fun nightlife complete with condos and apartments just feet away from its sister city of

Juarez, which was known as one of the most dangerous places on the planet.

Even before Juarez was known for its drug cartels, it had a history of horrifying violence against women, particularly in the early 1990s. Bodies were found in mass graves and the details were horrifying. Juarez, during this time, continued to deteriorate and crime became exponentially worse. Decapitation was a common word used in nightly telecasts of the local and national news outlets. It was hard to fathom a "vibrant" city in this milieu.

But the Progressives were not discouraged. Their path to revenue was through a tax base, real estate investments, and incentives to businesses willing to locate to a place of unknown potential. The tax base came in the form of hotel revenue and finding other ways for the City Council to have access to other tax resources, namely education funds. The citizens were promised that their own tax bills would not increase. Spoiler alert: That was a lie. If newer, more polished storefronts were made available, the Progressives had confidence that businesses would come. Real estate development was the necessary ingredient to make the plan succeed.[8]

Downtown El Paso's architecture, however, spoke in whispers of "what once was." With imagination, one could see that El Paso once had a vision and the buildings reflected a golden age influenced by the Art Deco movement. Henry Trost, one of Frank Lloyd Wright's contemporaries, built over 600 homes and structures in the city including libraries, museums, schools, and office buildings.[9]

Before El Paso had a historical society, many of Trost's structures had already been torn down. Luckily, not all of his art was destroyed before the preservationists saved the rest from the wrecking ball.

For vacant Trost buildings and other structures, the downtown plan envisioned condos, apartments and hotels. The thought of El Pasoans choosing to live downtown in high-end venues was foreign. However, other cities such as Fort Worth and Dallas had enacted such plans with success.

Slowly, parts of the plan were becoming a reality. But there was still an enormous obstacle, the poor neighborhoods of South El Paso, namely Duranguito and Segundo Barrio. These are some of the poorest neighborhoods in the country, but the plans for this area were to turn these depressed city blocks into art walks, trendy shopping, "mixed-income" housing, and a venue for sports and conventions. But getting this to happen was going to take getting the compliance of the current residents and businesses, along with the historical society and those who were highlighting issues of injustice.

Whereas Duranguito and Segundo were poor and in need of attention, there was history. Many immigrants began their US journey in South El Paso. A culture and pride developed, whereby it has become part of the folklore of the city.

Although most people growing up in South El Paso have a goal to leave it, they also romanticize the experience and see the values they learned by surviving the challenges inherent in a community devoid of money and access to what many citizens see as daily necessities. The Catholic Church and public schools offer chances to spring into middle class, and those two entities are held with high regard by the residents of these historic neighborhoods.

Sacred Heart, a Jesuit church in South El Paso, serves as a refuge for those seeking a better life. Sacred Heart offers a community center for the neighborhood and hosts many organizations seeking to provide aid in the community in the form of employment services, classes to become US citizens and to learn English, as well as access to health services. The schools of South El Paso are part of the El Paso Independent School District. Bowie High School stands as a symbol of pride and access to the world beyond the border. This home of the Bears, affectionately known as "La Bowie," serves as a beacon of hope to those who can see it from the other side of the border.

However, outside of South El Paso, Bowie was not viewed with high regard. Though undeserving, its reputation was that of a thug-and-drug school that had gangs with few students graduating and most not knowing English. At the same time, many in the city also "felt sorry" for Bowie students because of their challenges. Bowie provided the opportunity for other schools to feel good about themselves.

The reality of Bowie is quite different than the perception. The school has excellent discipline and the students are respectful. It is true that the students struggle more academically, due to factors that are easily observed. They are socioeconomically disadvantaged; these are the students who depend on free breakfasts and free lunches. Teenagers are expected to work in order to contribute to the household. English is the second language.

School is probably the only time and place when English is dominant. At all other times, Spanish is the common tongue of South El Paso. These are the barriers for academic advancement, but it doesn't mean that there isn't progress. Bowie class reunions exhibit amazing success from its alumni: civic leaders, teachers, lawyers, doctors and business professionals. The innate obstacles for a solid education are not barriers in the long run. It is the grist in that mill.

But NCLB did not consider the intrinsic obstacles in South El Paso. Instead, NCLB had a one-size-fits-all policy where schools had to meet an arbitrary standard in order to be labeled as acceptable. For schools that didn't meet those standards, the consequences could become severe. By 2006 (during the time of the El Paso revitalization plan), Bowie was on the verge of finding out what those consequences would be, with closure as a likely option.

For the Bowie community and its alumni, this was a travesty that had to be corrected. New superintendent Dr. Lorenzo Garcia saw it as a challenge, and it was one of the main reasons he was hired to lead the district. The Bowie faculty and staff were open to changes that needed to happen in order to keep Bowie open. Regarding Bowie's impending doom, Shapleigh said nothing publicly. City Council was mute. The *El Paso Times* simply did not report on it. At this early stage, El Paso's City Council, led by the Progressives already had plans in the making to take over Segundo Barrio and Duranguito.

Bowie High School: blight or flight?

For City Council, having a failing high school in the center of their redevelopment plan was necessary in order to make a land grab. For the redevelopment plan to become a reality, landowners had to agree to be bought out at the lowest price possible--not always an easy accomplishment. But the PDNG, supported by City Council members Susie Byrd, Beto O'Rourke and Steve Ortega, had a plan.

If there was not an agreement with the owners or the residents, then eminent domain would be used to justify the takeover. Generally, eminent domain is difficult to accomplish without the cooperation of the owners. However, if an area is declared "blighted," it becomes much easier. To be designated as blighted or condemned, the area must be considered a danger to health, particularly in relation to schools. In other words, if children are living in an area where there is no properly functioning school nearby, it is considered a health hazard.[10]

This was the plan for the Bowie area. If the schools of the neighborhood were to shut down, then the children of the neighborhood would have no proper school to attend. Perhaps their former schools would become charter schools, but those charters would not be considered neighborhood schools for students who lived in the area. Thus, the circumstances of replacing a closed public school with a charter school satisfy the condition of a health hazard, rendering an area as blighted.

However, it seems that City Council and Shapleigh had already considered replacement plans for lost educational opportunities. As stated earlier, Shapleigh had established *Equipo* Bowie with prominent El Pasoans—including redevelopment investors—signing to be charter members.

If Bowie closed, then *Equipo* Bowie could become the operating board for Bowie as a charter school and the area could still be labeled as blighted, paving the way for eminent domain.

The plan seemed to be going smoothly until Dr. Lorenzo Garcia took control of EPISD. The PDNG, Eliot Shapleigh and El Paso City Council had not considered that Bowie might improve significantly. Not only was Bowie improving significantly, but the entire district performed better on the standards set by NCLB and TEA. By the end of the 2008-2009 school year, Bowie had a clear path to get out of its trouble… and remain open.

The story of how Bowie and the district got out of trouble is a tribute to hard work and changing a mentality that sought to legitimize the idea that poor students can't succeed. For the record, poverty is not an excuse for students not to learn. But that part of the story was never told. Instead of celebrating the EPISD's accomplishments, Eliot Shapleigh and his entourage questioned the success, to the point of declaring, without any proof, that the district cheated in order to get out of its trouble.

6: Setting the stage for a scandal to emerge

When Dr. Garcia became the superintendent of EPISD in spring 2006, NCLB had been in place for almost three years and the district had 22 out of 90 schools in sanctions. No other El Paso County school district was in such trouble. In fact, few districts in Texas had managed to experience such a breakdown. There were many fires to put out and some schools required immediate attention. By the end of the 2005-06 school year, the district was showing a slight improvement with its elementary and middle schools. But that improvement was not being felt at the high school level.

Both Bowie and Austin high schools were facing restructuring if academics did not improve. Neither school had met the requirements of NCLB under the category of Adequate Yearly Progress (AYP). Because these schools were in desperate need, TEA provided substantial funding and state personnel to assist them.

But there were serious consequences if improvements did not happen: A clause in the improvement plans of both central city schools demanded the removal of a principal if academic standards were not met. At the end of the 2007-08 school year, neither school met standards, so both schools lost their principals.[1]

In response, Dr. Garcia placed two principals who were knowledgeable about NCLB and had demonstrated success at other Texas schools. Dr. Jesus Chavez became the principal of Bowie and Dr. John Tanner became the principal at Austin. These two had the unenviable task of significantly improving their schools in one year's time. Both schools had reached what was called Stage 5 AYP. There was no stage worse than that.

By the time a school reached that status, few options were left. Plain and simple, if there was not significant prescribed improvement by the end of the 2008-09 school year, TEA would begin restructuring procedures. If the schools met their goals, then they would still have to perform well for an additional year before exiting sanctions.

By May 2009, both schools had met their required improvement and all the work to remain open had been realized. The district celebrated the accomplishment. The *El Paso Times* and Senator Eliot Shapleigh did not. Zahira Torres, the educational reporter for the *El Paso Times*, wrote little on the two schools' accomplishments. Instead, she focused on how they were still in trouble and only had one more year to improve.

She wrote another article later in the summer of 2009 indicating that Austin had not met its goals and was going to be closed. The article was filled with misinformation. Tanner was allowed to write an op-ed that was buried in the back pages of the *Times* to counter what Torres had written, but not before the damage was done.

By September 2009, Shapleigh began to hint that he did not think that the results for Bowie were legitimate. He did this publicly in speeches, on his website and in some articles in the *Times*. At this point, he was only raising questions. At the district level, Dr. Garcia became more vocal about his strained relationship with the senator. He verbalized that he didn't understand why the senator was disparaging the district in stead of congratulating it for its accomplishments and, up to that time, the label of "cheating scandal" had still not emerged.

During the 2009-10 school year, Shapleigh continued to push his agenda regarding *Equipo* Bowie. He made it clear to Garcia that he wanted *Equipo* Bowie to have the decision-making power for Bowie, even if Bowie were to succeed. The more that Garcia resisted Shapleigh's requests that were increasingly becoming demands, the more the press was suggesting that EPISDs improvements were questionable.[2]

In May 2010, both Bowie and Austin had met the standards set by TEA and NCLB. Officially, they were out of trouble and it was a time to celebrate. But again, the *Times* and Shapleigh were critical. That same month, Shapleigh's demands toward Garcia became even more focused in a memorandum he wrote. His request was "non-negotiable" regarding *Equipo* Bowie's role in plans for Bowie High School. In response, Garcia made it clear that *Equipo* Bowie was not going to be the decision-making body for Bowie.[3]

In effect, Garcia had thwarted the plans of two powerful entities. He shut down Shapleigh's plan of *Equipo* Bowie. Second, Garcia halted the plans of the PDNG and the El Paso City Council regarding the downtown redevelopment. Who knows how many investors were involved in that redevelopment plan? Regardless of the number, he was now their enemy number one. At this point, Garcia did not know the ramifications of his success.

Chapter 7: Alleged cheating and an investigation

By June 2010, it was evident that Shapleigh was fuming and was no longer trying to persuade Garcia to change his mind about *Equipo Bowie*. Instead, he went on the attack. Utilizing press conferences, his clout with the El Paso media, and his own website, Shapleigh declared that Bowie High School had cheated in order to get out of state and federal sanctions. And he claimed to have the proof.

The Adequate Yearly Progress (AYP) scores of the NCLB Act were Shapleigh's primary focus. The system was complex and attention to detail was necessary to understand how scores were reached and how standards were either met or not met. For the purpose of this chapter, part of this complexity must be explained in order to understand the accusations that Shapleigh made.

The AYP scores at the high school level in Texas depended solely on the state test scores for 10th grade students. The battery of tests that each student took was called the Texas Assessment of Knowledge and Skills (TAKS). Every high school in Texas was focused on the success of their sophomores since their scores determined the accountability rating for the school on the federal level.[1]

Texas' exit level exams had been administered at the 10th grade level prior to the implementation of the No Child Left Behind Act. But the state had refined the system during the governorship of George W. Bush and that system became the model for NCLB when he became president.

Under No Child Left Behind, the exit level exams for Texas students moved from the 10th grade to the 11th grade level. With the federal AYP accountability grade level remaining at 10th grade, it created an unforeseen dilemma and the state came under scrutiny for not having a method in place to test all 10th grade students. Focusing on the 2004 and 2005 academic school years, a CBS *60 Minutes* report called "The Texas Miracle" addressed these very concerns in the form of repeat 9th graders missing the 10th grade test. This report was a full five years before any allegations were ever made by Shapleigh.

At that point, the 10th grade tests were used to measure student's academic ability in the 10th grade for federal accountability, but had no significance to the student personally.[2] In contrast, the 11th grade test was extremely significant because it determined whether or not a student would earn a diploma. In other words, the 10th grade test meant everything to the school and very little to the student, while the 11th grade test meant everything to the student and nothing to the school in terms of its AYP score.

The 10th grade tests measured federal accountability for student performance in language arts and math. The rating was based on the pass rate of the class as a whole.

But there were other metrics as well. The overall scores were disaggregated to evaluate how different segments of the school's demographics performed. This methodology intended to include separate pass rates based on race/ethnicity, socioeconomic status, special education status, and those who were not proficient in English.

Those students not proficient in English were known as LEP (Limited English Proficiency). For many areas of the USA, the LEP population is minimal. In El Paso, and indeed in most of Texas, LEP students are a focus for all educators considering the proximity to the border with Mexico. All these different demographics were referred to as subgroups. A school was AYP accountable for these subgroups if it met two conditions: 1. The population of the subgroup was at least 50 students at the AYP accountable grade level; 2. The overall subgroup population had to be at least 10% or more of the entire testing population of the school. Both conditions had to be met.[3]

Because of these parameters and because the scores determined the status of the school, all personnel were focused on ensuring that students were coded correctly in the state's database. Enormous attention was paid to the correct classification of students.

For example, a student might be attending his or her second year at a high school, but that does not automatically mean that student is a 10th grader. If he or she did not earn enough credits during the 9th grade year, then that student was still considered a 9th grader. If that same 9th grader performed well their second year at the school and managed to pass all their classes, then that student could very well have earned enough credits to be an 11th grader at the beginning of their third year of high school.

Thus, according to TEA guidelines, it was possible for a student to never be classified as a 10th grader because of the determination based on credits.

The student in the example above would have been classified as a 9th grader during the first year of high school. At the beginning of the second year of high school, this same student would still be classified as a 9th grader. But by the third year, this student would be classified as an 11th grader because he or she passed all classes the second year and perhaps even attended summer school in order to make up unearned credits.

Because of these caveats, there are trends that happen not only in Texas, but across the nation. It is a fact that the largest population of students nationwide in both actual number and percentage are 9th graders. This is true primarily because it is a transition year for students. It is the first year of high school which has been determined to be a difficult year for most people who are experiencing puberty and a change in social structure.[4] Further, high schools determine a student's grade status by the number of credits earned. As a rule, elementary and middle schools do not utilize such a method.

When studying a high school population, researchers find that the rule of thumb is that the 9th grade class is always the largest (often significantly so) and the 12th grade class is usually the smallest for various reasons, including dropouts or early graduations. Tenth and 11th grade populations tend to look like one another.[5]

With this explanation, most people understand the population shifts in a high school. Without this explanation, the conventional wisdom suggests that each grade level has about the same number of students in it. Shapleigh depended on the conventional wisdom interpretation for the accusation he made when saying that Bowie High School cheated to get its results.

Shapleigh's basic allegation was that Bowie manipulated the results of the 10th grade TAKS by ensuring that only good students would take the test. He alleged that Bowie "disappeared" students on the rosters and kept them from testing. His proof was using the number of students enrolled at the school. He took the numbers of the 9th grade class for the 2006-07 school year and then compared it with the numbers for the 10th graders during the 2007-08 school year. He highlighted that there were over 100 fewer students from one year to the next and concluded that those students were "disappeared" from the rolls at Bowie High School.

If one does not understand school populations, then Shapleigh's accusation sounds like it has merit. But when one knows how the population trends work, especially in Texas and especially at schools with high poverty rates, then that drop in the student number makes more sense.

However, Shapleigh depended on the public's lack of understanding. By using his logic, the state of Texas "disappears" about 65,000 students per year. By disappearing, Shapleigh alleged that personnel at Bowie High School and the district took these students off the rolls of the school.

Again, it is an accusation without merit. In Texas (and the US) it is virtually impossible to "disappear" a student. Each student enrolled has a state identification number that is tracked every year. Every student, every year must be accounted for. If a student goes to another school, that identification number follows them. One cannot just "disappear" a student.

The system was designed to account for all students every year. The purpose was to create a safety net so that no students would fall through the cracks. With this attention on student success, NCLB provided enormous revenue to struggling schools to help students with their academics. For schools in EPISD, this revenue was used for hiring more teachers and decreasing class sizes, hiring tutors, hiring consultants, increasing instructional time, extending the school day and the school week, and so on. Although Shapleigh was aware of these interventions, he never once indicated that the interventions contributed to the success of the once underperforming schools.[6]

A litany of officials from EPISD spoke to Shapleigh concerning his accusations against the district. Unsuccessfully, Dr. Garcia, Jesus Chavez, and Terri Jordan (EPISD's chief of staff) tried to explain the data to Shapleigh to no avail. Further, Garcia included staff members of the district's research and data department for the purpose of explaining the complex intricacies of NCLB and how that was implemented in Texas.

Alas, nothing could have convinced Shapleigh except for an agreement to his plan for *Equipo* Bowie. Since he did not get his way, he was out to accuse and make sure his accusation found an audience. In mid-June 2010, Shapleigh held a press conference to allege cheating at EPISD.[7] In front of the cameras, he held a stack of papers, claiming they contained the proof of the cheating scandal. But no written details were given to the public to see. Yet, Shapleigh had clout, and this led to many citizens believing that something was amiss in EPISD.

To combat this accusation, Lorenzo Garcia called a press conference of his own on June 23, 2010. Held at Coronado High School, the school where Shapleigh graduated, Garcia invited two principals to help him speak to the media: Dr. John Tanner, principal of Austin High School and Ms. Marielo Morales, principal of Coronado. Garcia, Morales and Tanner spoke to the accomplishments of EPISD's communities and the progress that had been made academically over the past years in the high stakes era of NCLB. Students stood in the background complete with placards showing school pride. All three speakers asked Shapleigh to stop making false accusations about the school district. El Paso media was there for the event but they didn't ask any questions of the speakers. Nonetheless, they reported on the event.[8]

"When the debate is lost, slander becomes the tool of the loser."

In response, the next day, June 24, 2010, Shapleigh announced another press conference on June 25 and during this one he was going to offer the proof on how Austin High School was cheating just like Bowie. He claimed that he would have Austin teachers and community members to help verify his claim. This press conference was detailed at the end of chapter two in this book.

Tanner attended this press conference and saw Shapleigh introduce his panel that was to verify his actions. Not one person worked at Austin or had ever worked at Austin. Not one person on his panel had any connection to the school. Tanner challenged Shapleigh on his claims to the point that the press that attended had serious doubts regarding Shapleigh's accusations.

Nonetheless, Shapleigh's homing in on a new target had just begun. Just five days later, Shapleigh's concerns had reached the US Department of Education (USDE). The USDE mandated for TEA to investigate EPISD with respect to Shapleigh's allegations, specifically, the disappearing students. As TEA prepared to investigate, Shapleigh pushed TEA to broaden its investigation of EPISD, especially with a focus on Bowie.

TEA complied. On September 20, TEA issued a report that cleared EPISD of any wrongdoing. Shapleigh's subsequent actions showed that he was incensed. He claimed that TEA was not taking the investigation seriously and that they needed to investigate again.[9]

TEA obliged and investigated again. On October 8, 2010, TEA again declared that there was no wrongdoing with EPISD. Important in this result was that TEA clarified that there were no "disappearing" students as Shapleigh had claimed.

Of course, The *El Paso Times* did not report this detail and Shapleigh continued this allegation for a few more years. In fact, neither the *Times* nor any other news media in El Paso has ever reported this result. Though TEA's result incensed Shapleigh, it only served to fuel his fire. Yet, one fact is clear: Shapleigh's accusation of "disappearing" students had no merit. He was discredited by EPISD and twice by TEA. As the investigation on EPISD continued, the USDE and the FBI also concluded there was no merit to this allegation, ever.

If you don't succeed the first time...

For a while, it appeared that Shapleigh's allegations were fading away. With TEA clearing EPISD of impropriety, many in the district believed that Shapleigh was satisfied. But that wasn't accurate. By December 2010, Shapleigh was again in the media alleging that TEA was remiss with their investigation. Now, not only was he targeting Bowie and Austin, but he also accused four other high schools. Using friends in high places—allegedly, requesting a favor from Hillary Clinton—Shapleigh persuaded the United States Department of Education (USDE) and the FBI to investigate his allegations of EPISD.

He wrote a letter to President Obama with his concerns.10 Given that the tenth amendment to the U.S. Constitution reserves education matters to the state, it was shocking that the FBI agreed to such an investigation. The federal government has no legal grounds to address "cheating" in a state-run education system, but that didn't seem to matter.[11] The FBI settled in for the long haul.

As we now know, Shapleigh worked diligently to get the FBI involved. With his authority dashed by TEA, Shapleigh's ambition appeared to morph into revenge. Apparently obsessed, Shapleigh became more determined to prove that a cheating scandal occurred. Attorney Richard Jewkes provided evidence in a sealed motion to the United States District Court for the Western District of Texas. Jewkes' motion revealed Shapleigh's manipulation to create a cheating scandal.[12]

Bringing in the federal government

Jewkes wrote the motion in order to be released from representing assistant superintendent James Anderson, one of the main defendants who was indicted and tried on this case. Highlighting the facts behind the deceitful origin of this investigation, Jewkes revealed that he rented an office in Shapleigh's building and that Shapleigh had asked Jewkes for advice in the latter months of 2010.

Specifically, Shapleigh wanted to know how to get a legal entity to take the charges he was aiming at EPISD more seriously. By this time, Shapleigh had exhausted his opportunities with any state entity, including the local district attorney. Jewkes advised Shapleigh to seek assistance at the federal level, specifically with the FBI as they were the only entity that could pursue such a complex case, given the revenue and personnel it would require. For this advice, Shapleigh paid Jewkes $1.00 as a retainer for his services.[13]

A few days after this encounter, Shapleigh invited Jewkes to a meeting he set up with two FBI agents, Thomas Murray and James Griego. For clarification, this was before the FBI was assigned to investigate.

During this meeting, Shapleigh allegedly presented his story to the agents, along with some documentation. Jewkes then divulged that a subsequent meeting took place again with the same participants. In this meeting, Shapleigh shared more of his evidence and findings of what he claimed were the disappearing students of Bowie High School.

It was after these meetings that Shapleigh formally asked for the assistance of the FBI. Amazingly, the basis for the request concerned "the disappearing students," despite the fact that this allegation had already been disproven and would ultimately never become a foundation for any of the indictments.

At the beginning of the federal investigation—December 2010—the USDE was the main investigatory entity working separately from the FBI. The investigation focused on grade level placement, specifically in and out of the 10th grade. No one was questioning whether students disappeared or not; rather, there was attention given to where these sophomores were placed.

In the USDE's final report, they found impropriety with two schools: Bowie and Coronado. At both schools, it was noted that some grade placements occurred erroneously. Bowie's errors were more numerous than Coronado's. In fact, Coronado had only three errors. But the USDE did not conclude that the errors at either school occurred because of cheating.

The USDE planned to give a report to include "best practices" that the schools should use in order not to make these same mistakes in the future. Although all of EPISD's high schools were investigated, these were the only two that were mentioned in the official report.[14] The USDE emphasized that these errors would be typical of any high school across the state of Texas. Specifically, the USDE asked TEA to provide guidance to all school districts in the state of Texas to prevent continued errors resulting from TEA's previous guidance and policies.

By June 14, 2011, the EPISD central office administrators and the school board were relieved with the report and they were verbally assured that the investigation was just about concluded with EPISD and the state of

Texas, with TEA receiving a corrective action plan to ensure it was complying with all federal and state requirements.

It was almost the end and Eliot Shapleigh was about to be told again—now from the United States Department of Education—that his allegations had no merit. Yet, as with all the bewildering twists in this case, that is not what happened.

Chapter 8: Adding timber to a dying fire

A bomb dropped just as the investigation was about to end. Whether intentional or serendipitously, the FBI discovered around May 2011 that superintendent Dr. Lorenzo Garcia had steered a $450,000 no-bid contract to his former love interest in Houston. The money used for the contract came from Title I funds, the federal source intended to serve economically deprived students.

The product did not significantly aid education and its value was not deemed to be worth the price of the contract. Furthermore, Garcia apparently gained financially from this transaction. The paper trail for this discovery appeared legitimate, and it halted the FBI's and the USDE's departure from EPISD.[1]

This turn of events allowed the FBI and Shapleigh to get something out of this investigation, even if it wasn't related to cheating. Special agents James Griego and Tom Murray were working with Assistant United States Attorney (ASUA) Debra Kanof. As a prosecutor, Kanof had a reputation for doggedly ripping through cases and defendants.

This no-bid contract allowed Kanof to gather the grand jury for the purpose of indicting Garcia. Garcia, aware of the evidence against him, didn't attempt to defend himself.

But keen and calculating, Kanof saw Garcia's quagmire as a way to keep the cheating scandal alive, and it worked. Kanof was successful in getting a grand jury to indict Garcia on the no-bid contract. Interestingly, he was not originally indicted for cheating.[2] Although Kanof had the evidence for the no-bid contract, the cheating evidence was non-existent.

Garcia's arrest

On August 1, 2011 Garcia had a planned meeting at EPISD central office for all the principals in the district. By the end of the day, Kanof and her agents had him under arrest. Former EPISD Assistant Superintendent James Anderson was at the meeting.

"That morning, people were circulating rumors that Garcia might be arrested. We found out later that FBI agents had been texting informants Mike Salcido and Michael Wormack," Anderson said. "It was a pretty typical meeting. Garcia shared a joke and presented his information. The meeting was over early, so we went back to Central Office to work on material for the media and information for the FBI."

Garcia called Anderson to Chief of Staff Terri Jordan's office, and the three of them gathered there.

"Terri was at her desk. As I am sitting there, I see a bald guy looking through the window. Terri gets up to investigate as Murray, Griego and three other agents come in," Anderson said.

"I'm thinking, 'here it goes,' so I put my hands on the table so that the agents could see them. Garcia stands up, they put the cuffs on him and empty his pockets. He tears up a little bit and asks if Terri could take his wallet and keys, so she took the items. He asks Terri, 'Can you call my attorney [Jim Darnell] and let him know that I've been arrested?'"

Anderson believes that the FBI had alerted the media and said that there were about 20 agents present for the arrest. However, this arrest would be less dramatic than the post Easter perp walk some of the defendants would undergo almost five years later in downtown El Paso.

The arrest forced Garcia to resign from the district. The 2011-12 school year was tense since the FBI was still upturning stones in search of a cheating scandal. They conducted many interviews with teachers and administrators in the district and, in some cases, it was more like an interrogation than an interview. Paranoia was high and trust between colleagues withered. The eye of the investigation was focused on Bowie High School and its principal, Jesus Chavez. Multiple audits were being conducted at Bowie and The *El Paso Times* ensured that EPISD and Bowie were spotlighted.

No longer was the cheating about "disappearing students." There was now a new focus from the FBI. It is important to note that the FBI agents had no background in education whatsoever. But that didn't stop them from accusing district employees of committing illegal acts that were not illegal.

The new cheating allegation was that the district was illegally offering credit recovery classes. At first, the agents believed that the mere offering of classes for students to recover lost credit was illegal. It took months for the agents to accept that not only was it not illegal, it was mandated by both a state and federal law.[3]

Once that was established, then the agents maintained that the way the recovery classes were implemented constituted illegality. Again, through agonizing explanations of education codes and laws, the agents were forced to reluctantly accept that the district was indeed following the law.

When Garcia resigned, EPISD chief of staff Terri Jordan replaced him as interim superintendent. Jordan had been a district employee for over 25 years and had risen through the ranks, starting as a teacher, moving to principal and ending up as the chief of staff for the district. She worked to make peace and wanted the FBI to end their investigation and allow the district to move forward. But pressure kept mounting on Jordan, and because of the constant allegations coming from the FBI regarding practices at the high schools, and at Bowie High School in particular, Jordan appeared to feel the need to prove that the district was responding to its critics.

On April 24, 2012, on the advice of Dr. Gary Brooks, her mentor and a paid consultant, Jordan held a press conference where she admitted that the district had some practices that needed to change.4 In this conference, she announced that Jesus Chavez, the Bowie High School principal, had been placed on administrative leave as the district researched the alleged questionable practices he was allowing at the school.

Though the press conference was intended to diffuse tension, it only fanned the flames and brought back to life a fire that was dying. Appallingly, it was later discovered that Brooks had been working with the FBI at the time he recommended the press conference to his protégé.5 At the beginning of June 2012, less than two months after Jordan's press conference, Lorenzo Garcia pled guilty to the no-bid contract. He also pled guilty to a charge of cheating that was never a part of the original indictment. He entered a plea bargain whereby he would pay a fine of $186,000 and serve three and a half years in federal prison.5

The backstory is that Garcia had no problem with pleading guilty to the no-bid contract, but he did not want to plead guilty to any type of cheating because, simply, he didn't cheat. But Kanof had boxed him into an offer that would reduce what would otherwise be a long prison sentence. At the time of Garcia's plea agreement, it was generally known that the initial offer entailed that if he had pleaded guilty to the no-bid contract, but not to cheating, Kanof was going to seek something in the neighborhood of 20 years in prison, a $450,000 fine, and an indictment against his current domestic partner, also an educator, and had formerly been employed by the district. If he pleaded guilty to both counts, however, then Kanof would only seek the deal Garcia accepted. Taking advantage of the human response to protect loved ones, Kanof not only used this tactic against Garcia, but would go on to threaten the sons of both defendant Nancy Love and potential witness Lupe Lucero in a similar fashion.

Remarkably, within less than a week of Garcia's guilty plea, a letter signed by many prominent members of the El Paso oligarchy/PDNG; Beto O'Rourke, Veronica Escobar, Susie Byrd, Steve Ortega, Dee Margo, Paul Foster, Woody and Joshua Hunt among others, was sent to the EPISD school board voicing their concerns with the issues in the district.[6]

Citing the guilty plea, misrepresenting that Garcia had pleaded to the debunked Shapleigh allegations and falsely lumping in two previous EPISD board members convicted a few years earlier on unrelated charges, the letter proceeded to demand a change in how EPISD board members were elected. The group insisted the board implement a majority election system and do away with the plurality system that had been in place for years. Their argument stated that the plurality system "protects incumbents" and cited an *El Paso Times* article from the previous month which indicated that two sitting board members were reelected though a majority of district voters did not want them back.

Given the enormous ramifications of the superintendent's guilty plea, why would the manner of board member election be the primary issue for such prominent members of the community?

It is easy for the average person to believe that Garcia would plead guilty if it entailed a significantly lighter sentence, but difficult to grasp the idea that he would plead if he was actually innocent of either one of the crimes. He pleaded, therefore he is guilty is the prevailing wisdom. To the legal mind and the average citizen, that act in and of itself indicates obvious guilt. Lawyers and judges see this every day and the uninitiated citizen generally believes in an inherently just system.

However, for those who have actually been caught in the catch 22 of that particular kind of pressure bordering on psychological torture—as were Love, Lucero and others—surrender in such a situation is akin to the decision to put a beloved pet out of its misery. The accused comes to a determination, often out of severe depression and anxiety, that there is no other way and that it is better to end the suffering and move on.

This particular case, including Garcia, has at least four other examples of individuals who capitulated to the insurmountable pressure of the FBI, the US Attorney and the overwhelmingly negative media exposure: Myrna Gamboa, Damon Murphy, Maria Flores and Vanessa Foreman. Gamboa, who pleaded in October 2014, did not expect to have to testify and, when called upon at the last minute, allegedly proclaimed that she had been made to sign a false statement and would not testify to what was written.

Only two of the remaining three were on the prosecutions witness list and were actually called to testify. All three, however, were later allowed to rescind their guilty pleas two years after the mistrial as the absurdity of the case finally arrived at its logical conclusion. It begs the question: Were these individuals actually guilty of a crime or simply convinced under pressure that they had done something illegal which, in actuality, would make them victims as well of a broken system that overwhelmingly favors the state?

With Jesus Chavez placed on administrative leave and Garcia admitting guilt to cheating, the case had new life. In fact, FBI agents Murray and Griego allegedly designated the EPISD Cheating Scandal as the "case of our career." With Garcia's admission, the agents freely told anyone they were interviewing that cheating absolutely occurred because the former superintendent had admitted to it.

Chapter 9: Renewed life, new allegations

El Paso's news media feasted on the fodder. Eliot Shapleigh (who was no longer a senator) gave a press conference where he said that the investigation was not over just because Garcia had admitted guilt. Shapleigh proclaimed that there were other "cancers" in the district that needed to be extracted.[1]

The *El Paso Times* was the most ardent media outlet to cover what was now deemed the cheating scandal. During this frenzy, the *Times* attempted to report on students who had allegedly been hurt by the scandal. A phrase emerged that was strategically placed in every subsequent article by the *Times*: "The cheating scandal had denied an untold number of students the right to a proper education."[2]

A real number was never attached to this statement, nor were there any legitimate examples of even one student who was hurt by EPISD due to misconduct. Nonetheless, the editorial staff of the *Times* called for all EPISD school board members to resign their positions, alleging that the board allowed such a travesty to happen under Garcia's leadership.[3]

> *"There is no fire without smoke, but there is often smoke with no fire."~Christine de Pizan*

Despite the frenzy, no evidence ever surfaced to indicate what the supposed cheating entailed and, remarkably, the general public believed the lie. There were copious clouds of smoke, but no fire. Without a fire, the cheating scandal was going to die, and if the cheating scandal was going to die, then the south side neighborhood of El Paso would not face eminent domain.

If that neighborhood didn't face eminent domain, then the El Paso Downtown Redevelopment Plan would be halted, if not scrapped altogether. If there was no redevelopment plan, then the developers were set to lose their investments. The dominoes could not be allowed to fall in that direction, so the cheating scandal had to continue.

Susie Byrd, a local politician on the El Paso City Council who was known to be extremely close to Eliot Shapleigh and best friends with Bob Moore, the editor of the *El Paso Times*, formed a Political Action Committee (PAC) named Kids First Reform EPISD. Purportedly, this was a group to represent El Paso's needs in the aftermath of Garcia's reign.

This "representative" group was comprised of over 40 middle-aged white women from the affluent west side. The PAC's donors included a who's who list from the PDNG with names that included Beto O'Rourke and his mother Melissa.[4]

No one knew it at the time, but this PAC was going to be cited as the group that was representative of the citizens of El Paso to justify changes made before the end of the calendar year. In hindsight, it is easy to understand why Byrd, a city council member, concerned herself with the school district. But at the time, it was curious as to why she wanted to involve herself in refueling an investigation that had no real evidence of wrongdoing. Nevertheless, she became a prominent figure in the movement to continue the investigation into EPISD.

At the last EPISD board meeting for August 2012, Byrd spoke during open forum.[5] She called for the board's resignation and then demanded that they keep investigations continuing on schools so that the community could know the full extent of the scandal. In particular, she called for full audits of El Paso High and Austin High.

This request came out of left field. Neither high school had ever been implicated in the alleged cheating scandal from any entity that had investigated the district; Shapleigh had been the only accuser and his allegations had been deemed groundless by TEA and the USDE. Echoing Shapleigh's sentiment, the *El Paso Times* had printed negative articles about Austin High and, like Shapleigh, they failed to provide any real evidence.

No one from the media questioned why Byrd was making these allegations and no one ever questioned the source or legitimacy of her information.

To give the media more fodder, another board meeting occurred in October 2012 where Susie Byrd was now on the agenda, along with El Paso County Commissioner, Veronica Escobar (who eventually became the El Paso congresswoman in the US House of Representatives, replacing Beto O'Rourke).[6]

Byrd, this time with Escobar at her side, addressed and accused the board members of being incompetent, once again demanding that they resign. In addition, she insisted that the board hire an auditing firm for El Paso and Austin High Schools to check for possible cheating. The words coming from Byrd's mouth were inspired by Eliot Shapleigh's now defunct website where he accused the district of denying an education to poor Hispanic students.[7]

Corresponding to this open forum presentation was an item on the agenda for that night: a proposal to hire an auditing firm.[8] It was a firm that came to be known simply as the Weaver Group and no other company was allowed a chance at the contract. Ironically, the Weaver Group won a no-bid contract that night much like the one that Garcia gave to his former lover. But instead of getting indicted for it, the board had the support of Byrd, Shapleigh, and The *El Paso Times*. During the deliberation, a board member asked why they needed an auditing group when they already had TEA, the FBI and the USDE in the district.

Byrd interrupted the discussion, blasted a board member with the words, "Why are you not wanting to be transparent!"

One didn't have to look far to ascertain why the Weaver Group was being recommended. Adam Jones, now a leader of the Weaver Group, was a colleague of Eliot Shapleigh.

The duo worked together on the state education committee when Shapleigh was a senator and Jones was part of the administrative elite of TEA. Jones retired unexpectedly from TEA in May 2012 and then became the head of the Weaver Group audit for EPISD in October 2012.

Financially, this contract was worth over $1 million to Weaver. Ironically, during his time as a TEA officer, Jones was the auditor overseeing TEA's investigation of EPISD that had exonerated the district in October 2010.[9] The mercenary character Jones demonstrated, first clearing EPISD when he was with TEA, then finding wrongdoing when he was on the payroll of the Weaver Group, seemed to be indicative of every investigator, politician and journalist who involved themselves in this sordid narrative.

After winning the no-bid contract, the Weaver Group set up offices in the main building of EPISD's central building. Weaver hired former FBI agents to conduct the audit and these auditors worked closely with the FBI agents who were investigating the district. Of course, that violated all ethical standards of an independent audit, but that was the process encouraged by the FBI/DOJ.

Simply stated, the Weaver Group was hired to establish a "factual" basis for the cheating scandal. Since Shapleigh's original allegation was null and void, there could be no indictment based on its lack of merit. Thus, Bowie High School was still open without any sanctions, which meant that the south side neighborhood could not be deemed as blighted and the land for the redevelopment could not be purchased.

With the FBI most likely orchestrating the Weaver audit, there was a motivation to uncover a deep cheating scheme in the district. To add drama and credibility to the audit, TEA was being pressured by the FBI/DOJ to comply with the cheating scandal investigation. At this point, TEA had already cleared EPISD twice of wrongdoing.[10]

It is presumed that, as a result of that, the FBI/DOJ began to accuse TEA of incompetence and, perhaps, corruption. Fearing for their own viability, TEA began to willingly comply with the narrative that had been scripted for them.

The drama continued to strengthen in December 2012 when Susie Byrd used her PAC to represent the alleged desires of the everyday average citizens of El Paso. That was the same PAC whose members had little in common with the El Paso population. Allegedly, the PAC claimed to the state authorities that something had to be done about EPISD's scandal. The Commissioner of Education was a new appointee from outside of Texas named Michael Williams.

Williams, a former federal prosecutor, bowed to the political and legal pressure and held a news conference to proclaim that he was replacing the entire elected school board of EPISD. The replacements for the elected officials were recommended by individuals with a vested interest in the downtown redevelopment project and appointed by Williams. Of the five appointed managers, Carmen Arrieta-Candelaria, Dee Margo and Ed Archuleta (a quorum) were known members of the PDNG.[11] To top it off, EPISD's academic accreditation was put on probation status by TEA. The increasing pressure caused Terri Jordan to resign from the district.

Vernon Butler, a retired educator who had worked most of his career in the El Paso area, was the interim superintendent who had been on the job for a few months by this time. Though Butler had moved to the Dallas-Ft. Worth area, he accepted the offer to run the district until a new superintendent was hired.

But Butler was no random choice. In fact, as with most of the actions taken in this case, the decision to bring in Butler was highly calculated.

Prior to Butler's hiring, long-time educator Ken George became the interim superintendent in the summer of 2012, when Terri Jordan relinquished her position as interim superintendent back to chief of staff. George, seasoned and well respected, had worked with many districts.

"The FBI and TEA came in and told Ken George to fire 14 specific people, but he refused to fire anyone without evidence," Assistant Superintendent James Anderson said. "So, they had to get rid of him."

Anderson contends that Butler was put into place by Jimmy Vasquez, the head of Region 19, Richard Dayoub from the El Paso Chamber of Commerce and the Hispanic Chamber of Commerce. All these people are associated with Shapleigh and Sanders and the Paso Del Norte Group. In essence, the PDNG pushed for Butler.

In addition, TEA Monitor/Conservator to the school board, Judy Castleberry, fully supported the decision to bring in Butler. She was not pleased with George's unwavering refusal to terminate pre-selected individuals. In fact, Castleberry herself pushed for her former TEA colleague Adam Jones and the Weaver Group to be hired and questioned why Ken Parker and the district had used "the same audit firm for the last ten years."[12]

When George refused to fire Anderson, Jordan and twelve others without evidence, in essence, he signed his walking papers. After a few weeks on the job, George was ousted. "TEA was violating everyone's due process rights," Anderson said. "Here's the head of the state telling the district what to do, without any investigation, when that should come from the school district itself."

This made it impossible for these educators to receive fair treatment and due process from the Texas Education Agency when it was the Agency who was bringing the charges and would, in turn, be in charge of any related hearings. Effectively, TEA would be both the accuser and the judge.

Butler was in EPISD's top position, and most likely, members of the oligarchy breathed a sigh of relief. It is important to note that after Butler completed his tenure at EPISD, he worked with the Weaver Group.

In a matter of 14 months, EPISD had been stripped of its leadership. The former superintendent was in prison. Interim superintendent Jordan had resigned, leaving education altogether and George was fired. Anderson was being pressured to resign or be terminated (he resigned). The school board was removed. Who was left running the district? The FBI/DOJ, the Weaver Group, and the consulting citizens of Susie Byrd, Eliot Shapleigh, Veronica Escobar, and Beto O'Rourke, none of whom had any background in educating students and all of whom had a stake in the downtown redevelopment plan. This complete overturn of personnel was accomplished with no concrete evidence to support the cheating allegations.

Lots of smoke. No fire.

The Weaver Group

December 2012 continued to be a stressful and eventful month. The Weaver Group began its interrogations of school employees before the Christmas break.

In response to Williams' decision to replace the elected school board, the board showed strength as they hired an attorney to represent them and they sued to fight their removal. It was a decision that would allow them to remain in place until their matter would be settled with a TEA hearing.13 However, by May 2013, the board was officially ousted.

By the end of January 2013, the Weaver Group had completed their investigation. Their next act was to present the results in writing of a complete forensic report to indicate if cheating occurred or not. No one was expecting an exoneration. Many people in the district were calling this audit a "witch hunt" that would allow Eliot Shapleigh to save face. At the time, no one—not even those being interrogated—knew how far the oligarchy would go to convince the public of a cheating scandal.

By the end of March 2013, the Weaver Group produced its report. The week after spring break, on March 26, eight campus administrators— out of a few dozen—who had been questioned by the Weaver Group were called into Central Office for a meeting with Robert Almanzan, the Associate Superintendent in charge of Human Resources. These individuals represented five of the district's 11 high schools, including Austin, Bowie, Burges, El Paso and Irvin.

The individuals included:

• Austin: John Tanner (principal) and Mike Salcido (assistant principal);

• Bowie: Juan Duron (assistant principal);

• El Paso: Kristine Ferrett (principal), Grace Runkels (assistant principal) and Adrian Bustillos (assistant principal);

• Burges: Randall Woods (principal);

• Irvin: Luis Loya (principal).

These eight were put on immediate administrative leave and told it was because of the findings in the Weaver Report. When asked what the findings were, they were told by EPISD Human Resources that they were not at liberty to discuss that information. Instead, the Weaver Report was being released to the news media, and it was there that the administrators could discover the allegations against them.[14]

No due process. No question and answer session to allow the accused to answer the allegations. In addition, the administrators were informed that they were on the agenda for the board meeting that was taking place on April 2, 2013; they were being recommended for termination based on the report that they were not allowed to view. The administrators were also informed that they were not going to be allowed time to speak in their defense to the board members or to the public at the board meeting.

In support of Principal John Tanner, Assistant Attendance Clerk Lupe Lucero and Principal's Secretary Danna Sadler found themselves victim to the terrorist-style interrogations and harassment that became the standard for the FBI/DOJ in this case. Using Lucero's son as leverage, the FBI attempted to intimidate her into lying to fit their narrative. Sadler believes the stress contributed to the early death of her husband. *photo courtesy of Austin Publications*

Keep them in the dark

From March 26 to April 1, those placed on administrative leave were left wondering what was going to happen, especially since they were not allowed to know the allegations against them.

The Weaver report was advertised as a "forensic" audit, indicating a thorough investigation. Considering that the audit examined a district with over 90 schools and more than 60,000 students, one would expect a forensic report to be in the range of 350 pages.

The Weaver Group managed to compile their report in 86 pages. Eighty-six pages for $800,000, which, before including the extra fees charged, ended up as a final bill of over $1 million. That is $9,302 per page for a report that emphasized Lorenzo Garcia's guilty plea in the very first paragraph as its primary evidence of cheating, offered a pittance of forensic evidence to support anything else and was replete with grammatical errors, misspelled names and allegations that had no facts to support what turned out to be rumors.

Large sections at the beginning of the report were simply copied and pasted to fill the pages at the back making the actual cost per page significantly higher. Some passages were used in more than one section. One of the teachers from Austin said, "The Weaver Report reads like a soap opera." As a professional publication, the Weaver Report was a disaster, but that didn't keep the oligarchs from using it.

The report highlighted 34 EPISD current and former employees who were alleged to be derelict in their duties or acted in ways that could be considered criminal. Bowie High School was mentioned prominently as was its former principal, Jesus Chavez, who had already resigned from the district.[15]

The allegations against Chavez were the closest the report had to any real scandal. His tactics to improve Bowie High School utilized uncommon practices but nothing he did was illegal, and he had all of his practices approved by TEA before he enacted any of them.

However, Chavez, for reasons unknown went to the FBI and DOJ and eventually "confessed" to wrongdoing. But even his confession didn't lead to his indictment, since there was nothing criminal about any of his actions. However, he reportedly told multiple people his goal was to use those agencies to seek retaliation on Terri Jordan and James Anderson.

The report concluded that there was an active scheme in the district that accounted for the academic improvement over the last four to five years among many schools. Though the report contained some truth, information was manipulated. Those who were not educators or aware of the law were not likely to understand the verbiage or the practices.

It is important to note that the methods used by EPISD high schools were legal and encouraged by the Texas Education Agency. In fact, these very methods were used all over the state, yet no other district was targeted. What the Weaver Group, and eventually the FBI and the DOJ, was calling a scheme was anything but. In fact, the methods were not only approved by TEA for every campus and district, but they were also mandated by law.

One of the most outrageous allegations was aimed at Dr. John Tanner, principal at Austin High School. It alleged that Tanner liberally reinstated credit for many students who had academically passed a class, but lost credit due to poor attendance. TEA allowed a principal to act in this manner (in fact, TEA highly encouraged the practice), but the Weaver Group claimed that Tanner committed a grave error of "not using a correct form to authorize the reinstatement of the credit."[16]

For the record, TEA did not require any type of form to be used for reinstatement and Tanner utilized a form that had been used all over the district for this purpose. [17] But the use of this form, according to the Weaver Report, provided grounds for termination and possible legal action.

The allegations aimed at the other administrators who were slated for termination were also without merit, but implied that something sinister had taken place in the district. As the story would eventually unfold over the next few years, the Weaver Report would be exposed for its slander, innuendo and ignorance about the public education system.

At the time, however, and to this day the news media of El Paso has not questioned anything coming from the Weaver Report, nor did it question the motivation of EPISDs' accusers, namely, Shapleigh, Byrd, Escobar and the rest of El Paso's governing officials. Instead, the media plastered pictures of those about to be terminated on the front pages of newspapers and as the lead stories on the local television stations.

As a popular principal, Tanner was committed to getting students into four-year colleges. Over the years, Tanner's students were accepted to many state colleges, as well as MIT, Emory and West Point. "Those who concocted this cheating scandal ended this process," Tanner said. *photos courtesy of Austin High School Publications*

Each administrator who was placed on leave (and informed of his or her impending doom) was told to seek an attorney. All of them did, and each attorney told their clients to expect termination at the April 2 board meeting. In addition, the attorneys told their clients not to attend the board meeting. These administrators were living in a nightmare not of their making.

On the morning of April 2, the city of El Paso had already been privy to the Weaver Report. The media's spin now focused on the board meeting that was to take place that evening.

What had been predicted as a cut-and-dry meeting where eight administrators were to meet their demise, resulted in an outcome that no one forecasted.

None of those set for termination attended the board meeting, as they all followed the advice of their attorneys. The auditorium was filled, standing room only, with throngs of people lined up outside the door. The number of chairs in the auditorium sat 350 people. However, there were at least 150 more individuals standing around the perimeter of the room and sitting in the aisles. There were more spectators outside the auditorium than were inside. TV monitors were placed outside the auditorium so that the overflow crowd could witness the meeting. Depending on who was reporting, the crowd estimate was anywhere from 800 to 1,500 individuals.

The board meeting began with open forum. At a typical board meeting, three to five people speak, with a time limit of three minutes per speaker. But this wasn't a typical board meeting. Pages and pages were filled with the names of citizens waiting to address the board. Miraculously, many El Paso citizens did not approve of what was happening, and they came to show their support to those being recommended for termination. Students, parents, teachers, and citizens from all walks of life signed up to speak.

It was a highly unusual event, considering that this was one of the last meetings where the school board was a valid and legal entity, and it was rumored that the night of April 2 was to be their last meeting.

Because the commissioner of education and TEA had lost trust in this board to do its job, Judy Castleberry, who had no familiarity with El Paso, was named monitor, and it was her job to ensure proper procedure was being followed at the meeting. Though Castleberry was condescending and contemptuous toward the elected board, she seemed to be professional and cordial with the interim superintendent, Vern Butler.

Throughout the night, students spoke of how the administrators were mentors and hard workers for their schools. Parents voiced the same accolades. Various citizens also cited that what they had read from the Weaver Report amounted to no evidence for the proposed terminations.

After 30 minutes of open forum, Castleberry interrupted and tried to retroactively invoke a 30-minute restriction. The audience was outraged. At this point, something extraordinary happened. The board found its voice and stopped fearing TEA, Castleberry and Butler.

The elected board members knew they were in their last days. Their appeal was denied, and they were going to be replaced by an appointed Board of Managers. But they knew they were elected by the people and they knew that what they did in the meantime still carried weight in the eyes of TEA and the law governing public schools. That night, they understood that it was their votes that counted, not Judy Castleberry's or Vern Butler's.

Board trustee Alfredo Borrego asked Castleberry for 30 more minutes so the public could finish speaking. Castleberry wanted to confer with the board president privately on the matter.

But instead, the meeting recessed, and she spoke with the entire board. When the meeting resumed, board member David Dodge made a motion to listen to all speakers who had signed up. The board agreed unanimously. The crowd cheered as Castleberry pursed her lips.

Open forum took four hours to complete. From the published minutes, 77 citizens spoke.[18] All were in favor of the administrators keeping their positions, except for one absent voice. Susie Byrd had signed up to speak, but most likely, when she saw the support for the administrators, she left the meeting. When her name was called, she was nowhere to be found.

Of those 77 speakers, 45 were specifically speaking on behalf of Austin High School. That community came out to support the improvements that had been made over a period of four years. Other speakers spoke regarding other schools. Still others spoke about their misgivings of the Weaver Report, especially considering a letter that had been printed in the *El Paso Times* by the former Chief Financial Officer (CFO) of EPISD, Ken Parker.[19]

Parker had recently retired from the district. Strong armed into hiring the Weaver Group in his last days on the job, he was disgusted by the group and their report. When Parker saw the injustice that was proposed for this board meeting, he wrote an open letter for the world to read.

The purpose of Parker's letter, published in the *El Paso Times,* was to expose the unethical, if not illegal, way the Weaver Group was chosen. He strongly suggested that the Weaver Group audit was merely a tool to justify the termination of at least 14 employees that TEA wanted out of EPISD, as per the recommendation of Eliot Shapleigh.

Shapleigh was no longer an elected official and had no title or employed position in the city that merited his input on any personnel matters in EPISD; however, in this political climate, that didn't seem to matter.

The community, in all its diversity, came out that night. They were students, teachers, parents, grandparents, and community members; they were Anglo, Hispanic, African American, Asian, and Indian; some spoke English perfectly while others struggled and some needed translators because they only knew Spanish. What they all had in common was their support for the administrators who had changed their schools for the better.

Students spoke about the changed environment of their schools from places of violence to places of higher learning. The following comments were some of the many.

"Our principal is the heart of this school."

"I have never seen a weekend go by without seeing Dr. Tanner's car in the parking lot."

"I have been a coach and teacher at Austin for decades and I have never seen as much peace and harmony at the school as when Tanner was there."

"Tanner was able to take a community of students from all different backgrounds and ethnicities and make it into a family."

Former students testified to how they went to college even though that had never been their plan until these administrators told them they were college material. The comments went on and on. Tears welled up when one student gave an account of how Tanner purchased clothes for him when he saw him wearing shorts in the winter.

"When he called me into his office, I thought I was in trouble for a dress code violation," the student said. "I couldn't believe that Tanner had figured out that I just didn't have the money for clothes. He bought me clothes and wanted nothing in return. Who does that?"

On Good Friday, 2013, students hold up a banner in school colors of brown and gold to get their principal, John Tanner, reinstated on campus. Built in 1929, Stephen F. Austin High School, created in an old Spanish mission architectural style, opened its doors to students in September 1930. In a twist of irony, the school, built by R.E. McKee Construction Company, originally intended to serve white students. Today, it is a school proudly teaching students of all races and ethnicities. *courtesy of Austin High School Publications*

Austin parent Dolores Tapia delivered one of the most memorable moments. Tapia was an Austin graduate back in the early 1980s and now she was a parent of Austin students. She was fair, but demanding, and only wanted the best in academic preparation for her children. Tapia was critical when necessary and complimentary when she saw good things happening. Overall, she loved the direction Austin was going under Tanner's direction, as did her children.

Simply put, Dolores Tapia is not an introvert. When she speaks, people listen. As she began to speak, she noticed that Vern Butler was not paying attention to her; in fact, he was having a private conversation with Judy Castleberry.

"Excuse me, sir," she called out, but Butler didn't notice. "Excuse me, sir… Mr. Butler…excuse me," Tapia repeated until she got his attention. "Are you not listening to what is going on? I am a taxpayer and this is a very important meeting. You need to be paying attention, especially considering how much we, as taxpayers, are paying for your comfortable salary."

The audience clapped and burst into cheers. Butler was red-faced and faked a smile. He then assured Tapia that he was paying attention.

At the end of open forum, the board met privately for over three hours. They returned to the public setting at 11:07 p.m. to announce their decision. Only one of the eight recommended for termination was actually terminated. The remaining seven were reinstated into their positions.

Clearly, the way the day ended was not the way the day had been planned. The board made its statement. But Butler and Castleberry's expressions indicated that this was far from over.

It was later learned in FBI and TEA discovery disclosures that the Weaver Group was told by TEA, months before the district even knew an audit was going to be requested, that they were going to get the job.[20]

Emi Johnson, a top official in TEA had assured them they had the job even before they were made an approved vendor for the school district. It is important that the public know that EPISD never wrote the contract for the Weaver Group.

It was secretly written by the Texas Education Agency and presented as if it were the work of the EPISD School Board.[21] It is documented that Judy Castleberry, Vern Butler and the FBI directed the Weaver Group about what to find before they even conducted the audit.[22] In essence, the conclusions were determined before the company ever set foot on district property.

Chapter 10: What should have been the end

The day after the board meeting, the seven administrators who had been reinstated went back to their jobs with no other notice than the result of the Board meeting the night before. Most campuses welcomed their administrators with open arms.

The Austin campus was especially celebratory. They planned a huge welcome back rally for Tanner in the football stadium, and it was attended by the school's population of about 1,600. The news media was there to cover the event.

Cameras were everywhere and the pictures and footage remained in the El Paso media for at least a week. Tanner could not get away from reporters. He gave interviews on the football field, in his office, and in the school's parking lot as he would arrive to and from work.

By the weekend, he couldn't go anywhere in town without being noticed. Even when he went to Sunday mass, a person he did not know approached him in the Communion line to offer his congratulations, as he let Tanner know that he had been praying for him.

For the most part, the media was playing nice and described Tanner repeatedly as "the very popular principal" or "the very popular and charismatic principal." Oddly, Tanner was the only one reinstated who was getting the press attention.

But by Friday, April 5, Tanner received a warning. An unnamed source informed him that this was far from over and that he had better be careful because his reinstatement had angered many powerful people and they had bonded in their fury. Tanner was told by a board member that Shapleigh was furious and wanted his head on a platter.

Until this reinstatement, it is important to note that neither Tanner nor Austin High School had ever been implicated in the cheating scandal. Outside of the Weaver Report, Austin had never been mentioned negatively in any official report.

But now, the plan for the cheating scandal was in tatters, and along with it, the redevelopment plan. With the reinstatement, the cheating allegations should have ended. Should have, could have, but didn't. While Eliot Shapleigh's ego may have been bruised somewhat, there was a bigger issue at stake.

The dismissing of the allegations and the reinstatement of administrators meant that there was no closing down of schools, no eminent domain for the purchase of real estate for the downtown redevelopment plan and no *Equipo* Bowie to run that high school.

In addition, the FBI/DOJ and the Weaver Group spent millions of tax dollars to prove, unsuccessfully, a vast conspiracy of an alleged cheating scandal that never happened. After nearly three years, only Lorenzo Garcia had been convicted of any crime, not by a jury of his peers, but rather by a plea deal he had accepted. The oligarchs had one hope left.

Chapter 11: Setting up the Hail Mary pass

"The minute that the FBI begins making recommendations on what should be done with its information, it becomes a Gestapo."~J. Edgar Hoover

As Americans, we grow up believing that the FBI is one of our sacred entities, a bulwark of truth and justice. Yet, in this case, that expectation was turned on its head. Scheming in a manner that they would later accuse the defendants of doing, three members of the DOJ—FBI agents James Griego and Thomas Murray, along with Assistant United States Attorney, Debra Kanof—began to spin a thread that would jeopardize the freedom and livelihood of educators who simply wanted to be good citizens. The very people who were supposed to protect the innocent and maintain the integrity of the justice system became the creators of the crime.

Protecting an abuser

It was a warm Thursday afternoon, Sept. 22, 2011, and Dr. Tanner was in his secretary's office around 3:30 p.m. using a device that placed messages on an outdoor electronic marquee.

Without warning, a senior student (whom we will refer to as Student X) entered the office. His personal story had been an uphill climb. When he began at Austin, he had come from a rough middle school where he had some disciplinary issues.

His older brother, with more serious issues, also attended Austin. During his freshman year, he was often judged by the faculty and staff as being "just like his brother." And this was for good reason: this student was no model citizen. His infractions were not serious, but they were annoying.

Yet for his flaws, he had potential, especially in math. His standardized scores placed him in the 75th percentile of the state, and that was before significant effort. There was more than met the eye. With positive reinforcement and acknowledgement of his talents, he became a regular on the Honor Roll, was on the baseball team and became a valued participant with the Mathletes (competitive math team). By the end of his junior year, he had been inducted into the National Honor Society, and by senior year, the student had his eyes on college.

Student X needed to get a good scholarship and financial aid to be able to seek higher education, and the possibility of that happening was real. By the end of his senior year, he qualified for the UTEP Promise where he was guaranteed full tuition. He graduated in the top 10% of his class and had received the recognition of being one of the best students in his graduating class.

The incident Student X was about to report on that early autumn afternoon involved Ruben Cordero, the automotive shop teacher. When it came to discipline, Cordero had a history with a lack of impulse control. During Tanner's second year at Austin, in the fall of 2009, Cordero was involved in an incident that resulted in a permanent discipline record in his file.

Cordero claimed that he thought a student was taking a controlled substance, which he believed justified him physically handling the student. He grabbed the student's throat, making the young man spit out what was in his mouth. It turned out to be a blue piece of chewing gum. The student's neck was bruised and a report was filed on Cordero. He kept his job, but he was warned that a future incident would result in termination.[1]

Student X was shaking as he entered the office.

"What's wrong?" Tanner asked with concern.

"Mr. Cordero almost ran me over," he replied.

"What?"

"Mr. Cordero tried to run me over," he repeated.

"With a car?"

"Yes, sir."

According to the official statement made by Student X, the baseball team was moving equipment, blocking the pathway, as Cordero was attempting to park a car into the garage. Again, Cordero's impulse control became an issue. The following is the statement written by Student X:

> *"At about 3 pm, the baseball class was walking toward the weight room, when Mr. C (auto shop) starts honking, we turn around and it was him in his Silverado, and an old Taurus car. We all moved aside to let them by, I was carrying a big blue baseball net, and moved to the side after the Taurus (driven by I don't know who) passed by and parked. We all bunched up to squeeze by. We all heard the engine being revved and tires skidding on the rocks. The*

truck driven by Mr. C hits the blue net I am carrying, making me stumble while the mirror hits my arm. He puts the truck in park, mumbles to himself, comes over directly to me and starts screaming in my face, 'Don't you hear me honking? That means to get the fuck out of the way, this is my fucken [sic] driveway, so you move. This car is breaking down and you are over here acting stupid trying to show off.' I replied with, 'I don't think it is right for you to try and run me over.' He then laughs and says, "If I wanted to hit you, trust me, I would have done it."[2]

After Student X described the encounter, Tanner called in a report to Child Protective Services and turned the investigation over to Mike Salcido, an assistant principal in charge of discipline. Salcido verified Student X's account through student witnesses and one adult witness.

Following protocol, the investigation was handed over to Chere Williams (pronounced Cherry), the district investigator at the Office of Employee Affairs. Immediately, Cordero was removed from the Austin campus and placed at Pupil Services at Central Office while he was under investigation. Within a few weeks, Williams conducted her own inquiry and concluded that Cordero did indeed commit the alleged assault.[3]

There's an old joke in education that asks, "How can a principal get rid of a bad teacher?" The answer: "You have to witness a teacher purposely run over a student in the school's parking lot." With a punch line for reality, Tanner had no doubt that a recommendation for Cordero's termination would be granted without hesitation. But he was wrong.

Nine months after the incident, on June 14, 2012, Williams called Tanner to her office for a meeting that included Cordero and his attorney. Presenting the full findings of her investigation, Williams found that Cordero committed the infraction and he was considered a serious danger to students. At this point, in a decision that seemed illogical, Williams gave Tanner two options: Tanner could either allow Cordero to return to Austin as a teacher, or he could pursue termination.

"I wondered if this was a trick question," Tanner said, "and I was seeking termination. Cordero purposely tried to run over a student, and everyone was lucky that it didn't happen."

As a condition of his principal's certification, Tanner had the legal and ethical responsibility to keep his campus safe.[4] Had he allowed Cordero to return to campus, Tanner could have faced charges for dereliction of duty, particularly since he already knew about Cordero's anger management issues. Not surprised by Tanner's decision, Cordero's lawyer tried to persuade the automotive teacher to resign instead of being terminated. Tanner left Williams' office confident about the termination.

Cordero was set to be discharged of his duties in August 2012, but that didn't happen. When Tanner was informed that the termination had been obstructed, he called Williams, demanding to know why. Williams told Tanner that he and Austin had lost some of her paperwork regarding Cordero and that was going to result in Cordero returning to campus. It was outrageous. However, the motivation behind this turn of events would not be explained until years later at the mistrial.

While Tanner saw Williams' claim as a stalling tactic or an attempt to blame someone for her mistake, luckily, Austin personnel were able to retrieve copies of the paperwork that Williams claimed had gone missing. But that didn't change a thing. Even with that resubmission, Cordero was still employed with the district, working for Mark Mendoza.

Mendoza was the head of Pupil Services. It was district protocol to reassign an employee who was under investigation for misconduct with students while the investigation was pending. This kept students safe and allowed the employee to maintain employment while he was being afforded his due process rights. Unbeknownst to anyone at the time, Mendoza was an informant for the FBI. It was learned through discovery after the mistrial that Mendoza was creating and manipulating data, which had been turned over to the FBI as official audits.

The year continues

The year bumped along with various reports related to the alleged cheating scandal, but nothing regarding Austin High. In this stressful climate, the Educators' duties didn't stop. Needs Assessment, a process that helps to prepare for the upcoming school year, was coming up. Decisions would need to be made regarding the budget and staffing of teachers.

On Monday, March 11, 2013, two days before Needs Assessment, Austin Assistant Principal Diane Thomas, who was in charge of curriculum and instruction, received an email from Teresa Thompson. Thompson was the acting chief financial officer for the district, having just replaced Ken Parker who retired from the position. Thompson's role with Needs Assessment was a numbers game only. She informed campuses regarding how many teachers they could and could not have, according to the budget.

The Austin faculty had already been informed that the school would have to cut three positions. In the email that Thomas received that Monday morning, Thomas was told by Thompson to prepare to cut six to eight more positions, so the administration would have to come up with ideas at the Needs Assessment meeting so that the cuts could be made.[5]

Two days later, on March 13, Thomas and Tanner went to the Needs Assessment meeting for Austin at Central Office. Thompson, along with many other district officials, was present, and by all accounts, the process went smoothly. There were few questions and everyone in the room signed off on the decisions that had been made. Some key decisions were made:

- Ms. Halliday, the speech teacher, would remain in her current position. Halliday was an eccentric teacher who became an FBI informant. She accused Tanner and other administrators of malfeasance over the years, all of which was proven to be false.
- The auto shop program would be discontinued, something administrators had been looking at for years. The program was expensive, and the students could take the class with more qualified teachers in a state-of-the-art setting at the district's Center for Career and Technology Education (CCTE) campus. Eric Winkelman, the CCTE director, had made this suggestion for at least three of Tanner's five years as principal at Austin, so it should not have been an issue.

A few other positions were cut, but no major surprises. It is important to note that it was the auto shop program that was cut, not the teacher. By this time, Ruben Cordero had been away from the campus for almost two years. There was every reason to believe that he was going to be terminated. Simply put, cutting auto shop was a good move for Austin and for the district.

After Needs Assessment was complete, Tanner and Thomas were relieved, but they knew that they had to get the information out to the campus in order to be ready for the following year. The conclusion of this meeting was less than three weeks before the April 2, 2013 bombshell of a board meeting that had removed Tanner and other administrators.

When the reinstatement happened for the seven administrators, the scandal should have died. But too many entities had too much to lose for it to go away. AUSA Kanof and her two agents, Murray and Griego, looked for another avenue. Though Halliday was not being displaced, she felt that the Austin administration was out to get rid of her, and well, Cordero was always ready for a fight. They were the perfect patsies.

The focus changes to retaliation

So Plan B, or the Hail Mary pass, was rolled out. The objective was to go after Tanner and Austin High School, in particular. Without seeking to become a public figure, Tanner had become one. He was all over the news and the press was reasonably positive about him at that point.

Plan B dictated diverting the attention from the alleged cheating scandal to another accusation altogether. The focus became retaliation, starring Jeannette Halliday and Ruben Cordero. The plan was to blame Tanner for retaliating against these two individuals because he "knew" that they were FBI informants.6 It was implied he was trying to get them off the campus to save himself. Though accused, Tanner was never asked by anyone—a superior, law enforcement or the media—for an explanation in defense of the actions he took.

Overall, the accusation didn't make sense. Tanner respected the law, and the FBI investigating his school made him that much more scrupulous. Nothing in his background indicated that he was a rule breaker or a vindictive individual—it was quite the opposite, in fact.

But Tanner was never allowed the chance to speak for himself. It was a developed plan, and moreover, it was protected by the oligarchy. The nightmare that he thought ended on April 2 took on new life. It was a scene out of Kafka's *The Trial*.

Alleged retaliation against Halliday

The accusation went like this: Tanner, along with Diane Thomas, retaliated against Halliday because they had planned to get rid of her through Needs Assessment because of her known cooperation with the FBI. What made it "clear" that it was retaliation was because Halliday "felt" that it was happening.

The reality was that Tanner and Thomas had been told by central office personnel that Halliday was protected and that any actions toward her, no matter how innocuous, could be interpreted as retaliation. For the record, there was never a plan to displace Halliday in any way. By Needs Assessment, Halliday was clearly on the Austin schedule for the following year. That was set in stone on March 13, 2013.

In May 2013, after the bombshell April 2 board meeting, Halliday told the FBI that she believed that she was a target of Tanner's retaliation. Note that her conversation with the feds occurred after it was clear that Halliday's position was secure at Austin.

Yet, Halliday seemed to believe that she was a target of retaliation. That fear was fueled by Austin counselor Liz Saucedo, who was alleged to be an extraordinarily close friend of James Griego, one of the main FBI agents investigating EPISD. On April 25, Liz Saucedo set up a meeting with Halliday to address the speech teacher's concern with the schedule for the following year. Allegedly, when Halliday told Saucedo that she was worried about her schedule for the following year, Saucedo answered by saying, "You need to know that they are trying to get rid of you."

"Who's they?" Halliday asked.

"Tanner and Thomas," Saucedo said.

In response to her fears, Janette Halliday, became an informant for the FBI. But it should be clear that Liz Saucedo intentionally planted this fear in Halliday's head. Her position had never been cut. This begs the question as to why would Saucedo do such a thing? Who told her to do it? Why was this being done after Tanner had already been reinstated at the April 2 board meeting?

The FBI was finding a way to keep the cheating scandal relevant. Clearly, there was no retaliation against Halliday.

Alleged retaliation against Cordero

If the alleged retaliation against Halliday was not false enough, then there was the allegation of retaliation against Cordero. Cordero had not been on the campus for nearly two years. He had been reassigned to Central Office because he was a danger to students.

He had already been recommended for termination and as far as anyone knew, he would never be allowed back at Austin High School or in front of any students ever again. Why would anyone think differently? He tried to run down a student intentionally.

"The truth that is suppressed by friends is the readiest weapon of the enemy."~Robert Louis Stevenson

But after Tanner was reinstated in early April, he began to see a different scenario unfold. In mid-May 2013, Tanner was informed by Patty Cortez, director of employee relations, that there was a grievance against him, filed by Ruben Cordero. The allegation was that Tanner eliminated the auto shop program because he was retaliating against the shop teacher because he knew that Cordero was an informant for the FBI.

The thought was so ridiculous, that when Cortez first told Tanner, he began to laugh. She told him that it wasn't funny, and it was a serious accusation. Tanner asked how it could be taken seriously since Cordero wasn't a teacher at the campus and was supposed to be terminated because he was a danger to students?

The director of employee relations said that Cordero's termination had not been determined, to which Tanner replied, "Yes, it has been. I have the documentation that was produced by your department. Your investigator, Chere Williams, concluded that Cordero tried to purposely run down the student. Your investigation clearly stated that he violated the code of conduct as described by TEA. Your department called CPS on him and CPS found validity in the complaint. What do you mean that it hasn't been determined?"

Tanner was understandably upset. He then asked Cortez, "When did Cordero supposedly become an informant for the FBI? Was this before or after he tried to run down the student?"

Cortez, who up to this point had been a friend of Tanner's, suddenly became cold, as she answered, "You are not allowed to ask that question and I am not at liberty to tell you."

"What do you mean?" Tanner asked. "I can't know when he became an informant to determine if there is any truth to this?"

"You heard me. You are not allowed to ask and I am not at liberty to tell you. You cannot violate his rights. It is illegal for you to even ask."

"His rights? The one who could have killed a student? His rights? What about my rights as the one falsely accused?"

Cortez ended the conversation and gave Tanner the meeting time and place for the grievance hearing for later in the month.

During the grievance hearing, Cordero's attorney was present via a phone call. This was not the same attorney that had recommended that Cordero resign his position. This was a new attorney from Austin, Texas from a firm that handled many educator cases against TEA.

Additionally, an attorney representing the school district was present, and Cortez was the hearing officer. Basically, she heard Cordero accuse Tanner, without evidence, that Tanner knew he was an FBI informant.

Tanner repeated that he had no idea, and that it wouldn't matter anyway.

"First, Cordero isn't a teacher on the campus and the program being moved was a separate issue. Secondly, Cordero is a danger to students. When did Cordero become an informant for the FBI?" Tanner asked.

"That is none of your business and you are not allowed to ask the question," Cortez said as a repeat of what she told him a few weeks previously.

The grievance hearing ended and Cortez said she would have her results within 10 days, as required by the guidelines of education law. Cortez did not have the results within 10 days. In fact, Tanner was never given the outcome of the grievance.

It would not be until February 2014—nine months later—that Tanner learned of Cortez's decision through an open records request of his personal information from EPISD. In that stack of information, there was a report that paraphrased Cortez's statement that there was evidence that Tanner was aware that Cordero was an FBI informant as per Cortez's conversations with Liz Saucedo, the alleged close friend of the FBI investigator.

At the beginning of June 2013, Tanner received a call from Robert Almanzan, associate superintendent of Human Resources. He called to inform Tanner that Cordero was going to be back on campus beginning in the fall. Tanner said, "Over my dead body."

"Why would you say that, John?"

"Where do I begin, Robert? First, we don't have an auto shop program anymore. Second, he was recommended for termination and I was led to believe that was going to happen. By the way, why hasn't it happened? Third, if he is fit to come back to campus, then I need a written statement saying such before I allow someone back that I know is a safety risk to students."

"Who told you that he was going to be terminated?" Almanzan asked.

Tanner interrupted.

"What the hell? Are you kidding me? You are going to act like this is brand new information? He has been at Central Office for two years because you all removed him from the campus because he was a danger. This is well-documented, Robert."

"Well, John, we don't have a place for him and CCTE won't take him. We need to put him somewhere," Almanzan answered, his voice becoming calmer.

"That place isn't Austin. Legally, he can't come back. And legally, you can't make me take him back."

Damned if you do, damned if you don't

If TEA or any regulating authority could prove that Tanner knew Cordero was a danger to students, but still allowed him back on campus, the Austin principal could have been held criminally negligent, especially if Cordero hurt a student again.

Tanner was damned if he didn't take Cordero back because then he would be accused of retaliation by the FBI, although the FBI knew that was false. However, Tanner did not know this was the FBI's plan until much later. He knew something sinister was happening, but he couldn't imagine it was as bad as it turned out to be.

Weeks and days—even a single day—became important in this case. It wasn't until June 2017 (at the time of the mistrial) that Tanner and his attorneys discovered why they were never given the date when Cordero went to the FBI as an informant.

In his grievance, Cordero claimed that Tanner had retaliated against him for being an informant one week before he had ever spoken to the FBI. Additionally, Cordero filed his grievance the very day he would have been put on the board agenda for termination.[6]

Who and what led Cordero to make such an allegation? Tanner already knew that Cordero's original attorney had advised him to resign because the deed he committed was so damning. But Tanner and his legal team believed a plan was set into motion by the FBI with the help of Mark Mendoza, director of pupil services.

Mendoza started working with the FBI when they entered EPISD in December 2010. Cordero, when removed from Austin in September, 2011, was placed in Mendoza's department at Central Office. Over the next two years of working together, Mendoza and Cordero had plenty of time to become acquainted. It would be a logical conclusion that Mendoza arranged with Cordero to save his job by claiming retaliation.

Helping Cordero solidified Mendoza's loyalty to the FBI and it created a way for the FBI to keep the cheating scandal alive.

At that point, EPISD's Board of Managers and legal team were seeking to terminate Tanner for retaliation against Cordero. Tanner's attorney, Tiger Hanner, filed a records request for documents that EPISD then gathered. EPISD's legal team discovered that Cordero became a witness for the FBI a full week after he'd made the claim in order to save his job.

It is clear that these documents would have cleared Tanner and others of any retaliation. Instead of providing those documents, Bruce A. Koehler of EPISD's legal team sought guidance from AUSA Debra Kanof as detailed in their emails to each other:

From: BRUCE A. KOEHLER
Sent: Thursday, September 05, 2013 01:21 PM Eastern Standard Time To: Kanof, Debra (USATXW) Cc: Murray, Thomas J.(EP)(FBI) Subject: Open Records Request to EPISD from John Tanner's attorney

> *Dear Debra, Similar to the Diane Thomas Open Records Request, the El Paso Independent School has also received the attached request from John Tanner's attorney. I understand that there is an active federal investigation involving John Tanner. As such, I enclose a copy of the Public Information Act request to the El Paso Independent School District from his attorney. We have previously provided to you responsive documents relating to the investigation conducted by EPISD in to allegations about activity at Austin High School. Would the release of EPISD's investigative file (apart from records previously reviewed and signed by Tanner) interfere with the detection, investigation, or prosecution of a crime? If so, an exception to disclosure may apply under Section 552.108 of the Texas Government Code. Please let me know. If you have any questions, please do not hesitate to call.*

Thanks, Bruce. Bruce A. Koehler Mounce, Green, Myers, Safi, Paxson & Galatzan, P.C. P.O. Box 1977 El Paso, Texas 79950

Kanof Responded:
From: Kanof, Debra (USATXW)
Sent: Thursday, September 05, 2013 11:30 AM
To: BRUCE A. KOEHLER
Subject: Re: Open Records Request to EPISD from John Tanner's attorney

> *Sorry I have been slow in responding. I am on leave. I do believe the release would impede the FBI's investigation on both individuals. Unfortunately, part of the conduct under investigation*

may include intimidation of witnesses, which may rise to a felony obstruction of justice. Please seek the exceptions. Thank you

Koehler then responded in kind:
From: BRUCE A. KOEHLER
Sent: Thursday, September 05, 2013 05:25 PM Eastern Standard Time
To: Kanof, Debra (USATXW)
Subject: RE: Open Records Request to EPISD from John Tanner's attorney

Thanks Debra. We will need to provide your response to the Texas Attorney General's office. I wanted to make sure that is acceptable. It is possible the AG would release to the requestor. Let me know.

Bruce. Bruce A. Koehler Mounce, Green, Myers, Safi, Paxson & Galatzan, P.C. P.O. Box 1977 El Paso, Texas 79950

Kanof's direct response:
From: Kanof, Debra (USATXW) Sent: Thursday, September 05, 2013 11:15 PM To: BRUCE A. KOEHLER Subject: Re: Open Records Request to EPISD from John Tanner's attorney
Yes. Its ok.

Koeler: From: BRUCE A. KOEHLER
Sent: Friday, September 06, 2013 3:38 PM
To: 'Kanof, Debra (USATXW)'
Subject: RE: Open Records Request to EPISD from John Tanner's attorney
Thanks Debra. I understand this applies to both the Diane Thomas and John Tanner requests, correct? Thanks, Bruce

Bruce A. Koehler Mounce, Green, Myers, Safi, Paxson & Galatzan, P.C.
P.O. Box 1977
El Paso, Texas 79950

And later Koeler sent this:
From: BRUCE A. KOEHLER To: Kanof, Debra (USATXW) Cc: Murray, Thomas J.(EP)(FBI); S. ANTHONY SAFI Subject: RE: Open Records Request to EPISD from John Tanner's attorney Date: Monday, September 9, 2013 10:53:58 AM

Debra, This is to confirm my conversation with FBI Special Agent Tom Murray, who indicated that he conferred with you this morning, and the answer to my last question is yes and that the your office is requesting that EPISD withhold the referenced documents in both the Thomas and Tanner Open Records Requests. Thanks, Bruce

Bruce A. Koehler
Mounce, Green, Myers, Safi, Paxson & Galatzan, P.C.
P.O. Box 1977
El Paso, Texas 79950

This withheld exculpatory evidence later became the reason the retaliation charge was dismissed with prejudice after the mistrial. Based on the aforementioned emails, it was clear as of June 2017 that the following people knew about this date discrepancy from its inception:
1.Agent James Griego (FBI agent)
2.Agent Tom Murray (FBI agent)
3.Debra Kanof (AUSA)
4.Bruce Koehler (attorney for EPISD)
5.Tony Safi (lead attorney for EPISD)
6.Clyde Pine (attorney for EPISD)
7. Vernon Butler (interim EPISD superintendent)
8.Dee Margo (former president of the Board of Managers; current mayor of El Paso)
9.Patricia Cortez (director of employee relations who collected the documents) 10.Robert Almanzan (associate superintendent of Human Resources, who has since left the district to work in HR at El Paso Electric)
11.Chere Williams (district investigator) For so many to be aware of this clear injustice highlights a very powerful force that encouraged withholding of evidence that would have exonerated five innocent people.

An unholy trinity: the weak, the fearful and the corrupt

Through power and intimidation, the oligarchs were able to summon an unholy trinity of sorts: the weak, the fearful and the corrupt. Each of the names above fits one or more of these categories. Without these characteristics that one would find in the medieval Seven Deadly Sins, the oligarchy would not have been able to continue.

But the truth is, the 11 knew that the defendants were innocent, yet they kept the truth hidden. If they followed the news, the 11 knew that the educators were facing prison time, but they did nothing. The 11 looked out for themselves and allowed for those they knew were innocent to be publicly shamed, professionally discredited and financially ruined. The 11 bear a deep responsibility.

"Silence in the face of evil is itself evil."~Dietrich Bonhoeffer

Interim superintendent Vern Butler's role deserves special attention. Initially, Tanner believed that Butler didn't know what he was doing when he put Cordero back on the Austin campus and that he was merely following the orders of the FBI agents. After all, Butler presented himself as an upright man of God. For years, Butler put forth the following mantra: "First, you do what is right for the students. There is no rule after that." But there was no place for that mantra regarding the Cordero reinstatement.

Butler had power and clout. If he had said something was wrong, most likely people would have listened, but instead, he was compliant and complicit with the scheme.

Further, in the position of the top educator for one of Texas' largest districts, Butler had a duty to be informed about the legal happenings of the district. EPISD attorneys Tony Safi, Bruce Koehler and Clyde Pine were certainly aware of the legal issues and it was incumbent upon them to share that information.

In addition, Texas state law mandates that Human Resources share any information about an employee before termination can take place. Finally, all terminations must go to the school board and Butler would have to be informed. Therefore, on many levels, it is safe to say that Butler knew all the following information when he put Cordero back on campus:

- That both the district and Child Protective Services had found Cordero culpable of child endangerment.
- The district was about to terminate Cordero with good cause. The district's legal department had already cleared the way for that action.
- There was a timeline that exploded all accusations of retaliation. Instead of revealing these facts, Butler actively hid them.

Diane Thomas's interview with the FBI

On June 10, 2013, the FBI called Austin Assistant Principal for Guidance and Instruction (G&I), Diane Thomas, for an interview. Her position was integral to the school and was as stressful as the principal's position. Basically, she oversaw the master schedule and worked to ensure that the counselors were abiding by all district and state mandates for academic instruction.

For a school with as many needs as Austin High, the job required at least 60 hours per week. Thomas had been in education nearly 25 years at the time and had already worked at Austin for nearly a decade. However, she had held this particular position for less than a year, but she was dedicated to her craft and wanted Austin students to have the best education possible.

When she was called for the FBI interview, Tanner warned her not to go. After Tanner's experience with the Weaver Group and because of almost losing his livelihood, he no longer trusted any investigator. Tanner also believed that the FBI was trying a new tactic to keep the cheating scandal alive by utilizing the Cordero grievance.

Those wanting a cheating scandal had their efforts thwarted when the EPISD school board reinstated the seven administrators, including Tanner. They were most likely working desperately to salvage their plans. Tanner strongly believed that using Diane Thomas was part of their strategy.

They don't want the truth: they want you repeat what they have contrived as the truth

However, trusting soul that she was, Thomas believed the worst was over and thought Tanner was paranoid. She naively thought that her interview with the FBI would bring the entire cheating scandal investigation to a close. She said, "All I have to do is tell the truth and everything will be OK."

Tanner warned her to look at others in the district who had believed the same thing but found out quite differently later. Tanner said, "They don't want the truth. They want you to agree to what they have contrived as the truth." Thomas went to the interview but took her attorney with her.

Rarely does the FBI allow an interviewee to have an attorney present. Often, if the interviewee insists on the presence of an attorney, the

FBI refuses to conduct the interview. Under no circumstances will the FBI allow an interview to be recorded. If there is an insistence on a recording, the meeting will not occur. Oddly, Thomas' attorney was allowed.

Thomas was not prepared for what happened. She was interviewed by Griego and Murray for six hours. For six hours, they tried to get Thomas to say that Tanner told her that Austin needed to get rid of Halliday because she was an FBI informant. For six hours, they tried to get her to say that Tanner eliminated the auto shop class because he knew Cordero was an informant for the FBI. In addition, they were accusing Thomas of trying to allow an ineligible student to graduate illegally.

> *"I am answerable to a higher authority than you. I will not lie."~Diane Thomas*

Though she may have been naive, Thomas was not weak. At every juncture, Thomas would not admit to what she was being coached to say. Agent Murray became aggressive by making faces and exhibiting anger when Thomas would not give him the answers he wanted. Agent Griego, playing good cop, told Thomas that if she complied, all would go well for her. Thomas answered that she was complying because she was telling the truth.

At one point, Murray told her, "You are answerable to us." Thomas replied, "I am answerable to a higher authority than you. I will not lie."

Tanner saw Thomas after she met with the FBI. It was around 7 p.m. in the evening at the school. They were both busy with end-of-year tasks and the upcoming graduation. Thomas was distraught and she was instructed that she could not tell anyone, especially Tanner, anything. She only let Tanner know that she had to continue the interview the next morning.

The next day, June 11, she returned for her interview. This time it was only 20 minutes. It wasn't until June 2017 (at the time of the mistrial) that Tanner and the other defendants discovered exactly what had occurred at that meeting. The only thing Tanner knew was that they threatened Thomas when Murray said, "You will see what happens to people who don't cooperate with us."

The morning of the so-called second interview, the FBI presented Thomas with a confession form admitting that she was acting to get rid of Halliday and Cordero under Tanner's alleged directive. Further, the confession said that Tanner gave that directive to Thomas because he knew that Halliday and Cordero were informants for the FBI. Thomas refused to sign it.

In June 2017, defense attorneys revealed that the confession form was written by the FBI agents *two weeks before* their first interview with Diane Thomas.

By the end of June 2013, Thomas was removed from the Austin campus by EPISD administration and reassigned to Central Office. She was directed not to speak to Tanner. Tanner was not privy to the exact actions of the FBI, but he knew that the FBI was after him. He believed this was the oligarchy's reaction to his being reinstated with so much public support.

Tanner is removed

On August 15, 2013, Tanner was called into EPISD's Central Office and was informed that he was once again on administrative leave, due to an ongoing investigation regarding his alleged retaliation against Halliday and Cordero. The news media was informed, and once again, Tanner was all over the news.

Considering the manipulation of the FBI and of Kanof, it is not surprising that the media did not report on any aspect of the Cordero angle. In fact, the *El Paso Times* has never reported on Cordero's abusive behavior or the EPISD and Child Protective Service's findings that Cordero was a danger to students. Further, they have never reported that Cordero had been convicted of battery against a family member. He was only mentioned as a victim of retaliation.

Of the hundreds of reports about this case, Cordero was only exposed in one media story, and only for a few minutes. On Sept. 5, 2013, television station KTSM broadcasted a report on the late news. This news report covered the demonstrations at Austin High School by Tanner's supporters.

Outspoken and active, they made clear that they wanted Tanner reinstated as the principal of Austin. Prior to the demonstration, a KTSM news reporter, Jackie Crea, had obtained the district report detailing Cordero's criminal actions toward Student X and she reported that she had the document. Crea also interviewed Student X, who by this time had graduated from the school. The student confirmed the story and expressed support for Tanner to be reinstated.

That was the only time the report aired. It was never to be seen again and it was not available on the web. When Tanner's attorneys tried to subpoena that broadcast, KTSM claimed that the file with the report was corrupted and could not be retrieved. Contacting Student X, EPISD officials, and Tanner's attorney Tiger Hanner, Crea had done her due diligence and checked sources. Yet she never received a lead story again in El Paso and soon after, moved to a news station in Houston. When contacted by Tanner's defense attorneys to verify the broadcast, Crea said that she didn't remember the story. Even after the conclusion of the case with all charges dismissed, Crea remains reticent to comment.

By mid-August 2013, both Tanner and Thomas were on administrative leave, and with their removal, Cordero was reinstated to the Austin campus. Though Cordero was never reevaluated as to whether he was fit to return, he arrived with no paperwork and no official signatures to signify that he had been evaluated and determined as safe for students.

Mark Tegmeyer and Nancy Love, the two remaining administrators at Austin, were incensed. Fulfilling their moral and legal duty to keep the campus safe, they actively resisted the shop teacher's return.

Tegmeyer submitted a grievance against the district and Love consulted with law enforcement to see what could be done to keep this danger off the campus.

While Tegmeyer and Love received support from the campus community, they did not get backing from the district. Within weeks, Tegmeyer resigned from Austin and took a job in another district at a lower salary so as not to be part of the corruption of Superintendent Vern Butler, Robert Almanzan and those conducting the investigation. Love asked to be reassigned to another campus and her request was granted.

Love's testimony before the grand jury

Nancy Love was subpoenaed to testify before a Federal Grand Jury on September 26, 2013 regarding the alleged retaliation and the cheating scandal at Austin High. At this point, Love did not seek the advice of an attorney. She saw no need as she was still confident in the system at that time. Love fulfilled her civic duty to testify and she told the truth.

But Debra Kanof was running the Grand Jury and Kanof did not like what Love had to say. After her testimony, Kanof told Love that she had committed perjury. Love had a son who went to Austin High School and Kanof claimed she lied to protect him. Kanof went so far on this allegation that she eventually declared Love's son as a witness against his own mother.

Love's son was 18 at the time and he was served a subpoena in Austin High School's parking lot.

Assistant principal Nancy Love, along with her son Ryan, attended the rally. Ryan was a senior and valedictorian for the class of 2014. Because he spoke out against what was happening, the FBI targeted him, going so far as to declare him a witness against his mother. Love was forced to hire an attorney for herself and another for Ryan, despite the fact that he was only a high school student who dared to call the DOJ into question. *photo courtesy of Austin High School Publications*

Tegmeyer's interview that didn't happen

Also, in October 2013, after he had left Austin in protest, Tegmeyer was contacted by the FBI. The agents wanted to have an "interview" with him regarding Tanner. Tegmeyer agreed to the meeting but stated that he wanted his attorney present and wanted the meeting recorded. Agent Griego said he would get back with him soon. Tegmeyer was already aware of the FBI tactics in this case and in other cases and did not want his words misconstrued. He also knew that the FBI would never agree to the conditions.

Three weeks later, the FBI returned the call to Tegmeyer's attorney. They informed the attorney that the interview was no longer requested and that Tegmeyer was now a target of the investigation.

"I didn't understand what being a target of the FBI meant at the time. I knew it was serious, but I hadn't done anything. I was nervous, but at the time, I couldn't imagine where it would go," Tegmeyer said. "When my attorney gave the letter to me in 2013, it didn't sink in how acerbic and nasty Kanof was. She was just ugly. I was nervous for three years. I didn't hear anything until the spring of 2015."

(For clarification, Tegmeyer received the aforementioned letter in 2013. In spring 2015, Tegmeyer received another letter informing him of a probable indictment. That indictment did not occur until April 2016.)

It was ludicrous that Tegmeyer was now labeled a target. He had only been in EPISD since March 2010, his arrival almost simultaneous to the time that Shapleigh had made the allegations against Austin. Further, he was a new assistant principal who was learning the job, under the nose of the TEA monitors who were assigned to Austin to ensure that the school was implementing best practices in order to meet all state and federal mandates.

The only individuals who ever said Tegmeyer cheated were Kanof and her minions, Murray and Griego. Not the Texas Education Agency. Not the USDE. Not the Weaver Report. Not the Office of Inspector General report.

But Tegmeyer knows why he came under the gun.

"I became a target of the investigation because of my friendship with John Tanner," Tegmeyer said. "I have become convinced that they wanted me to try and turn on John. It's all a psychological thing."

Leading off the March 2013 rally to reinstate the administrators who had been removed, Austin Assistant Principal Mark Tegmeyer spoke to the students, faculty and staff. "Though the press was there, I never spoke to the them specifically. I speaking to the community, telling people that we needed some kind of justification," Tegmeyer said. "We didn't see any reason why the administrators had been removed. They were denied due process, and the school district needed to listen to the community, which was crying out for justice." At the time, Tegmeyer who had been at the school for three years, had no idea that he, too, would become a target for the FBI and DOJ. *courtesy of Austin High School Publications*

A life overturned

Tanner was trying to survive, trying to find answers, trying to figure out what life would be like outside of education, so he was not fully aware of what was happening with Tegmeyer and Love at this time. Instead, in the back of his mind, Tanner hoped this nightmare would end with him remaining as principal at Austin, but the signs were pointing in a different direction.

It was now December 2013 and the elected board had been removed. Upon the recommendation of Susie Byrd's PAC—Kids First, Reform EPISD—a new Board of Managers was appointed by Michael Williams (a former federal prosecutor), who served as the appointed Commissioner of Education for the state of Texas.[7]

Williams had publicly stated that EPISD had a culture of cheating and that he had listened to the El Paso business community instead of the constituents in making the decision to remove the board.[8] Not one member was elected by the district's constituents and all were members of the business community. The unelected Board of Managers all lived on the west side of El Paso and all touted that they were going to make EPISD great again. Dee Margo, a Republican and prominent El Pasoan, was the chosen leader for this board, and this was largely due to his wife's political connections. Curiously, Margo also held over 10,000 shares in the Borderplex REIT.[9]

At the EPISD Board meeting in December 2013, Tanner and Thomas were on the agenda for a proposed termination.[10] This time, open forum was not allowed. Tanner's supporters were still present, but not in the numbers seen in April. While the news coverage before the meeting was minimal, after the board meeting, it exploded.

The board—which included three PDNG members—unanimously agreed to recommend termination for Thomas and Tanner from the district for allegations related to retaliation. (Interestingly, at the next Needs Assessment for Austin with Tanner and Thomas out of the way, the auto shop program was discontinued at Austin. The reasons were the exact same as Tanner's reasons the previous year.)

Thomas was given the option to resign from the district, and she did so by the end of March 2014. Discouraged, Thomas had not fared well at the TEA hearing, which was later discovered to have been rigged against her. TEA is supposed to function as an independent entity, but at Thomas' hearing, TEA officials were illegally taking their cues from the FBI.

This is critical because the five TEA attorneys associated with the EPISD scandal no longer work for the agency. Perhaps this is due to indications of unethical behavior in this case regarding their work with the FBI.[11]

Tanner was forced to resign by the end of May 2014, having taken the option to wait on a TEA hearing until he was free from any FBI action. Thomas did not follow that process, as she likely did not anticipate that she was going to remain a primary FBI target.

At the time, neither Tegmeyer nor Love had reason to believe that they were going to become FBI targets. After all, they had absolutely nothing to do with any allegations of the cheating scandal. Their names had never been mentioned regarding the scandal and neither educator was working in the district when the contrived "cheating scandal" was birthed years earlier.

But they had both been hired by Tanner, and they were known to be loyal assistant principals and ones who refused to bear false witness. Desperate to take down Tanner, the FBI targeted those closest to him and turned them into defendants. Evidence wasn't needed. If there was a real retaliation case, it should have been filed against the government, as Kanof and her agents victimized those who wouldn't turn on Tanner.

Chapter 12: Changes in the district

With all of the former Central Office administrators gone—either due to resignation, termination, or pleading guilty to a cheating scandal that never existed—EPISD completely changed just prior to Tanner's removal in August of 2013.

Without the elected Board of Trustees, the new Board of Managers gave the district a new format for conducting business. At best, it became a formal process. At worst, it was dictatorial with little influence from the public allowed. Dee Margo was the new Board president who set the new tone.

The best description of Dee Margo comes from a quote attributed to Barry Switzer: He was born on third base, but he tells everyone that he hit a triple. Margo has been an insurance agent in El Paso for his entire professional career and lives a life of affluence. To hear him tell the tale, he did it all by himself. But the truth about Margo's wealth is that he married into it.

Margo is an Oklahoma native who came from an upper-middle-class family. His grades in school were high enough and his talent in football was good enough to land him at Vanderbilt University.

While at Vanderbilt, he met his wife, Adair Wakefield. Adair came from an affluent family in El Paso. Her social circle included her best friend Laura Welch Bush. With this backing, Margo went from third base and scored a run.

With the power and influence from his wife's family, Margo landed a job in his father-in-law's insurance company and used his connections to become a known personality in the El Paso area. Margo is an outspoken Republican in a city of Democrats.

He has longed to be a civic leader with authority, but he was rarely given the opportunity due to two things that don't sit well with general El Paso voters: Republican political leanings and public perception that he was arrogant.

However, Margo has had his bright moments. On one occasion in 2010, he beat Democratic incumbent Joe Moody in the election for state representative. But not to fear, Margo's representation of El Paso, or lack thereof, angered the voters to the point that when he ran again, Moody came back and won the contest, overwhelmingly.

When EPISD was restructuring because of the alleged cheating scandal, Margo was chosen by the appointed Texas Education

Commissioner, Michael Williams, to the Board of Managers of EPISD. It seemed an odd choice. The commissioner was to appoint citizens of El Paso who represented the community and it had been made clear that Margo was not the choice of the people. But Margo was appointed, despite no apparent support from the citizens of the city.

Where are we going to get the day laborers?

Before Tanner was removed from Austin, he had one encounter with Margo after he was appointed to the Board. Ironically, Tanner was chosen to be a district representative on a panel of principals appointed to help familiarize Margo with the needs of the district before he took his position on the board.

At this time, Tanner did not know that Margo had ties to the American Legislative Exchange Council (ALEC), a far-right conservative think tank whose mission is to give corporations a voice in politics. However, ALEC has a more nefarious agenda item: to defund public education in America to the point of collapse. ALEC emphasizes that education should be privatized, as it costs the taxpayers too much to educate the population.[1]

Further, ALEC strongly supports vouchers and charter schools as the tools that will break down the public education system. (Other notable members of ALEC include Texas Governor Greg Abbott, former Texas Governor Rick Perry and Secretary of Education Betsy DeVos.) Despite the fact that Margo and his children attended public schools, he was strongly aligned with ALEC.

"We met in Margo's office in December 2012 shortly after the names of the Board of Managers were announced to the public," Tanner said. "Margo wanted to speak to some school principals to discuss what they thought the direction of the district should be."

In the meeting, Margo asked, "What are some things the district should focus on?"

Tanner was very direct with this question and answered forthrightly, "We need to have our students focus on attending a four-year university as a first option."

"No, you're wrong," Margo responded and was just about ready to change the topic. "Well, sir. I'm not wrong. In fact, it is imperative for those of us with large Hispanic populations…."

Tanner tried to answer but was abruptly interrupted by Margo who stepped toward Tanner and pontificated in a loud voice.

"No, you're wrong. People down in Austin do not agree with you and that's not what they are saying."

Again, Margo was intent on changing the subject, but this was a major initiative in Tanner's philosophy of education on the border.

"What people in Austin are you talking to? Obviously, not the same ones I speak to. Not the educators."

Margo was clearly irritated.

Tanner went on to explain his position, "Texas is already a majority Hispanic state and Hispanics have the lowest educational attainment in the state. It needs to change, and we need Hispanics in four-year schools."

Tanner wanted to continue the discussion and to explain what accomplishments were happening at Austin High School.

But Margo had enough. He cut off Tanner abruptly and exclaimed, "Then where are we going to get the day laborers?!"

Perhaps the limited orbit of Margo's world became most evident at the EPISD Teacher of the Year banquet in May 2013. It was one of his first speaking engagements after being officially appointed to the Board of Managers. His speech focused on his own accomplishments in life and did not include any congratulatory comments toward the teachers who were being honored. He went on to express how the community needed to acknowledge the accomplishments of students who were accepted to prestigious universities in the country.

Did he mention the students from Austin who that year were accepted to MIT, Emory, and Baylor? No. Did he mention students from another district high school who were accepted to Princeton, Columbia, and Harvard? No.

He only mentioned three students, two of whom were his own children who were accepted to Vanderbilt. Granted, a great accomplishment, but he did not mention that perhaps his own children had an advantage because of their parents' legacy at Vanderbilt. Perhaps his children weren't destined to be day laborers.

Complying with the oligarchs

Theoretically addressing the needs of EPISD, the new Board of Managers had the task to hire a superintendent for the district that would replace the interim, Vernon Butler. On paper, the new superintendent was to have all the qualifications one would expect for the position: experience in education, preferably a doctorate in education, and superintendent certification earned through the state of Texas. The job notification was published and qualified applicants applied.

Margo went to Austin, Texas and came back with an announcement that he had found the perfect candidate, Juan Cabrera, an Austin attorney, who had taught middle school history for one year in the distant past. Cabrera did not have a doctorate in education. He did not have a superintendent's certificate. How could Cabrera meet the qualifications required of every other superintendent in that state? Simply put, he couldn't. But he did have some credentials that Margo did not share with the public.

Cabrera, a fellow Republican, was allegedly friends with Rick Perry, the Republican governor. And Margo and Perry were friendly with the American Legislative Exchange Council (ALEC). Forging through the Board of Managers, Margo's cherry-picked candidate was handed the job. Juan Cabrera became the new superintendent of EPISD. He looked like an El Pasoan, but he really wasn't one. Cabrera's connection to El Paso was his brother, Rick Cabrera, an executive and anchor with the local TV news station, KVIA, the most watched news program in El Paso at the time.

Cabrera was hired right after Tanner had been placed on administrative leave; thus, the two men never met. That did not stop Cabrera from commenting negatively about Tanner or complying with the wishes of Margo and the FBI. Cabrera expressed full agreement to get rid of Tanner and never requested to meet him.

New leadership speaks with the Austin community

When Tanner was put on administrative leave in August 2013, he wasn't provided with reasons and any questions he asked were not answered by his superiors at EPISD. Most of the information he discovered was in The *El Paso Times* and through the rumor mill. The Austin community was outraged and they came to Tanner's defense hoping that if they put up another fight, he would be restored to his position. Their efforts were even stronger the second time than the first, but to no avail.

There was a community meeting at Austin High in the gymnasium in October 2013. Cabrera, knowing that there was going to be media present and many questions asked, opted not to attend. The place was packed and the new Board of Managers were there to inform that community about what was happening.

This new board made it clear that they were not there to hear the concerns about Tanner being removed. That did not stop the community from asking questions, nonetheless. But those questions were not answered and finally Margo stopped any inquiry as he blustered with the pomposity of the Cowardly Lion when he sang that he was king of the forest, "Your beloved principal will not be back! Just get used to it."

It took until June 2017 at the mistrial to realize that the Board of Managers—especially Margo—knew that the allegations of retaliation were false at the time he disparaged Tanner to the Austin community. A significant reason for the mistrial was that the prosecutors kept the defense from having evidence (the timeline indicating that Cordero claimed he was an informant for the FBI when he wasn't) that conclusively exonerated Thomas and Tanner from retaliation.

Margo, president of the Board, had to know this. Yet, he willfully encouraged the termination proceedings, apparently having never contemplated that Thomas and Tanner would eventually have access to this information.

Margo was rewarded for his work on the Board of Managers with an endorsement for mayor from the *El Paso Times*, compliments of Bob Moore, the editor. The *Times* covered Margo with praise and showed his picture prominently daily. The other candidates were discredited and rarely named. Even with his press coverage he had to endure a runoff with an opponent, David Saucedo, whom the *Times* barely covered. Margo won the election in June 2017.

Interestingly, Margo was a major investor in the Borderplex Alliance REIT. This alliance is just the renaming of the Paso Del Norte Group. In Dee Margo's biography, he's listed as a member of the PDNG. Once Margo became mayor, he hired Rick Cabrera, from KVIA, the brother to the superintendent he had picked, to manage his business finances. Later, Rick Cabrera was appointed by Margo to manage the city finances pertaining to the downtown redevelopment plan.[2] As mayor, he was able to further the plans of the PDNG.

Reinforcing the narrative

With the Board of Managers taking the lead in the district, along with a new superintendent who was uneducated about public education, the narrative of the cheating scandal was being solidified in the arena of public opinion. The new board, the majority of whom were members of the PDNG, did not hesitate to confirm that a "cheating scandal" occurred, despite no concrete evidence.

The FBI and DOJ yelled loudly that there was criminal misconduct and their voices were amplified by all El Paso's media. Any scenario used as evidence had zero credibility. But the stories were written to tug on people's emotions rather than provide facts to support the allegations.

Using the scandal methodology to sell papers and get advertisers, the *Times* used catchphrases instead of hard evidence. This is evident when reviewing those the *Times* claimed to be alleged victims of the scandal and the alleged motives behind the victimization. Using the ethics of tabloid journalism, the *Times* had reached a point that they didn't need evidence to prove what they were writing. They blamed without facts, and they reported without research or verification.

The *Times* wrote stories on alleged victims who shared common characteristics. They were students who were in the district who had failed many classes and had ultimately dropped out. When they wanted their education to continue, they were denied enrollment at their regular high school because they were older, adult students. But they were all offered a full education by the district at a campus for older students that offered a completely valid high school diploma.

One of the students the *Times* highlighted as a "victim" of the scandal wanted re-entrance to Bowie as a 20-year-old male who had just been released from prison after doing time for a felony assault conviction.

The *Times* reported that this adult student had enough credits to graduate in the spring of 2008. Had that been the case and the cheating real, the school would have fallen over backwards to graduate him, because that was the only way he would have improved their AYP rating. Once he didn't graduate, he remained a mark on the school permanently.

He would not have impacted any other category of data because the time period and initial accusations of the cheating scandal involved manipulation of freshmen, sophomores and juniors between fall 2007 and spring 2010. Furthermore, the article purposely failed to highlight that the school personnel that denied him admission to a school that had 13 and 14-year-old students, worked diligently to get him into a school for older students. The student ended up attending that school and received a high school diploma from EPISD.3 At no point was he ever denied his education.

Finding victims became an issue for those selling the scandal. EPISD placed ads in the paper, on TV and on billboards throughout the city looking for "victims" of the scandal. The district even had personnel go door to door to find victims. After a well-publicized search that lasted at least four months in a district of over 63,000 students no student was identified as a victim of the "cheating scandal." No student was found to have had their rights violated.[4]

Yet, the media had a scandal to sell. Instead of using quantifiable statistics that could be verified, the *Times* chose to use the qualitative phrase of "the untold number of students denied the right to a proper education." It is a phrase to cause outrage of readers' emotions without facts to support the claim.

But the methodology worked. With enough entities proclaiming a scandal occurred without the other side of the story being allowed to have any airtime, the lie told a thousand times became the perceived truth. At the same time, the focus school of the "cheating scandal" was successfully transferred from Bowie High School to Austin High School, due to the manufactured allegations of retaliation.

By Christmas break of the 2013-14 school year, the cheating scandal was back on track by those who fabricated it five years earlier. Thomas and Tanner were on their way to uninvited new life adventures. Tegmeyer had left the district and Love was at another school, creating a complete turnover of administration at Austin at a moment so critical that even the most seasoned administrator would have been at a loss regarding how to continue the impressive progress that had been made over the previous four years.

In the five years Tanner was at the helm, the number of graduating seniors applying for and being accepted into at least one four-year university had risen from 17% to 92%. Violence in the community and school was down significantly and pride was up. Further, the new administration was understandably apprehensive to do much of anything innovative out of fear that it would be construed as felonious behavior.

What no one knew at the time and what was withheld from the defense team was a classified FBI document (now unclassified) that was written on September 20, 2013. In part, it read:

> *CHS [Confidential Human Source] reported Tony Connors, an attorney in Austin, Texas who often represents unionized teachers, advised that Texas Governor Rick Perry is "deeply involved" in trying to prevent the US Department of Education (DOE) from investigating the Texas Education Agency (TEA). Perry fears a DOE investigation of TEA will spread to all Texas independent school districts and reveal the issues currently under investigation within the El Paso Independent School District (EPISD) are*

actually present throughout all Texas independent school districts.[5]

Shockingly, the CHS worked for the FBI. This report revealed that the methodology used at EPISD was employed all over the state of Texas under TEA supervision. Further, Rick Perry, the governor of Texas, was completely aware of that fact. Perhaps Perry was afraid that an FBI investigation into TEA because it could unravel Texas' approach to education and force The Lone Star State to accept the Obama administration's education plan, Race to the Top, which Perry feared would federalize US public education.[6]

Instead of allowing that to happen, TEA and possibly Perry himself allowed EPISD to become a scapegoat for the entire state, instead of fighting the feds on false charges of cheating. The report above acknowledges that in the state of Texas, EPISD was following the mandates set out by TEA; ergo, there was no cheating on the district's part. The FBI knew this and TEA knew this. Nonetheless, they opted to continue, apparently indifferent to overturning the lives of innocent individuals by destroying their reputations, ruining their careers and crippling them financially.

By January 2014, Tanner and Thomas knew that they had done nothing wrong, but the power of the press continued the narrative of a cheating scandal to where any other point of view or opinion was not allowed or tolerated.

At the time, Tanner believed that the worst was over for Tegmeyer and Love. They had fought the good fight but ended up leaving Austin High and continuing their educational careers at different schools. Tanner knew that Thomas was going to continue to face trouble unless she was pressured to make false statements in lieu of losing her livelihood, full career and certification. Tanner would have understood if Thomas cooperated given the hell the FBI/DOJ had put her through.

But Diane Thomas was and is an extraordinarily strong woman who held onto her integrity. For her, lying was never an option for the purpose of saving herself. She ultimately did lose her education career and certification through the rigged process of the TEA hearings. She and her attorney opted for a TEA hearing hoping that she would not lose her certification.

Tanner, as well as others, also had certifications pending investigation, but, unlike Thomas, Tanner opted to postpone a TEA hearing until after he was finished with the FBI investigation. Tanner knew he was in for the long haul and he followed his attorney's advice to postpone any TEA proceedings.

Thomas' attorney had advised her to submit to the hearing, as no one thought the FBI would keep pursuing her. Naively, Thomas and her attorney believed that TEA would hold a fair hearing.

But as with everything else in this case, this hearing was greatly influenced by the FBI. The government's involvement was verified years later when discovering the vast amount of evidence withheld from the defendants.

In that evidence, it was discovered that the FBI was heavily involved in all TEA hearings for any EPISD employees during the time of the fabricated cheating scandal.[7] Agents Griego and Murray made their wishes clear for EPISD defendants to lose their credentials.[8] They did this through their conversations with TEA lawyers and with the hearing officers as well.

Of course, this was completely illegal as it did not allow for a fair and impartial hearing. Instead, the hearings were a mere formality where the final decision had already been made before any witness or defendant took the stand.

Thomas' hearing officer was Patricia Palafox, a prominent El Pasoan from a prominent El Paso family. She had close ties with Eliot Shapleigh as she served on several municipal committees with him.[9] Many of these committees had direct ties to the work of El Paso's City Council. When requested to be a hearing officer, her duty for impartiality should have dictated a decline. Palafox ended up accepting all allegations against Thomas for retaliation.

In a travesty of justice, Thomas was not allowed to use exonerating evidence to clear her name. However, this was the same evidence, in part, that had her charge thrown out in federal court with prejudice.[10] Thomas was disgusted with the proceeding and decided not to waste any more time or money on a TEA appeal process. Ultimately, her certification was revoked without any evidence.

Tanner was disgusted by the process and knew that Thomas had been a victim of outrageous injustice. But Tanner also believed her ordeal was over. In his mind, the FBI was only out to get him. He saw the FBI's tactics toward Thomas as a bullying technique to remind her unequivocally of the power they exercise over those who don't comply with their designs. But even Tanner didn't believe that the FBI would continue to target Thomas. She had only been an assistant principal for a few months.

Basically, she was still in training. But that didn't matter to Kanof and the FBI agents.

Chapter 13: Parameters of the fabricated scandal change again

I strongly believe that the Founding Fathers of our country got it right: power corrupts, and any time you have too much power concentrated in one place, it tends to get abused, so checks and balances are always needed.
~Dean Ornish

After Tanner was forced to resign, with his brother's assistance, he began another career as a nursing home administrator in Olympia, Washington. He knew he would never get a job in education in El Paso or Texas, for that matter, and he and his wife agreed that it was time to leave. *The Times* and the local news stations provided constant reminders of what was, for Tanner, the most painful period of his life.

The fear of indictment was a constant reality for Tanner, but there was also speculation that if there had been no indictment by the summer of 2014, then there would be no indictments at all. Rhetorically, how could there be any indictments when nothing happened? But Tanner's attorney cautioned him about becoming too optimistic. His attorney did, however, contemplate the possibility that the FBI/DOJ might allow the statute of limitation to run its course with a deadline of August 2018.

The summer of 2014 was rather quiet in El Paso regarding the cheating scandal, but as soon as the new school year began, the *El Paso Times* revved up the rhetoric again. There was significant anger from El Paso politicians because Lorenzo Garcia had been released from prison almost one and a half years earlier than his sentence.

When the announcement of the early release happened in December 2013, Beto O'Rourke wrote a letter to the federal Bureau of Prisons addressing Garcia's early release, which made *The New York Times*. O'Rourke demanded that Garcia remain in prison…even though the deal had been legally completed. That article enhanced the lie of disappearing students that was fabricated by Shapleigh.[1]

Now that Garcia was free, those forcing the idea of a scandal were adamant that the investigation must continue. Old names from the scandal became news again. One such person was James Anderson.

Relishing a moment of joy with his son Daniel, seven years old, at Universal Studios Orlando, James Anderson says this was "the calm before the storm." "Daniel has been dealing with this stress for over half of his life, from the age of seven to 16. The FBI was folowing him around his middle school the week before my arrest," Anderson said. "But despite this, Daniel found his purpose through helping special needs children learn to ride horses. His teaching of horse therapy helped him, too." *photo courtesy of James Anderson*

With the goal of being the youngest superintendent in the state of Texas, Anderson was unapologetically ambitious. In his young career, he was on his way to achieving that goal. At 22, Anderson became a high school math teacher in 1998, and before he reached the age of 25, he was already an assistant principal at the high school level. By the time he was 28, he was a principal of a middle school. Two years later, he was the principal of Andress High School in EPISD.

Anderson took over Andress at a time that school was experiencing both academic and disciplinary challenges. During his tenure there, Andress cleaned up discipline and got out of academic trouble. After almost three years there, Anderson's aspirations called out again when EPISD's Central Office advertised an opening for an assistant superintendent. Anderson got the job and his pathway to a superintendent position appeared unobstructed.

When he arrived at the job, EPISD was riding high. The schools were getting better and the reputation of the district was improving both in El Paso County and in the state. But this was going to be short-lived. Soon after Anderson arrived at Central Office, Shapleigh began his allegations against the district.

Anderson's new role was immediately laden with stress. It was his job to address alleged improprieties at Bowie High School regarding a principal who was once his colleague. Anderson had to initiate standard operating procedures for high schools that should have already been established beforehand, but his predecessor, Damon Murphy, had failed to do so. Anderson was strict about data practices and read TEA guidelines with conservative eyes.

A year before Garcia was indicted in August 2011, Anderson became concerned about the allegations that were aimed at Bowie and its principal, Jesus Chavez. Anderson had questions about the allegations and he believed that a full investigation of Bowie and Chavez was warranted. Anderson contacted TEA in June 2010 for the purpose of investigating Bowie and Chavez. He was repeatedly told that TEA would not investigate. Anderson had a gut feeling that this could come back to haunt him, so he kept all phone records of his contacts with TEA.

Anderson's intuition proved to be correct. Emi Johnson was his contact at TEA. He specifically asked Johnson for TEA to conduct a full investigation into EPISD in order to satisfy Shapleigh's constant accusations. Johnson clearly told Anderson on a few occasions that TEA would not conduct any investigation. Unknown to Anderson at the time, Johnson had already approved an investigation at the request of Lorenzo Garcia, the superintendent.

Even though he tried to get help from TEA as he was complying with the FBI investigation underway at EPISD, Anderson became one of the fed's major targets. Even though the FBI and the news media were adamant that a cheating scandal had happened, they never clearly stated what that scandal entailed.

Nonetheless, the FBI accused Anderson of not doing enough to stop the scandal, despite the fact that it was never fully defined. However, through emails and phone logs, Anderson was able to verify his communication with Johnson.[2] In numerous interrogations with Murray and Griego, Anderson submitted documentation regarding how he was contacting TEA and how TEA was not willing to comply with the requests. Murray and Griego accused Anderson of lying and threatened to conduct a lie detector test on him. Anderson was completely willing to take that test, but the FBI never followed through on the bluff.

What wasn't known at the time but discovered through information withheld by the agents and AUSA was that Emi Johnson was working with the FBI to frame the fabricated cheating scandal on EPISD.[3] While Johnson was telling Anderson that she could not assist him in an investigation, she minimalized Anderson's contacts with her to the FBI agents.

As per the fears alleged by Rick Perry, Johnson was complying with the FBI so they wouldn't implicate TEA in a federal investigation. Apparently, a willing participant in the effort to scapegoat EPISD, Johnson became the key contact for the USDE and the FBI.

Through interoffice emails provided in discovery after the mistrial, it was evident that she was working diligently to secure Anderson's removal, as it was her job to approve or "scrub" all data passed on to these two entities. It was Johnson who reached out to her former supervisor, Adam Jones, to inform him of the opportunity to perform an independent audit (The Weaver Report) of EPISD.[4]

Thus, by 2014, Anderson's name began re-emerging in the storyline of the EPISD cheating scandal. He had been gone from the district for nearly two years and had managed success as a real estate agent. He had tried to stay in education, applying for jobs ranging from teacher to administrator.

Anderson was even offered a teaching position in a nearby district. But as he pulled into the parking lot to sign his contract, he received a phone call that the district had decided to eliminate the only math teaching position in their small high school. It appeared that the FBI was making sure he was blackballed.

Other individuals related to Anderson began getting airtime again. Myrna Gamboa, Vanessa Foreman, and Maria Flores were three people falsely implicated in the scandal. Gamboa and Foreman were school directors and Flores was a former associate superintendent. All had already resigned or had been terminated from the district due to the interrogations of the agents. Again, there was no evidence, but the accusations from the FBI were loud as they were continuously fed to and reported by a compliant media.

In November 2014, the attorneys for Gamboa, Foreman, Anderson and Tanner were called by AUSA Debra Kanof. Kanof told the attorneys that she was offering a "blue light special" to their clients. She was going to allow them to make a plea deal, whereby they would admit to a felony for cheating in exchange for a $5,000 fine and a five-year probationary sentence. It is critical to note that Kanof offered this before any charges were written against any of the clients. She was hoping for the innocents to fall on their own swords.

Kanof got one taker for that offer. It was Myrna Gamboa. Gamboa had been on the FBI's radar from the beginning of the investigation in

December 2010. Her job title was school director for Bowie High School and other schools in South El Paso. She was determined to create order in a school that was only known for chaos in its administrative offices. When she was approached to be interviewed by the FBI, she complied without hesitation, like so many others. Her interview led the FBI agents—who knew nothing about education—to conclude that Gamboa was cheating so that Bowie would appear to be improving higher test scores.

Over the course of the years that they interrogated and intimidated Gamboa, they lied to her about what other colleagues said about her. They lied because as government agents, they can do that without repercussion. At the time the "blue light special" was offered, Gamboa had already lost her career and reputation. She was married and had a child who was still in grammar school. Allegedly, Gamboa was distraught to the point that her family believed that something had to change so that Gamboa could move on with her life. Therefore, Gamboa agreed to a plea. She was given a $5,000 fine and a five-year probation sentence.[5]

Gamboa, who complied with the FBI/DOJ, is the only individual who was convicted and served her full sentence.

Once again, in the post mistrial discovery, it was shown that the USDE auditors had reviewed her work in its entirety and had told the FBI that it was proper and in the normal course of her position.[6] Ideally, her plea agreement, given under extreme stress, should have been overturned.

It was not until June 2015 that Kanof again contacted the attorneys for Tanner, Foreman and Anderson, telling council that their clients were going to be indicted. Tanner remembers telling his attorney that he didn't think it would happen and that it was just another scare tactic. "How can you have evidence of a cheating scandal when there was no cheating?" Tanner asked to his attorney. By the end of June, no indictments happened. Kanof informed the attorneys that she had scheduling conflicts and would have to work on it later.

For his part, Tanner remained concerned, but still not convinced of any indictment. After all, only one indictment had ever been enacted and that was against the former superintendent for a no-bid contract and over four years had passed since that had happened. As always, he wondered how an indictment could happen without evidence. The only other conviction was Gamboa and that was because of the psychological stress and intimidation she endured, not because of any evidence.

However, by the fall of 2016, the old accusations were back. The media and the investigation focused again on Cordero and Tanner's retaliation towards the hotheaded shop teacher. It was a trend: once the case began to die down, an old alleged infraction was relit and the narrative was off again. As ridiculous as it seemed, Cordero, who five years earlier tried to run down a student, was being used as an example of someone who was a victim of the cheating scheme.

Paranoia validated

April 2016 was a beautiful month in the city of Olympia, Washington and the Pacific Northwest. Tanner and his wife dared to hope that perhaps this nightmare was over. They had even discussed how there was really no possibility of an indictment given that six years had passed since the FBI started its investigation, despite having zero evidence.

Tanner had settled into a new career as his wife transferred her teaching skills to the public school system in Washington. They had purchased a home and were settling into the idea that they could start over again.

But then Tanner's phone rang on the night of Thursday April 21, 2016. It was his attorney, Jim Darnell.

"John, you've been indicted." Tanner took a deep breath and settled into the reality quickly, having known for a few years that this might be on the horizon.

"Who else? Teri Jordan, Anderson, Murphy, Jesus Chavez?" Tanner asked, as those names as they were the most mentioned in the news articles of the contrived debacle.

"No," Darnell answered. "Well, Anderson and Murphy, yes. But also, Tegmeyer, Love and Thomas."

Tanner was dumbfounded. It was inconceivable that those top educators of Austin High were indicted. They didn't have anything to do with anything. They were indicted because they wouldn't lie for the FBI so that Tanner could be completely framed without any hope of a defense. The surreal nature of the event was just beginning. Nothing could have prepared the innocents for what was going to happen on Wednesday, April 27, the day of initial court appearance.

Chapter 14: El Paso media

An analysis of the media is required to fully understand how this case got so out of hand. In the isolated city of El Paso, the news media had carte blanche to report—or not report—anything they wanted. There was no regulation. There was no accountability. There wasn't even a half-hearted attempt at either.

"The media's the most powerful entity on earth. They have the power to make the innocent guilty and to make the guilty innocent, and that's power. Because they control the minds of the masses. The press is so powerful in its image-making role, it can make the criminal look like he's the victim and make the victim look like he's the criminal. This is the press, an irresponsible press. It will make the criminal look like he's the victim and make the victim look like he's the criminal. If you aren't careful, the newspapers will have you hating the people who are being oppressed and loving the people who are doing the oppressing."~ Malcom X

Fake news. It's a common term used in today's journalism. This inherent insult that is meant to shock and awe the average citizen has lost its impact. It is news agencies of reporting fake news—and many times they are correct. Likewise, left leaning news agencies and many liberal politicians point to conservative news agencies and politicians and accuse them of fake news—and often they are correct as well. Suffice to say, we do not have objective news in the US. We have become consumers of predetermined news; in short, we listen to what feeds our political and ideological needs.

This lack of objectivity in news consumption fosters a lopsided truth that leans to the consumer demand. Arguably, this has aided the deep divisions we now experience across the map in terms of political affiliation. No longer do we as a nation even try to fool ourselves into believing that our news media is fair and balanced. And if we do, we certainly shouldn't.

Was there always such a bias to our news organizations? It would be akin to using a golden age motif to assume that at one time the news organizations of the US were all fair and balanced. However, it is probably safe to say that between 1949 and 1987, the news was probably fairer and more balanced than it is now.

That is because the US had a law called the Fairness Doctrine whereby the news media (those with broadcast licenses) were required to "present controversial matters of public importance and do so in a manner that was honest, equitable and balanced."[1] The free press was obligated to uphold the First Amendment by reporting honestly and being fair to both sides of an issue. This requirement was abolished in 1987 during the Reagan Administration.[2]

What happened from there has led to our current news media. Without the legal requirement of being fair and balanced, long respected news outlets chose to report only one side of an issue while allowing reporters of basic news stories hard to know when the term was first used, but it has become very popular in the Trump era. Trump and his supporters accuse left-leaning to add their opinions to the events of the day. Naturally, that creates a bias.

Often that bias creates an environment where those who are reporting the news are also those who are telling the public how to interpret what is being broadcast. Basically, our newscasts tell us what to think and how to think. If a viewer disagrees, then he or she can simply switch the channel.

Nullifying the Fairness Doctrine did not endanger freedom of the press; instead, it perverted it since members of the press no longer had to monitor content or methodology. From the time we lost this doctrine, slander and defamation of character has become common practice.

Simply put, legal ramifications are few, if any, despite ruining the lives of citizens through exaggeration, hyperbole, omission of truth or lying. Slander and defamation lawsuits are myths in today's publishing world. The press is heavily protected and can print most of what it wants—including lies—and continue on comfortably knowing that lawsuits from average citizens are almost nonexistent.

There are many people who claim—perhaps rightly—that Fox News was born out of this abandonment of fair reporting. Fox might even agree with that analysis.

But it becomes the chicken or the egg question. Did biased and unbalanced reporting lead to the creation of Fox or did Fox on its own start reporting in an unbalanced manner in order to attract an audience who wanted news reported in such a manner? The answers are probably yes and yes.

Today, if we want balanced news, what are we to read and/or watch? At least in the US, that is almost an impossibility. CNN is biased to the left and Fox is biased to the right. When watching either one, discriminate viewers understand that they are not getting the entire truth.

———

By watching both, one can only hope to get the full story, but there are no guarantees.

This trend of accepted bias in news reporting trickled down to local news media in cities across the country. Local TV affiliates mimic the biases of their parent companies. Nearly extinct are independent local newspapers. Most city newspapers are owned by giant conglomerates and as satellites they report in the same manner that is dictated to them.

One could also argue that local news is more biased or intimidated in favor of the wealthy and powerful of a city or region because they have to be more careful about who they report on and how. There is also a higher likelihood that local newspaper editors and TV executives have close ties to those powerful individuals whom they cover. The revelations after so many years about Judge Roy Moore of Alabama may be just such an example.

In Chapter 10, the news station, KTSM, featured prominently. It was the only TV station that reported anything—albeit it only once—that gave a hint to the defense's side. But the report was quickly silenced, and the reporter developed an amnesia to her featured news presentation.

Who was controlling the "free press"? Why was there an obvious agreement with all news sources in El Paso to silence the defense's side of the case? Moreover, why was there a concerted effort to ensure that those accused remained visible in concocted situations designed to make them look like criminals while also rendering their voices mute?

Another TV news station deserves mention: KVIA. At that time, the news station had a joint venture with the *El Paso Times* whereby they promoted each other and would report each other's news. When seen holistically, one cannot conclude that it is a mere coincidence that one of the major players at KVIA, Rick Cabrera, is the brother of the handpicked EPISD superintendent, Juan Cabrera. From the time Juan set foot in El Paso, KVIA praised him.

And how could it be just mere coincidence that the one who picked Juan—Dee Margo—also hired Rick to manage not only his personal business finances, but the finances of the downtown redevelopment plan? That is the same development plan that is set to profit if EPISD schools in that area are closed or converted into charter schools.

Rick's reward was a profitable job with Margo, where the other lead anchor, Estela Casas, was given the Executive Director position at the University Medical Center and El Paso Children's Hospital Foundations appointed by members of the PDNG, to include former Board of Managers appointee Carmen Arrieta-Candelaria. Quid pro quo seemed to be the name of the game.

Ethical standards of local newspapers have been compromised by the removal of the Fairness Doctrine. Fair and balanced reporting doesn't sell papers. In addition, local papers are losing readers to online news and the 24-hour news broadcast.

To survive, local papers have resorted to blood, scandal and rumor as headlines to attract readers and advertisers. If it bleeds, it leads, so to speak. Integrity and honest, unbiased journalism has breathed its dying breath, having been sold to the highest bidder in exchange for tabloid-like stories that used to be relegated to publications such as the *National Enquirer*.

The *El Paso Times* has not been immune to this trend. For many decades in the 20th century, the *El Paso Times* was one of two newspapers in the city. The other was the *Herald-Post*. There was enough demand in circulation that the city could support the *Times* in the morning and the *Herald-Post* in the evening. As readership declined for local newspapers, the *Herald-Post* finally shut down leaving a growing city with only one English newspaper.

But even without the competition of the *Herald-Post*, the *Times* continued to struggle financially. In an all-out effort to remain relevant, the *Times* began to focus on investigative reporting in the late 1990s.

From a paper that used to report on local events with attention to community initiatives, successes and events, it switched to finding scandal and innuendo in most of its stories.

Yet, the *Times* wasn't closely covering the stories that were really important in the community and surrounding areas. For example, the drug cartels began to become very powerful in the 1990s as the crime rate in Juarez was making international news. Most El Pasoans discovered what was happening in their sister city by reading the *New York Times* rather than The *El Paso Times*.

But if a wealthy El Paso school managed to have a student achieve a rather innocuous feat; that became a front-page news story with the student—most likely the offspring of a wealthy businessman or influential politician—along with a prominent photograph.

To keep circulation going, the *Times* tended to cater to the wealthier citizens who were more likely to buy the paper. That modus operandi led to being controlled by the wealthy and powerful citizens of the city. Beginning in the 2000s, it became difficult to find an article in the *Times* that is critical of anyone with substantial political or economic clout unless he or she was the target of the oligarchy. Thus, The *El Paso Times* became the key influencer of everyday El Pasoans' attitudes and opinions, ensuring the agenda of those who truly held the power.

Journalist Bob Moore was fully on board. Moore was a part of the *El Paso Times* beginning in 1986, a year before the Fairness Doctrine dissolved. He reported for the paper until 2006 when he returned to his native Colorado to be an editor for a small-town newspaper there. But he returned to El Paso to become the editor-in-chief in 2011, coming in at the time that EPISD was being falsely accused of cheating.

Interestingly, Moore took over the *Times* when EPISD had been cleared of wrongdoing twice by TEA and cleared by the USDE. But the *Times* and El Paso's City Council, along with Eliot Shapleigh, seemed determined to use the press to their own advantage. It is fair to contemplate that perhaps there was a concerted effort by Shapleigh, Byrd and others to bring Moore back to El Paso for the purpose of exploiting the scandal that was losing steam.

Journalists Code of Ethics

With the knowledge of the Journalists Code of Ethics (https://www.spj.org/ethicscode.asp) in his metaphorical back pocket, why did Moore agree to violate it? After all, he was clearly aware of its basic tenets. A summary is listed here:

1. Seek Truth and Report it
Ethical journalism should be accurate and fair. Journalists should be honest and courageous in gathering, reporting and interpreting information. Journalists should:
 • Take responsibility for the accuracy of their work. Verify information before releasing it. Use original sources whenever possible.
 • Provide context. Take special care not to misrepresent or oversimplify in promoting, previewing or summarizing a story.
 • Gather, update and correct information throughout the life of a news story.
 • Diligently seek subjects of news coverage to allow them to respond to criticism or allegations of wrongdoing.
 • Avoid undercover or other surreptitious methods of gathering information unless traditional, open methods will not yield

information vital to the public. • Be vigilant and courageous about holding those with power accountable. Give voice to the voiceless.
• Support the open and civil exchange of views, even views they find repugnant.
• Recognize a special obligation to serve as watchdogs over public affairs and government. Seek to ensure that the public's business is conducted in the open, and that public records are open to all.
• Label advocacy and commentary.
• Never deliberately distort facts or context, including visual information. Clearly label illustrations and re-enactments.

2. Minimize Harm

Ethical journalism treats sources, subjects, colleagues and members of the public as human beings deserving of respect. Journalists should:

• Show compassion for those who may be affected by news coverage.
• Avoid pandering to lurid curiosity, even if others do.
• Balance a suspect's right to a fair trial with the public's right to know. Consider the implications of identifying criminal suspects before they face legal charges. Consider the long-term implications of the extended reach and permanence of publication. Provide updated and more complete information as appropriate.

3. Act Independently

The highest and primary obligation of ethical journalism is to serve the public. Journalists should:

•Avoid conflicts of interest, real or perceived. Disclose unavoidable conflicts.
• Refuse gifts, favors, fees, free travel and special treatment, and avoid political and other outside activities that may compromise integrity or impartiality, or may damage credibility.
• Be wary of sources offering information for favors or money; do not pay for access to news. Identify content provided by outside sources, whether paid or not. Deny favored treatment to advertisers, donors or any other special interests, and resist internal and external pressure to influence coverage.

4. Be Accountable and Transparent

Ethical journalism means taking responsibility for one's work and explaining one's decisions to the public. Journalists should:

- Explain ethical choices and processes to audiences. Encourage a civil dialogue with the public about journalistic practices, coverage and news content.
- Respond quickly to questions about accuracy, clarity and fairness.
- Acknowledge mistakes and correct them promptly and prominently. Explain corrections and clarifications carefully and clearly.
- Expose unethical conduct in journalism, including within their organizations.
- Abide by the same high standards they expect of others.

While we cannot pinpoint what motivated Moore to abandon the journalists' bible of behavior, we can review and find violations at almost every point occurring under his tenure as editor in chief of the *Times*. The violations were both frequent and flagrant. Why did Moore only allow the voice of the accusers? Was he influenced by his close friendship with Susie Byrd and Eliot Shapleigh? (Byrd often publicly claimed that she and Moore were best friends, and that she would often lunch with Moore and Shapleigh. Sometimes the main reporter of the scandal, Zahira Torre, would join them.)

Rest assured, Moore did not know the accused in the case. He had little contact with Anderson, and no contact with Tanner, Tegmeyer, Love or Thomas. There was absolutely no attempt to reach out to them. In fact, the *Times* never reported (a) evidence that would exonerate the falsely accused; or (b) shed light on the unethical behavior and methodology of EPISD, TEA, the FBI or the DOJ. In fact, it seems that he actively worked to omit evidence that would have caused the public to raise questions about the validity of the cheating scandal.

There is, however, an intriguing line of thought that takes its cues from an earlier case. Was Moore motivated to continuously report this false story because of the challenging financial situation of the *Times*? As proposed throughout this book, El Paso's City Council needed the cheating scandal to happen so that the downtown redevelopment plan would become a reality. There is evidence to support this theory, and it was a tactic used in the highly publicized cheating scandal in Atlanta. The public is now discovering that much of the Atlanta cheating scandal was a scam, which reads as a blueprint for the alleged El Paso scandal.[3]

El Paso's "progressive" city council proposed many high-priced community projects that included massive parks with water features, large Olympic swimming pools, and a AAA baseball park. The price tag was high, especially for one of the poorest cities in the US. To approve these projects meant significant debt for decades with a high likelihood of huge property tax increases in a city already enduring the weight of some of the highest property tax rates in the US.

Many citizens went to City Council meetings to challenge the proposals for so many high-ticket items, but those concerns were met with denial and minimization of the concerns and they were not reported in the local media. The *El Paso Times* editorial board, headed by Moore, overwhelmingly supported the ballot initiatives and assured El Paso that the revenue was available to cover the costs of the items.[4]

In particular, Moore enthusiastically supported the proposal of the AAA baseball stadium. The proposed location for the stadium was in the downtown area on the land occupied by a ten-story City Hall building that was about 30 years old. For the stadium to be built, City Hall had to be demolished. These two expensive proposals—tearing down a building and building a stadium—didn't consider the cost to purchase land and the construction of a new City Hall. The destruction of City Hall meant that the functions performed there would have to find a new location.

For the City Council to advance its plan, it needed a temporary space for City Hall functions. Bob Moore came to the rescue. The *El Paso Times* building was sold to the city of El Paso (while Beto O'Rourke and Susie Byrd were on the Council) at three million dollars above market value.[5]

That sale provided revenue to keep the financially struggling newspaper running. But this quid pro quo compromised the *Times* with what it could objectively report in a fair and balanced manner. And the functions of City Hall could not fit in the old *Times* building.

When the *Times* reported on EPISD, nothing about it was fair and balanced. The only slant allowed was the one given by Shapleigh, the FBI, and the prosecution. No other viewpoint was ever printed. The only people interviewed were the accusers. It's not that the *Times* didn't have access to the facts. They did. It's not as if there was a lack of credibility to the accuser's narrative. There was. Three examples emphasize the point.

First, the *Times* has never reported that Shapleigh's original allegation about the district hiding students was false—a fact revealed for the first time in October 2010 from TEA. The *Times* wouldn't print that. Shapleigh's allegation of "disappearing students" was again shown to be false when even AUSA Debra Kanof clearly stated during the trial that Shapleigh was wrong in his original assertion. The *Times* did not report that.

In Garcia's indictment and of the educators that followed, Shapleigh's allegation was never used because it was false, but the *Times* included continued to report the falsity anyway.

Second, the *Times* has never reported on shop teacher Ruben Cordero's attempt to run down Student X. Instead, it has been reported that Cordero was a victim of retaliation.

Though it is known that the all facets of the local media received the factual report on Cordero's behavior involving child endangerment, that content has never seen the light of day in the *Times* or in most other local media. In addition to receiving the report of the investigation and findings from EPISD, reporters from the *Times* also heard explicit testimony about this incident at the trial of the Educators. To this day, the *Times* has yet to report on the incident.

Still pertaining to Cordero, the *Times* has never reported information that they have had since the mistrial. One of the main reasons that the mistrial occurred stemmed from the prosecution knowingly withholding a timeline that proved retaliation against Cordero could not have happened.[6]

The charge of retaliation claimed that personnel (Tanner, Tegmeyer, Love, and Thomas) at Austin High School targeted Cordero because they knew he was an FBI informant. The withheld information exonerated the accused since it showed that Cordero claimed he was an FBI informant seven full days before he had ever had any type of contact with the FBI. This fact has emerged at least three times in various court settings and the *Times* has been there for each occurrence. They have never reported what is clearly and freely public information.

Third, *Times* reporter Zahira Torres ran an article that disparaged James Anderson in favor of Emi Johnson, though the facts were clearly on Anderson's side. It was titled "Unheeded Warnings" and it ran on December 2, 2012.[7]

This story revealed Moore's and Torres' complete bias and manipulation of the facts. Although the byline is credited to Torres and another reporter, Anderson believes that Moore was influential in the direction of the reporting, as he was present for Anderson's interview and

Moore himself asked questions for the story. There is little doubt about Moore's influence.

The article claimed loudly—but without evidence—that a cheating scandal occurred and that TEA failed to catch it. The reporters again alluded to Shapleigh's allegation of disappearing students that had already been debunked fully and completely two years earlier. The accusation toward Anderson at this point inferred that he did not do enough to stop the cheating scheme. Anderson defended himself by stating that he took the charges of cheating very seriously and he wanted TEA to investigate the allegations. Because Anderson had documented everything, he was able to prove that he called TEA contact Emi Johnson when he said he did and he provided evidence of letters to TEA (Emi Johnson) from his colleague, Terri Jordan, asking for help and for an audit.[8]

Johnson initially told the *Times* that Anderson had never contacted her. When the *Times* filed an open records request to get the phone records of both TEA and EPISD, the *Times* discovered that Anderson was telling the truth and Johnson was forgetful to the point of incompetence or caught in a few lies. Nevertheless, the story supported Johnson by insinuating that Anderson may have called TEA, but that there was a discrepancy in what he actually said in his conversation with her. The *Times* indicated that they believed Johnson.

What the *Times* omitted from this report and future stories was that Anderson's actions triggered the Office of the Investigator General (OIG) to audit both EPISD and TEA. Despite that impending investigation, Anderson was still forced out of EPISD due to the *Times'* insistence (fueled by the FBI) that he did not do enough to stop what was now being called—without question and without evidence—the cheating scandal.

After the OIG completed the audit of both entities, they concluded that EPISD followed all directives of TEA and that if there was any entity doing wrong, it was TEA and not EPISD. The *Times* (neither Torres nor Moore) has never reported this.[9]

This OIG report connects directly to the FBI report of September 20, 2013 (cited in chapter 11) that alluded to Governor Rick Perry's concern that TEA would be investigated because all districts in Texas were using the same standard operating procedures as EPISD as ordained by TEA. Why wouldn't Moore or Torres report this? If EPISD wasn't the culprit, then it would mean that Garcia was unjustly convicted of cheating. But more than that, if EPISD was off the hook, then the downtown redevelopment plan remained in jeopardy.

When investigating how the *Times* arrived at this story, Moore's role becomes more curious. He crossed the boundary—and stomped on it repeatedly—from being a journalist whose job is to maintain objectivity to becoming the carte blanche mouthpiece of the government.

Moore's lack of objectivity is evidenced from his press releases that are highly influenced by those he was receiving from the FBI and AUSA. As he crossed that line, Anderson's integrity became the target of Moore's and Torres's attacks.[10] The *Times* ran over 700 stories regarding the cheating scandal and *not one of those 700 included an alternate point of view* from the educators.

Clearly, that runs against the idea of investigative reporting. Without evidence, the *Times* convicted the accused. Even today with the FBI case having completely cratered, the *Times* continues to use pictures of the educators, while they were forced to wear prison attire, four years after the event. It is interesting to note that Moore quit The *El Paso Times* in September 2017. This was less than three months after the innocents endured a federal court case that ended in a mistrial due to outrageous prosecutorial misconduct. (The *Times* has still not published in detail what that misconduct entailed.)

At the time Moore left the fledgling paper, the defense attorneys were learning just how much prosecutorial misconduct had taken place; there was more information withheld than what was originally given. Was Moore aware that the truth of the alleged cheating scandal was going to come to light? Perhaps he wanted to be dissociated from the *Times* when the depth and scope of the truth would surface. It would be interesting to discover if he had any personal financial interest in the Borderplex REIT.

Zahira Torres, a homegrown journalist, took his place as editor, and it was she who was the originator of the fabricated cheating scandal. It was her highly questionable investigative skills that led from an allegation of misconduct to a full-blown cheating scandal without any evidence to justify it as such. But she was published so often that the public stopped questioning her accusation. It is interesting how Zahira Torres entered the profession.

Torres began her career at the *El Paso Times* writing obituaries. Eventually, she wrote a few human-interest stories. She was known for significant grammar and syntax issues with her writing, but she improved with time. Her dedication landed her with the position as the *Times'* education reporter. In that position, she looked for ways to criticize the schools she was covering, and she seemed to have a particular interest in

Austin High School. Tanner says he patiently tried to work with Torres during his tenure there, but resolution proved futile.

A telling incident occurred on August 28, 2008; it was Tanner's first day with students as principal of Austin High School. Tanner saw this as a big day and he wanted to begin his tenure there with a good start. Torres contacted Tanner because she said she had received an anonymous report that Austin High School was in chaos because it didn't have schedules for its students. The simple fact is that the accusation wasn't true and that should have ended the phone call. But Torres pressed and practically insisted that the anonymous report she received was accurate. To be transparent, Tanner invited Torres to the campus to see for herself.

The accusation echoed one from a few years earlier in August 2004, however, when Cheryl Felder was principal of Austin. At the time, Felder instituted an enormous change in the school's schedule from a traditional to a block schedule. Felder was granted the permission to change the schedule, but the work to change it didn't happen.

Thus, on the first day of school in 2004, Austin students and teachers did not have schedules. Teachers were instructed to pull random students into their classrooms and try and teach something-anything- to them; this procedure lasted almost a month. The school was in total chaos and was not put back into general order until the end of the first semester. In truth, for that school year, Austin never fully recovered. Not only was the catastrophe covered by the local media, but it hit the state media sources as well. It cost Felder her career as a principal; she was reassigned to a central office position in the Department of Pupil Services. Therefore, when Torres accused Tanner of not having schedules, he took the matter very seriously.

Torres accepted the invitation and arrived on the campus by midmorning. Tanner walked her throughout the school and demonstrated that classes were in process and the school year had begun with schedules. Torres still wasn't convinced, even as students showed printed schedules to her. She intimated to Tanner that he could have staged this event for the benefit of the reporter. In order to be completely transparent, Tanner gave Torres free reign in the school and left her alone so she could get her story. She stayed at the campus for about three hours and then approached Tanner in his office.

"Well, they do have schedules," Torres claimed.

"Good. I am glad you saw that and am glad we have this resolved," Tanner responded.

"Yeah, but why did someone call me with that allegation?"

"I don't know."

"Well, why are there so many people lined up at your registrar's door?"

"Those are the students who didn't come to register during the summer."

"Why didn't they register?"

"I don't know. You would have to ask them."

Torres then went back to inquiring why someone would make such a call. Tanner continued to respond by saying, "I have been more than transparent with you and even gave you open reign on the campus so that you could satisfy your questions. I don't know what more I can do."

With that, Torres left the campus. In an article that evening, Torres reported that she had received an anonymous call. She admitted that the students had schedules, but then threw in a zinger, "However, things looked rather chaotic."

Torres continued to write negative and false articles regarding Austin without ever correcting blatant errors. In summer 2009, Torres wrote that Austin was about to be closed down by TEA. The fact was that Austin was getting out of academic trouble and was not in jeopardy of closing down.

Torres then decided to write a "feature" story on Austin in fall 2009 that read more like an exposé. In that article, she claimed that the school had one of the highest teenage pregnancy rates in the United States. There was no truth to this at all. Although the school had many issues, a high teenage pregnancy rate was not one of them, especially in comparison to the rest of the nation. The error was pointed out, but Torres never published a correction.

For the fabricated cheating scandal, Torres repeatedly used Shapleigh's narrative even after the allegations were proven erroneous. As no evidence of an actual scandal surfaced, Torres switched to emotion in her articles, insinuating that many students were hurt by the scandal. The catch phrase she used (and is still used by her, Moore, and the current *Times* staff) was "an untold number of students were denied the right to a proper education."

If taken at face value, an untold number means that they are not telling the number. It doesn't say an unknown number. The actual value is known if one examines the evidence acquired through this investigation: *that value is zero.*

At no point could the investigation by the *Times*, the FBI, the DOJ, EPISD, the USDE or any other entity provide even one name of a student who was denied a proper education. If any student could have been identified, then the Office Civil Rights (OCR) would have acted. Shapleigh tried to get the OCR to act on this case, but they declined.[10]

Because of her work and recognition on this sensational story, Torres landed prestigious positions with the *Denver Post*, the *LA Times* and the *Chicago Tribune*. Her resumé looked great and these three journalistic pillars took a chance on her.

However, when reviewing her work at these three entities, one learns that Torres rarely had a byline of her own on reports involving investigative journalism. For those stories, she was often part of a team of writers, and she did not receive top billing. When Torres left the *Chicago Tribune* to return to El Paso, she claimed it was because she missed home. It is hard to fathom that one would choose to leave the career and income of a journalist at one of the best newspapers in the world to return to *The El Paso Times*. That simply doesn't happen. As in the articles Torres writes, the public probably wasn't given the whole truth.

Just as the timing of Moore's departure from the *El Paso Times* was curious given its proximity to the mistrial, so was Torres' departure. She departed from the *Times* a day before the federal court announced that the charges against Tanner and Anderson (and three others who had already pled guilty) were being dismissed. One can only assume that she was avoiding the fallout from her unethical and inaccurate reporting.

Moore and Torres received a few journalistic awards for their work on this case. No Pulitzers, but some minor awards that they flaunted as verification that something nefarious had happened at EPISD.

But in the end, no awards or accolades received can mask the cover-up that was implemented by Moore and Torres and disseminated with equal malice by every local television station. They never attempted to investigate all sides of the story. They refused to give a balanced view or allow the other side a voice. They didn't merely omit facts that were contradictory to the narrative they created, they actively buried it. Clearly, they are reflective of today's journalistic infection of fake news.

Chapter 15: The Disgraceful Debra Kanof and Her Crew

Debra Kanof is a Monster

Literature and film are replete with monsters of all sorts—there is Grendel and his mother, Frankenstein's monster, and the Brothers Grimm, Shakespeare and Disney have presented monsters aplenty. But rarely do we think of monsters making the jump from fiction into reality. AUSA Debra Kanof, however, does just that.

In a publication about Lady MacBeth, Alyah Scott defines a monster as one who "has cruel intentions in which she has full knowledge of the harm she's causing, and commits her actions for no good cause, but rather her selfish desires."[1]

"The real world is where the monsters are." ~Rick Riordan, The Lightning Thief

The case of the fake cheating scandal that convincingly ended Kanof's high-profile career was defined by the corrupt tactics she used for her entire life. This is not a prosecutor who went after the bad guys. When seeking her victims, she avoids mobsters, murderers and drug dealers; instead, she targets individuals who are thoroughly unprepared for the criminal justice system because they have never even considered committing a crime. In a *Twilight Zone* reality, Kanof seems to show a particular pleasure in watching her victims flounder under the weight of psychological and exorbitant financial pressures.

Of the many cases that illustrate her pathological approach and complete disregard for evidence, truth and human decency, two stand out as an introduction to what she eventually wreaked on dozens of innocent lives who used to work honorably at the El Paso Independent School District.

Dove and Noble

In the late 1980s, Kanof victimized two women: Gayle Dove and Michelle Noble. While reading this, keep in mind that these two were eventually exonerated completely, but only after Kanof ruined their lives.

What Dove and Noble endured cannot be rectified. The damage done is irreparable.

Dove was a daycare worker at the YMCA on El Paso's east side. She was a longtime El Pasoan whose husband was a respected high school band director. She was also the mother of a teenage daughter. In addition to her job, she was a volunteer at the local zoo. She had many friends and was loved in the community. As for her criminal record, there wasn't one. In every way, Dove was a model citizen.

Similarly, Noble, five years younger, was the wife of a military soldier and she took the job at the YMCA for some extra income during her husband's station in El Paso. She was known to be extremely meek and a devoted mother to her two children. Again, there was no criminal record.[2]

Dove and Noble's nightmare began in February 1985 when a parent called El Paso's Department of Human Resources (DHR) to file a complaint of sexual abuse that "might" have happened to his son at the YMCA. The father was not certain of it even at the time of the report. As per the investigation of a social worker, it was discovered that the two-and-a-half-year-old boy had many adult handlers in his life beyond the YMCA and his parents. There was also a babysitter who was with him often. The social worker admitted that there was no physical evidence or even circumstantial evidence to indicate anything wrong occurred. But the parent of the alleged victim was outraged that the daycare had not been shut down.[3]

Because of the parent's emotional outrage, an investigation ensued regarding the YMCA. The daycare was observed multiple times with no reports of any indecency or any fear from the children toward their caregivers. But as the investigation continued, the parents of the children began to talk to each other and investigators began to talk to the parents. Parents then began to interrogate their own children.

Most parents were supportive of Dove and Noble, though some began to have doubts. But the entire situation took a different turn when parents of a YMCA student took their three-year-old daughter to a doctor who determined that the child's hymen had been broken. The little girl exclaimed to the doctor, "Please don't hurt me like he did." The "he" in the statement was never identified, but the investigators alleged that it was from the daycare even though no males worked there. Further, no males were ever investigated or indicted in this case.[4]

This unverifiable statement put the entire focus of abuse on the daycare center and no one else, even though there were other adults besides the daycare workers who took care of her. What ensued was an investigatory process outside the lines of standard policies and procedures of a criminal investigation.

In sum, a social worker and a police detective worked together on the case and interviewed children and their parents as co-workers on the case. Such a joint endeavor was not supposed to be allowed, as the investigative process of social workers and detectives is different because they have different goals. At best, a detective can ask a social worker to investigate after the detective has conducted his/her own investigation or vice versa. But working together is seen as collusion and a conflict of interest.[5]

In this case, that procedure became even more compromised since the male detective and female social worker began an extramarital affair during the investigation, which lead to divorces on both sides. With their investigations, it was noted that they were eager to get children to say abuse was happening. By and large, the children were not reporting abuse until they were asked repeatedly. Years later, some of the children admitted that they lied because they didn't want to get in trouble with the investigators.[6]

Debra Kanof was the prosecutor for this case and was told how the investigation was being conducted. To his credit, the male detective told Kanof that he and the social worker were a team with in the investigation and that they were romantically involved. He asked Kanof if this was OK and legal. The detective alleges that Kanof answered, "Don't worry about the legalities." Not only did Kanof not worry about the process of the investigation, she was not worried about the legalities of how children were being recorded for their interviews for court.

Numerous video tapes showed children being cajoled into telling outlandish stories of "monsters" threatening them while they were forced into either fondling the genitals of Dove and Noble or being fondled themselves by their teachers and by other adults the teachers had brought into this molestation ring (other adults who were never found or identified). All the molestation was allegedly occurring at Dove's house, which was close to the YMCA. Allegedly, she would take the daycare class on an excursion to a nearby park, but then redirect the children to her house where all the alleged abuse would occur.[7]

Kanof defended her manner of handling the case because she claimed to be an advocate for children, claiming that she would do anything to stop a child from being hurt. She claimed to believe the emerging practice to trust everything a child says as the complete truth. Even if what the child was saying was not logically possible, Kanof believed it was best to err on the side of believing what the child was saying, even if that violated the rights of the accused.

Kanof shared this belief with her close friend, Yolanda Aguilar, a director at the Department for Human Services in the division of child sexual abuse. Aguilar zealously held this belief to a point that had observers questioning her methodology. In one interview, Aguilar kept asking a child the same questions repeatedly regarding alleged abuse with the daycare personnel. The child would continually answer "No" or "I forgot" to Aguilar's questions, never one time confirming any abuse. The child finally was exhausted and fell asleep in Aguilar's arms. Aguilar's conclusion was that the child was "terrorized" and exhibited "avoidance behavior."   Some viewers of the tape in the courtroom process said that it looked like the little child was playing possum so that the big lady would "bug off."[8]

Both Dove and Noble were indicted and Dove's indictment was handled with what would become standard Kanof flare. It was a media sensation whereby Dove was arrested at the El Paso Zoo while she was doing her volunteer work.

Noble had been warned and she turned herself in a few days later, albeit with cameras rolling. Kanof kept her story going through a compliant media, including a willing *El Paso Times*. Although there were many people willing to speak in favor of Dove and Noble, those voices were never heard by the El Paso public.

Questionably, Kanof began interviewing the children and their parents. She even chaired a support group for them. When asked why she was doing this and noting that it could be construed as a conflict of interest, she said it was to control the parents and to protect Dove and Noble from those parents since they could have turned into a lynch mob.

Sam Callan was the judge that allowed such outlandish behavior of this now disgraced prosecuting attorney. Callan admitted to allowing Kanof to run the show and he gave her just about anything she wanted including the stomping of the defendants' rights. He was quoted as saying, "I just let Debbie (Kanof) shear the law off the page. An appeals court can rule later on what the law is."[9]

With this complete control of the courtroom along with her influence on the media, Kanof was able to convict Dove and Noble without one shred of evidence. It is unfathomable to imagine, but no search warrant was ever issued and there was no search conducted on the house where all the alleged abuse occurred. This means there was no physical evidence: no pictures, no cameras that recorded kids doing sexually deviant behavior as was suggested by the prosecution; no costumes that the "monsters" wore; no markings on the skin; no descriptions of the bodies of the alleged offenders. No evidence other than emotional outrage spewed by Kanof.

The *El Paso Times* reporter on this case became suspicious of the prosecution and began to question everything that was happening especially with Noble. This reporter could not find any evidence to substantiate the claims. However, when he reported this to his colleagues and the editor of the *Times*, they were more interested in how many times they could write "hineys" or "vagina" from witness' statements in order to sell more papers.[10]

But the reporter couldn't get it out of his head that the kids could say where Dove and Noble lived because they passed by their houses daily, but they couldn't describe what was inside the homes. The reporter kept asking why the police did not search Noble's home to look for video cameras, or film, or receipts or even vestiges of the children's fingerprints. Why couldn't the prosecution produce anyone who had ever seen classes of children walking near Noble's home? There were so many questions, but also an editor who would not allow them to become print on a page.

At the end of the trial, Noble received life plus 311 years in prison. Dove received life plus 60 years. Noble was granted a new trial in 1988 after already serving two years in prison. However, Kanof was no longer the prosecutor, and during Noble's second trial, the media flipped and showed her in a sympathetic light. Judge Callan was still the presiding over the case, but he took a different stance and began to treat the defense with equal justice. Parents and children were called back to the stand and the truth was allowed to surface without objections being sustained for the prosecution. Noble was acquitted. In fact, some of the jury members wanted Kanof herself investigated as to why there was an indictment in the first place.[11]

A few months after Noble's acquittal, Dove's verdict was overturned and she was allowed to leave prison and return home. However, she had to wait over a year with the charges still hanging over her to see if she would be retried. Finally, the prosecution dropped the charges.

Years had passed since the initial accusations, and even though both Dove and Noble were ultimately exonerated, it was not before having their lives turned upside down, including financial ruin. They never went back into education and elected to stay away from the public eye. They would never be the same.

Kanof, for her part, was rewarded instead of reprimanded. She was elevated to the position of federal prosecutor after her convictions on Dove and Noble. One could argue that she was just a zealous young lawyer who was trying to do right. But there are grounds to dispute that. During the trial against Dove and Noble, Kanof proclaimed herself as the champion of children's rights when she said fighting abuse for her was not just a job, "it's a passion." She even touted her work with the National Committee for the Prevention of Child Abuse and the El Paso Shelter for Battered Women.[12]

But those resumé bullet points don't seem to reflect her actions when it came to the "cheating scandal" of EPISD. To try and prove a cheating scandal that didn't happen, Kanof made deals with two individuals, who in reality did put children at risk.

The first was Fernando Parra, a charming young man with questionable values. He was associated with former county judge of El Paso, Luther Jones, who was convicted for corruption in a high profile case. Parra also held a job at EPISD in the department of Special Education, even though he did not possess a degree in education, nor did he have the certification for the job. However, he became the unofficial personal driver for Lorenzo Garcia; during that time, Parra learned much about Garcia's extramarital affairs.

When Parra was being investigated for his connections to the EPISD case, his district computer was confiscated by the FBI. Unexpectedly, child pornography was found on it. This made headlines and Parra was held in jail and eventually was indicted for child pornography.[13]

Being in such a compromising position with private knowledge about Garcia's personal affairs, Parra was an excellent potential informant. In exchange for his cooperation, Kanof arranged for Parra to be released on bond after residing in El Paso's County jail for over five months.[14]

Ultimately, Parra pled guilty to possession of child pornography and received a one-year, unsupervised probated sentence instead of a 20-year prison sentence.[15]

Parra continued his life by enrolling into a graduate program at the University of Texas at El Paso (UTEP) where he earned a Ph.D. Kanof seemingly aided Parra's entrance into the program.

As a self-proclaimed person of "passion" when it came to fighting child abuse, Kanof *minimized child pornography* charges on a man who admitted guilt to the crime. Kanof was certainly aware that researchers who study this topic proclaim that these offenders are difficult to rehabilitate given their high rate of recidivism. This is one example of how

Kanof does not prosecute to get criminals out of society; she prosecutes to win cases at all costs, truth be damned.

But Parra was not the only questionable person she lauded for the sake of her own prosecutorial reputation.

Kanof was completely aware of Cordero's propensity toward violence with students. When reviewing what happened with Student X, a conclusion can be made that it was only the luck of Student X's quick reflexes that kept him from getting seriously injured or killed. But Kanof, along with the two FBI agents ensured that this danger would be in front of students once again. This had nothing to do with advocating for students; it had everything to do with winning, no matter the cost.

Compean and Ramos

With more experience as an AUSA, Kanof refined her craft for framing innocent defendants. This was evidenced with her handling of two border patrol agents. The case of Jose Compean and Ignacio Ramos is another extreme example of how far Kanof will go to get a conviction regardless of the clear evidence that the accused are innocent.[16]

This saga began in February 2005 when border patrol agents Ramos and Compean were in Fabens, TX tracking down an individual who was reported to them as a drug smuggler.

When the agents saw the smuggler, Osvaldo Alderete Davila, they went in chase. As Compean was running toward Davila, he fell. When Ramos saw this, he did not know if his partner had been shot or not. Ramos saw Davila running away and Ramos fired at Davila. Davila got away and ran to the Mexican side of the border where he was picked up in a vehicle and fled away. At that point, there was no indication that Davila had been shot.

When searching Davila's van, the border patrol agents found 750 lbs. of marijuana with a street value of $1 million. At this point, a supervisor was present, along with other border patrol agents at the scene. As per protocol, this was an event that required a report to be filled out by Compean and Ramos, but they didn't because they thought since a supervisor, a higher-ranking agent, was present, there was no need (and the supervisor never asked for a report).

A few weeks went by with nothing to report on this case. The van of marijuana had been inventoried and it seemed to be the end of the story. However, Davila, the Mexican drug smuggler, was friends with a US border patrol agent in Arizona. Davila told his friend what had transpired.

That border patrol friend tried to find the report on what happened, but it did not exist. This friend then told Davila that he should report the incident. Davila's mother made a call to the Department of Homeland Security and complained that her boy had been shot by some border patrol agents. She claimed her son was unarmed and was just an innocent person who was being targeted by the agents.[17]

Homeland Security went into action and as they investigated, so did Kanof. This case fit her personal criteria. First, Compean and Ramos were two upstanding citizens with stellar reputations and strong family ties.

Second, whereas they made a middle class living, they did not come from money and affording a full defense team would be a challenge.

Third, this case had the makings to attract the attention of the media and she knew she could frame it in a way that made the agents look guilty. Finally, if she could suppress key evidence, she knew she would be able to use emotion to sway a jury.

Along with Homeland Security, Kanof contacted Davila, the drug dealer, and offered him immunity for his testimony against the border patrol officers. In addition to immunity from his drug offense, Kanof also obtained a travel visa for Davila to the US where he could come and go to the country as he pleased. Adding insult to injury, Davila was encouraged to file a $5 million lawsuit against the Border Patrol. There was speculation that Kanof and US Attorney Johnny Sutton would help him find an attorney for this purpose.[18]

In his testimony, Davila described himself as an unfortunate individual who was only transporting drugs to get money for medicines for his mom. He claimed he was unarmed that day and that he was shot in the butt by one of the officers. Indeed, the bullet was retrieved from his butt and sent to a ballistics expert.

While having immunity and a visa, Davila was caught again for drug smuggling. This time it was with 800 pounds of marijuana worth well over $1 million. But he wasn't arrested or charged with the offense. Kanof and her boss, Johnny Sutton, kept the arrest from happening and sealed the evidence of the drug smuggling.[19]

By this time, Kanof had already successfully indicted the border patrol agents and was able to do so without a completed investigation that was supposed to be conducted by Homeland Security. When the case went to trial, the sealed evidence of the drug smuggling was not allowed into testimony and the jury never heard about it until after the trial was concluded.

By September 2006, there was considerable attention given to this case on a nationwide basis. Many petitions in favor of the agents were sent to numerous government officials. At this time, officials from Homeland Security gave a report to Congress for the purpose of justifying the indictments of the agents. In their testimony to Congress, Homeland Security claimed the following:

- Compean and Ramos confessed to the crime
- Compean and Ramos knew that Davila was unarmed
- Compean and Ramos were wanting to "shoot some Mexicans" on that day

The presentation did not sit well with members of Congress and subsequently they asked for proof of the statements. What probably caused the most doubt was the accusation that the agents wanted to "shoot some Mexicans" that day. It is not hard to tell that Compean and Ramos are Mexican-American and they have family on both sides of the border. It wouldn't make sense for them to have that motivation or to use such vernacular. Homeland Security never presented any more evidence to Congress to substantiate their claims. After the trial, Homeland Security admitted that they gave incorrect information to Congress. Another term for incorrect information is a lie.[20]

As Kanof was getting ready to go to trial, she allegedly and unsuccessfully tried to invoke the death penalty as a possible outcome. In order to get witness testimony outside of Davila's against the agents, she exerted extreme pressure on the other agents who were present on that fateful day in February 2005.

If they didn't testify to the story she wanted, she threatened to indict them with the same charges as Compean and Ramos. After the trial, these other agents testified to Kanof's actions and their lies about their co-workers. Though their testimony indicated otherwise, all agreed that they did not actually see what had transpired during the ordeal between the agents and Davila. But to save themselves, they bore false witness against their brothers on the patrol.[21]

During the trial, Davila was presented as a defenseless victim who was shot for no reason. His drug deals didn't make it to the jury's ears. As for the bullet that was found in his backside, Kanof had an expert witness conclusively verify that it was from Ramos' gun. Even Ramos saw that as being a possibility.

In an interview post trial, most jurors said that when they were given instructions, they believed that there were given only one option by the judge and that was to come up with an unanimous verdict. Both Compean and Ramos were found guilty with Ramos getting 11 years and Compean receiving 10 years of prison.[22]

As the case was being prepared for appeal, many events happened whereby one would think that the appeal would be granted. First, there was a public outrage against the verdict. And this outrage was not politically motivated.

Citizens who were liberal, conservative, and everything else in between were calling for justice. Members of Congress as conservative as John Cornyn and as liberal as Dianne Feinstein pressured President George W. Bush to immediately grant a pardon.

Second, three jurors made it clear that they would have said not guilty if they hadn't been under the impression that they had to have a unanimous verdict. All the jurors said that having the information of Davila's second drug trafficking event would have made a difference.

Finally, on further analysis of the bullet, it was not conclusive that it came from Ramos' gun. In fact, an ammunition specialist did not believe it could have come from Ramos' gun.[23]

But the appeals court did not overturn the verdict and the agents went to prison. They had to remain in solitary confinement for two years because their physical safety was in jeopardy from other inmates due to their status as law enforcement individuals.

After serving two years in prison, President George W. Bush commuted their sentences, but did not give a full pardon. Many people question Bush on his harsh stubbornness to not grant the pardon.[24] Most likely, he did not want to embarrass the officials from Homeland Security, the department he created.

Nonetheless, this was a case that exposed Kanof and her methods. Perhaps the justice system didn't fully listen, but many of "We the People" took notice of her underhanded ways that kept defendants from having a fair and impartial trial. Led by John Cornyn, Republican in Congress, the people wanted an investigation of Kanof and her boss, Johnny Sutton. The belief was that they are the only two in this case, other than Davila, who committed crimes. [25]

The contrived EPISD cheating scandal case fit Kanof's criteria: (1) there was no evidence for cheating; (2) there were many innocent individuals who did not know how to defend themselves when being accused of actions that were preposterous; (3) the defendants did not have wealth and finding defense teams that would have the same resources as the government would be terribly costly; and (4) the probability of media exposure was high and this was going to be her last big case before retiring. She allegedly mentioned to her friends and colleagues that she wanted to leave with "a bang."

It would be interesting to discover how Kanof became the prosecutor for the alleged scandal. Shapleigh knew Kanof as a contemporary in the legal community of El Paso and most assuredly was aware of her reputation for obtaining convictions in highly publicized cases. Shapleigh consulted with Richard Jewkes about the case and Jewkes was associated with the FBI agents who worked often with Kanof.

Jewkes was Anderson's first appointed counsel who recused himself because he had already been retained by Shapleigh. Shapleigh used Jewkes for the purpose of creating a prosecutorial team for charges that were yet to be invented. According to Jewkes, Kanof wanted this case.

Superintendent Lorenzo Garcia was Kanof's first victim, but she was having a tough time making any type of cheating charge against him. TEA had already debunked Shapleigh's original allegation, and there was really nothing else to pursue. But Kanof's luck changed when it was discovered that Garcia had created a no-bid contract for his former lover in the amount of $450,000.

This contract and its details were developed by an attorney outside of EPISD's legal team. That attorney was Luther Jones (who served six years in federal prison for public corruption and was disbarred) and he had a close relationship with Fernando Parra, the person who had child pornography charges trivialized by Kanof in exchange for the information he had had on Garcia.[26]

With this substantial charge involving school revenue, Kanof had leverage and she used it to get a guilty plea from Garcia. The no-bid contract of Garcia was a crime with direct and clear evidence. Garcia never denied it happened. The possible prison sentence was 20 years and the fine for the crime was the cost of the contract, $450,000.

Kanof purportedly offered Garcia a plea deal whereby if he would accept guilt to both the no-bid contract and the cheating scandal, then she would only seek three-and-one-half years in prison and reduce the fine to $186,000. If Garcia refused to plead guilty to cheating, then there was no deal. She had her ace in the hole.

Garcia felt that he had no choice, so he pled guilty to both charges even though he would claim on many occasions afterward that he had no idea what the "cheating scandal" entailed.[27] But Kanof used that plea to make a blanket claim. Garcia's guilty plea allowed the FBI/DOJ to claim a cheating scandal occurred without having to prove it. Thus, Kanof and her agents were able to tell those they were interviewing that it was already an established fact that there was cheating because Garcia said so. His plea provided the leverage to keep the scandal alive and to continue the deconstruction of EPISD.

But it was even bigger than that. If Garcia had not compromised himself with the no-bid contract to his former lover, he would have never pled guilty to cheating. He would have been in the same boat as all the other superintendents in the state of Texas. EPISD did what every other district was doing and not because administrators thought they were doing wrong. All the districts were following the mandates of TEA. If that truth had been common knowledge, then there would have been no cheating scandal and that alone would have placed the entire downtown redevelopment in jeopardy. The OIG's report declared as much by saying that although EPISD was not following the correct procedures, they were following TEA guidelines.[28]

Hence, at Kanof's behest, the FBI/DOJ seemed to pressure TEA with threats of an investigation that could lead to indictments at the state level. This motivated TEA to focus solely on EPISD and Garcia, thereby allowing EPISD to be the scapegoat for the common practice of all Texas districts. When Garcia's arm was twisted to plead guilty, that allowed TEA to separate itself from EPISD and avoid an FBI/DOJ investigation into their agency and the rest of the districts in Texas.

Garcia, however, was not enough for Kanof. She wanted more. In order to satisfy this hunger, Kanof used her tried-and-true tactics of power and fear to render guilty pleas and false testimonies from innocent people who were compromised by their life situations. As in the case of Compean and Ramos, Kanof threatened district employees with indictment if they did not tell the story she wanted to hear. And just like both previous cases, Kanof involved herself in the investigatory process.

Director of High Schools Vanessa Foreman was another individual who found herself in a compromised position. As an educator for over 20 years, Foreman had experienced significant success as an elementary school principal. Her dedication to the students of EPISD led to a promotion as a director for a high school that needed significant improvement in its academic performance. At the time the FBI was beginning its investigation into the district, Foreman was becoming acquainted with the standard operating procedures of high schools.

When the FBI called Foreman for an interview, the agents, along with Kanof, had already formed an opinion. As Foreman walked into the interview/interrogation room, the FBI had a mugshot picture of one of her colleagues and insinuated to Foreman that they could arrest her right then and there. Foreman did not back down to their intimidation. Instead, she challenged the FBI agents with their extreme ignorance regarding education law and protocol. She became so enraged at the FBI agents' behavior that she walked out of the meeting.

This seemed to spur on Kanof's anger and infuriated the agents. Payback involved targeting Foreman because they didn't like her, not because they had any evidence of wrongdoing. Ultimately, however, their constant bullying tactics led to Foreman's termination from the district. For Foreman, a single mother, the threat of indictment and multiple years in prison brought her to her knees, and she ultimately accepted a plea deal.

Interestingly, Foreman wasn't informed that she had been indicted until the day after she had secured an Equal Employment Opportunity Commission (EEOC) attorney to represent her against EPISD and TEA. Even more curious was the fact that her alleged indictment did not come down until after April 20, 2016, the day the five educators were indicted. Such a quick turnaround, and to receive an indictment at this curious time begs the question as to whether Foreman truly saw a copy of the actual document that day. Was she just the recipient of a common FBI tactic of lying in order to obtain compliance with the details to be filled in at a later date?

Foreman had much to lose by risking a courtroom trial. Like Gamboa, she agreed to plead guilty to fraudulent charges so that she could avoid prison time. For Foreman to have that guarantee, she would have to testify against the five educators. Her plea secured, Foreman's sentencing was put on hold until after their trial.

This same tactic was used with two more individuals, Maria Flores and Damon Murphy. Flores, an associate superintendent, became the scapegoat for the entire state of Texas regarding standard operating procedures for special education. Her actions were not only approved, but also mandated by TEA.

But when the FBI said EPISD's methodology was an illegal procedure, Flores became the fall guy for the state. As the main support for her grandchild with special needs, Flores already had her retirement benefits and could not afford to spend time away from her grandchild in a criminal trial. Associate superintendent Damon Murphy, a special target for Kanof and the agents, also succumbed to a plea deal due to his severe personal fear of losing his freedom.

In all, Kanof had absolutely no evidence to show cheating. But she did possess the power given to her by the federal government. She didn't use that power to get justice for victims who were harmed by the defendants since those victims didn't exist; instead, in a perversion of justice, she used it to win cases and feed her insatiable ego. It would be interesting to see if she had any personal investment in the Borderplex REIT.

As the mistrial would reveal, Kanof would stop at nothing to win the case even if it meant purposely hiding evidence that clearly exonerated the defendants which is exactly what happened. But Kanof had considerable help in her minions, Griego and Murray.

Kanof's Crew

Both Griego and Murray were in their late 40s to early 50s and were special agents. That should elicit a raised eyebrow for anyone who knows the protocol of the FBI. By their age, they should have already achieved a higher rank of agent or have been promoted into management. But after years in the department, they were still at a position usually reserved for those young in the industry. They were veteran gumshoes.

Second, they lived in El Paso, Texas right next to one of the most dangerous cities in the world, Juarez, where there are all types of investigations happening because of drug cartels that jeopardize the safety of our country. Yet, these two investigators were assigned a cheating scandal of a school district. Not the stuff that defines stellar careers. Not the stuff of FBI legends. Even if the accusations against the district were true, not one person being targeted was "dangerous." No allegations of violence, drugs, embezzlement or any real danger at all. Instead, these agents were being paid taxpayer money to harass educators.

Recipients of their interrogation techniques say that Griego and Murray were known to emphasize their clout by repeating, "We are the FBI." Along with this statement, they also exercised their power using intimidation and playing good-cop, bad-cop. It seems Murray, who apparently had a penchant for throwing things was usually the "bad cop."

The power given to the FBI/DOJ merits discussion. Simply put, the FBI/DOJ is above the law, no matter how much they will say otherwise. They are allowed—even encouraged—to behave in a manner that would land the average person behind bars. For example, they can lie all they want, and are encouraged to do so.[29] The stated purpose is so that they can get to the truth, but the reality is that they lie in order to trick people into statements that will fit their version of what they will advertise as the truth.

In the EPISD case, defendants were told by Kanof and the agents that their co-defendants had turned on them. There wasn't a shred of truth to their accusations, and they knew it, but it was done to make the defendants so distraught that they would plead guilty to something they didn't do just to avoid an outrageous prison sentence. Ultimately, Murphy, Foreman and Flores succumbed to those techniques. The pressure was too much and they were made to believe that there was no way out.

In truth, there is rarely a way out once the FBI/DOJ has made its decision. It's true that in the Western District of Texas they have a 99.2% conviction rate.[30] Their never-ending revenue and scare tactics often break victims, who go on, so to speak, to fall on their own swords. Rarely do their cases go to trial and this is true across the country. Most defendants and key witnesses who either become defendants (or bargain not to become one) make deals so they don't have to face the possibility of having to spend unthinkable prison sentences for crimes they most likely didn't commit.

In the EPISD case, Tanner and Tegmeyer faced a total possibility of 60 years in prison. Anderson was looking at 40 years. However, if any of them took a plea bargain, then all they had to face was one felony conviction and a mere five years of probation with a $5,000 fine. It must have been unbelievable to the prosecution that none of them would take that "deal."

While prevarication in the name of a perverted justice is encouraged among the FBI and DOJ, that's certainly not the case with those they are investigating. If anyone lies to the FBI, they can be charged with perjury and face 10 years in prison. It doesn't even have to be a deliberate lie. It can be an honest mistake on the part of the person interviewed, but if the FBI calls it a lie, then it is a lie. Worse yet, if potential witnesses and/or defendants tell the truth, but it doesn't correspond to the FBI's narrative, then the FBI can accuse and threaten that person with perjury unless they change their story and tell the FBI's manipulated version of the truth. [31]

Those who have become FBI targets know well just how far-reaching the organization is. They can follow you. They can listen to your phone calls. They can jeopardize your employment and livelihood. They can get access to your finances. They can put a GPS tracking device on your car without your knowledge. They can invade your life and it is completely legal. With the FBI, your Fourth Amendment right prohibiting an illegal search and seizure, realistically, does not exist. In addition, they can keep defendants from talking to co-defendants and potential witnesses thereby obstructing a defendant's ability to prepare a proper defense. However, they can speak to whomever they want whenever they want; if a person doesn't want to speak to them, then they can use coercion and threaten with actions like indictment and the fear of prison. They can record you in secret, but you cannot record them.

They will not allow any of their interviews to be recorded and rarely do they allow a third party to be present at one of their interviews.[32] The law empowers the FBI to do this so that they can "control the narrative of a case." FBI agents will write what transpired in a meeting after a meeting is concluded. The narrative is written on what is called a 302 form; it is solely written by the FBI without input from those being interviewed and the narrative is a result of memory and scant notes a detective takes during an interrogation. By law, what is written on the 302 is considered the truth and anyone who contradicts the 302 puts him or herself in jeopardy of being charged with perjury.[33]

Most US citizens are completely unaware of the breadth and depth of the FBI's powers and how they are immune to the law. Prior to the case that would shatter their careers and identity, the educators say that they, too, once trusted their government and took it for granted that their inalienable rights would be protected and respected by the FBI.

Especially early on, some, like Thomas, had no problem speaking to the FBI totally believing that the truth would set them free. Instead, the FBI in at least two instances had already completed their 302s before they ever interviewed their targets.

But this doesn't happen in a vacuum. It's fed to us culturally. Television crime shows train—brainwash—the public into believing that the government is always right. In most cop and lawyer programs, the defendant rarely is a good guy and almost never wins. Our media plasters our computer and TV screens with accused suspects as if they have already been convicted with the accusation alone being enough to condemn. Before the public knows the facts of a case, people are already asking for heads to be chopped. After understanding the true nature of the FBI/DOJ and their propensity for absolute power, authority and corruption, victims of their tactics view their surroundings quite differently.

Those who have been victims of these FBI tactics often liken the agents to terrorists. It's akin to an older brother bullying his younger brother by twisting his arm to the point of severe pain and saying it will stop "if you say the sky is red." The little brother may very well say the sky is red even though he and his brother know it is blue, but the little brother needs the pain to stop. The little brother's dignity and integrity may be gone, but his arm is free again. In the EPISD case, Garcia proverbially professed the sky to be red. Anderson, Tanner, Tegmeyer, Love, and Thomas refused by maintaining that the sky was blue. For telling the truth instead of agreeing to the contrived FBI script, their pain continued and increased.

It is important to remember that no one accused in this case was accused of any financial irregularities or any type of child abuse, the most common reasons for educators to lose their careers. None of the charges contained concrete information, and to this day, the defendants still don't understand the charges that were lodged against them. It is nearly impossible to ascertain exactly what the accusations were. But not having actual and definable accusations never stopped the agents from interrogating teachers and telling them that they were criminals for following the mandates sent out by TEA.

One such example was on accelerated instruction (a methodology most often used in summer school). The agents told teachers that accelerated instruction was illegal and part of the cheating scheme. The agents just thought this because… who knows? It wasn't merely a bad interpretation of the law. They just made it up. When it became clear to them that accelerated instruction was not against the law, but instead, was mandated by law, they never offered a correction or an apology. But they did imply without evidence that those in authority over the teachers were somehow personally benefiting financially from the process.

This begs the question: "Why?" Why were the agents committed to creating a cheating scandal? When referring to the Richard Jewkes' letter, were the agents perhaps given an assignment to find a cheating scandal? Not only did they have the backing of Eliot Shapleigh and Secretary of Education Arne Duncan, but also a possible directive given by FBI Director Robert Mueller and supported by his successor, James Comey. Thus, when one ponders why they abused their power in such a colossal manner, it is because they simply could.

Monsters.

Chapter 16: The day of the initial court appearance

The indicted had absolutely no idea what to expect in the wee morning hours of Wednesday, April 27, 2016. After the indictment, five of the six (Tanner, Tegmeyer, Love, Thomas and Murphy) had agreed to surrender themselves at the FBI offices on Mesa Hills Boulevard at 6 a.m. that morning. James Anderson was out of town at the time and, as a result, would pay the price a few days later for not being there.

What in normal circumstances should have been a routine processing, reading of the charges and release became a 19-hour circus marathon that was a deliberate and staged event. However, in this case, for Kanof and the FBI, a plea of guilty was imperative and they believed the treatment given on this day would guarantee at least five more bargains. Confession from enough of them would put pressure on the rest, legitimize a scandal and a narrative that was beginning to lose steam and potentially expose the truth about those who concocted and perpetuated it.

"Don't trust everything you see;
even salt looks like sugar."

The Shapleigh-Kanof-Margo-Moore confederation would point to the images produced that day time and again over the course of the next three years to reinforce for El Pasoans the idea that the scandal was legitimate. They depended on the public to follow the dictate, "If you see it, it must be true," and showing the public spectacle of these high-profile indictments was proof of guilt.

Surely, the images of the defendants—tired, bewildered and shell-shocked—would discourage any objective onlooker from peeking behind the curtain to see who was pulling the levers and why. A principle objective of the indictment and perp walk was to publicly humiliate and intimidate these six individuals to the point that they would beg for a plea deal just to end the nightmare and, in turn, substantiate the accusations of the Shapleigh coalition.

That morning, only Tanner, Love and Tegmeyer encountered each other upon arrival. Eventually, all were led away to separate dark, windowless, wood-paneled rooms to contemplate their fate and grasp for some sense of sanity. The early morning was spent waiting until finally agents took their fingerprints and DNA samples, asked routine questions and relieved them of any items that might assist in suicide (ties, coats, belts or shoestrings).

Sometime around 8:00 a.m., the educators were led out to the parking lot where each was placed in a separate car with a contingency of FBI agents accompanying them. The convoy left with military precision as if it were a caravan of soldiers en route to some secret location. What normally would have been a beautiful April morning was marred by the excruciatingly long, stressful drive from the west side of El Paso to the Old Federal Court House downtown. Darkness had descended on those handcuffed in the back seat of the nondescript sedans.

The arrival in downtown El Paso was uneventful. The caravan parked in front of the county courthouse, constructed from reflective, mirror-like materials, and the prisoners were escorted through the cool morning across the street into the Old Federal Courthouse. Passing through that marvelous 1930s neo-classical entrance with the famous Tom Lea mural Pass of the North, the defendants were taken, one-by-one, in the small, outdated elevators to the second floor with its cold, nondescript cubical offices of Pretrial Services. There they were processed again and assigned to an officer whose job it was to make sure they complied with the bond that would be imposed on them.

Each educator went through the security door dividing the waiting room from a hallway with several separate cramped offices to sign paperwork, assess their financial ability to pay for legal defense, give their first verified urine sample (witnessed by an FBI agent) and be given the rules they were expected to follow for an indeterminate amount of time. Handcuffed in the cramped sitting area waiting for the next one to finish their time in the cubical down the locked hallway, they sat and waited for that part of the process to be over. Each was flanked by two FBI agents at their side as if they were a public threat.

Tegmeyer was one of the first to emerge and his guardians inadvertently began to escort him toward the elevator. Agents Murray and Griego were waiting in the hall in front of the elevators on what resembled an old church pew and stopped the escort.

"Where are you guys going?" Griego asked them.

The young agents nodded toward the elevators to which Murray responded, "No. We're taking them all over together."

With that, it was back into the cramped waiting room to sit uncomfortably with hands cuffed behind their backs for another half hour.

When the time came, the defendants were herded into the Grand Lobby. As employees were being scanned to clock into work, the educators were held in line, each sandwiched between two agents. But if one wanted to see what was happening inside, one didn't have to be in the lobby. The windowed doors removed all confusion as to why the two greenhorn agents had been halted. Every local media outlet had cameras and reporters stationed in front of the courthouse awaiting the "perp walk" about which they had obviously been informed.

For the five who self-surrendered, an already stress-filled morning which had ironically been relatively calm up to that point, was about to get ugly. What they were about to endure was a practice that had been discontinued in the years after El Paso had built a new federal courthouse. Defendants were now regularly transported by vehicle from one building to another, but an old tradition was resurrected that day specifically for purpose of instilling fear and humiliation on the innocents.

Once the doors opened and the flood of agents and handcuffed prisoners appeared, camera shutters clicked in loud succession like machine guns in a battle. Reporters scrambled to shove microphones and recorders in the stone-silent faces of the accused, trying to get sound bite answers to inane questions.

Stephanie Valle, a reporter from KVIA Channel 7, posed a question to Murphy and Tanner that summed up the media angle for this day and the years to come. After all, the media had a role to play as the confederation's spin doctors.

"Do you have anything to say to the EPISD taxpayers?" she quipped.

The defendants kept walking.

As the group had to cross two main streets in order to get to the county jail where they were being taken, the traffic lights and crossing signals allowed the media plenty of time to photograph and report back to the talking heads at the studio about what was taking place.

Upon reaching the jail, the educators-turned-prisoners descended the ramp down to the loading dock, reporters and photographers in tow, and disappeared into the bowels of the basement floor, leaving the havoc outside. From the basement, they were taken upstairs to be processed into the jail, have their mug shots taken and exchanging their clothes for El Paso County Detention Facility blue coveralls and crocks.

The next step was the transfer to the federal holding facility across the street. Instead of simply loading them into the van from the basement loading dock, the five were paraded back up the loading dock ramp to a passenger van parked on the street. This gave the media one more shot of the five in jail attire and, once again, accomplished the two goals of the day: humiliating and intimidating the accused while burning the images of handcuffed educators into the psyches of the El Paso public via the media spin.

At the federal holding facility, men and women were separated and lined up face first toward the wall. An overzealous officer threatened violence if they turned their heads or spoke. They were shackled about the ankles to complete the handcuff couture, making it impossible to scratch a nose or elbow. Tanner was yelled at specifically when he stated under his breath that this treatment was completely unnecessary. Once everything was in order, all were escorted upstairs to Judge Torres' court room a little after 1 p.m. for the reading of the charges and setting the bonds.

Magistrate Judge Miguel Torres' courtroom was filled with defendants in the front of the courtroom, with family and local media occupying the gallery. Once all defendants, not just the educators, were present, the charges were read and an acknowledgment of understanding was required. The charges ranged from being undocumented immigrants to drug trafficking to the five EPISD administrators charged with fraud, mail fraud, conspiracy to commit fraud, retaliation against a federal witness and perjury.

Unsecured bonds were set at $30,000 for all except Diane Thomas, whose bond was $20,000 as she only had the count of retaliation against her. It was at this time that the defendants were instructed that they could no longer speak to one another and other conditions of the bond were set. However, once they were escorted back to the county jail, the government separated the group by gender and kept them in cell blocks for the rest of the day.

Tragically, Thomas was the only defendant who also owned firearms and did not yet have an attorney. The government conveniently failed to inform her that the list of firearms she was to hand over had to include serial numbers. As it was too late in the day for her family to retrieve those numbers and get them back to the court in time, she would remain in jail for the night and she would be released once those were turned over the next day.

After remaining in holding cells in the basement of the federal courthouse for a few hours, the transfer back to the county jail took place around five o'clock with no fanfare this time. Now it was a matter of surviving until they were released. News of the educators' identities had circulated quickly around the city and in the jail, and as they waited in the central area to be assigned a holding cell, prisoners began to taunt them from other holding areas. One specific taunt was from a seemingly disturbed young man who shouted, "They say you guys stole money from kids! Wait 'til we get you upstairs!"

Sometime around eight p.m., the two women were taken to a holding cell as were the three men. The men were put in a cell block by themselves with about six open cells and three iron picnic type tables bolted to the floor with the seats welded to the mainframe. Though it was cold and sterile, being placed in there alone eased their minds somewhat, given the threats that were being shouted at them before.

Sometime around 10 p.m., a young man was placed in the cell block with them. At the time, the placement seemed innocuous. Perhaps there wasn't room for him elsewhere. Maybe he was causing problems given the mental instability he was displaying in the cell block with the three. As he entered, Murphy, Tanner and Tegmeyer observed him while sitting at one of the immovable tables in the main corridor. He then entered one open cell to lie down, complain about the bed and move to another. He spoke nonsensically at times and his agitated behavior and demeanor was a clear indication that he was a disturbed soul.

Upon reflection afterward, however, it became obvious why this poor individual was placed into the relative solitude of the trio after their already harrowing day. It was to give them a foretaste of what was to come should they be convicted. It was the government's way of letting them know the possibility of serving time with individuals such as this, should they decide to fight the charges. It was designed to make them question the possibility of surviving should they not win acquittal. It served the same purpose as the day's circus: intimidate them into ending it all with a simple guilty plea.

After about a half hour, the young man was removed from the block just as unexpectedly as his arrival. By midnight, all but Thomas could change back into their own street clothes. Sometime after one in the morning, their belongings were returned to them and they were released. Exhausted and dazed, they were greeted by their families and drove through the dark, quiet streets that looked much as they did when they had arrived at the FBI offices just short of 24 hours earlier. The treatment of these five, however, was a pat on the back for compliance compared to what James Anderson received for not being available for the government's public humiliation scheme.

Anderson had attempted to turn himself in a week earlier as he had planned a trip to California to visit his mother, but the FBI intake office would not process him. Unknowingly, they had planned a show for April 27 and Anderson would be one of the stars whether he liked it or not.

140

On advice from his counsel, he was instructed to leave town for his commitments and turn himself in the following Monday. Because he followed this advice, an example was made of Anderson to emphasize the power of the federal government and its tactics of psychologically beating its foes into submission.

Anderson turned himself into the county jail the following Monday. He was handcuffed and put into a cell. In the hour that it took for the FBI to arrive to retrieve him, the media had been contacted and had a gauntlet of reporters and cameras prepared for him as he was led from the jail to the nondescript sedan that was to take him to their offices on the west side.

As an added bonus to Anderson's ordeal, upon arriving at the FBI offices, Tom Murray and James Griego, the two agents in charge of the cheating investigation scheme, stripped searched him down to his undergarments and photographed him in this state. This is treatment is generally reserved for drug addicts, drug mules or violent criminals; in Anderson's case, this was completely unnecessary and served only one purpose.

Murray, Griego and Kanof were the power and anyone who challenged that power would pay dearly. Anderson and the Austin administrators all paid dearly. With Anderson, however, they seemed to take even greater delight in being particularly sadistic.

The media was still there when he arrived for the walk to Pretrial Services in the old federal courthouse and from the courthouse back to the county lockup. The rest of that day until about two the next morning was spent in a standing room only drunk tank awaiting intake into the federal portion of the El Paso jail system, where they brought ten sandwiches for about 30 individuals and Anderson went hungry.

Finally, at about 2 a.m. after receiving his coveralls, he was taken to an upstairs federal unit of the jail, escorted into a dark cell with approximately 10 beds and only one top bunk unoccupied. Carrying his mattress, a roll of toilet paper and a razor, as is required of inmates, he took the unoccupied bunk. At about 3:30 a.m., the alarm for breakfast sounded. In the light, he could see that he was rooming with about 20 other inmates, all presumably South American, based on their dialect.

It was lights out again after breakfast concluded at about 4 a.m. A half hour later, the guards came for Anderson, holding flashlights and Taser sticks. He was to gather his mattress and supplies and be escorted to another unit. The new unit had two sides and he was specifically placed in the section on the right. Once again, he set up his bunk in the dark where he lay awake until the lights came on again at 7 a.m.

Anderson was later taken to court to have the charges read. At the time, an entire group of inmates were being taken to the courthouse. Instead of taking him by bus with the rest, the media was alerted and he was walked across the street once again to the sound of rapid-fire camera shutters and reporters who were barely old enough to vote.

The sadism continued when the Kanof and the FBI agents fought to deny him bail and he was forced to spend four days in the county lock up. He returned twice more to the court to argue against the fed's insistence that he remain in prison with no bond until the time of trial over a year later. Anderson had told the jailer that he was concerned for his safety as he had charged individuals as a principal at Andress High School in northeast El Paso. He was told not to worry, and that it had been taken care of and that he would be "separated." "It had been taken care of" turned out to mean that the jailers "separated" him for about five minutes and then lumped him in with the rest, surely on orders from Murray and Griego.

The minute he was placed with the general population of the federal jail prisoners, he was recognized from the news coverage and began to be surrounded. A student from Andress that he had charged with gang activity and possession drugs was in the mix. Multiple inmates had threatened him because they understood from the local media that he and the others had hurt Mexicans. Anderson spent the next four days convincing gang members with names like Little Puppet, Snoopy and John Mark that the news was lying to them.

Anderson had to explain that the authorities were accusing him and the others because Hispanics were doing well; he and the others had worked hard to help them overcome an unjust system, and it was because they were doing well that these people were saying that there was cheating. Interestingly, Anderson's rapport with the fellow inmates was ruining the plans of Griego, Murray and Kanof. By the time he was released on Thursday morning, he had won the protection of Little Puppet, Snoopy and most of the population.

Interestingly, Snoopy, an MS-13 gang member, was the first to reach out to Anderson asking if the allegations about Tanner were true. He had been a student of Tanner's and was enrolled in high school and community college through Tanner's support. He was working toward earning college credit when he was arrested selling automatic weapons to undercover federal officers. He was said he had wanted to better himself and get out of the life, but was arrested before he could do that. He knew Tanner very well from his time at Austin High School and none of the stories made sense to him. This was incentive enough to give Anderson the protection he needed for his time at the jail.

Over the four days there were many incidents that could be addressed in an entire book by itself. During that time, the media rebroadcast the story daily and it was shown on the jail televisions. Suffice it to say, Kanof and the FBI put Anderson in harm's way for a reason.

If we examine the sadistic show of power inflicted on Anderson and the marathon of humiliation imposed on Tanner, Tegmeyer, Love and Thomas (the Austin four) in juxtaposition to the gradual disintegration of Kanof's case over the next three years, only one conclusion can be drawn as to the purpose of this spectacle: Kanof had no case.

Therefore, she and Murray and Griego did with these six what they did not do with Garcia, Gamboa, Flores or Foreman. With the help of a complicit media, they made sure there were unforgettable images of these six being led in handcuffs and jail attire. They influenced opinion and prejudiced the jury pool just in case these individuals were audacious enough to try and make it all the way to trial.

Bob Moore's seven-page feature in the *El Paso Times* the next day in white, or reverse print, on a black background, along with the special reports issued by every local television station showed well enough the narrative they chose to perpetuate. For the average El Pasoan, this was explosive news and a dying narrative was brought back to life. The El Paso media never corrected that narrative, even as the government's case fell apart and Kanof's impropriety and Shapleigh's impossibility became blatantly obvious. This behavior attests to how completely Moore and the rest of the El Paso media outlets shirked their First Amendment responsibilities and their journalistic integrity to protect themselves in a sadistic and gross miscarriage of justice.

Chapter 17: Leading up to the trial

Under normal circumstances, a trial date is set within three months of the arraignment. No one believes that a trial will really take place that quickly, but in an attempt to satisfy that requirement, a date is usually set to meet that standard. Often, a defendant will ask for a continuance of the trial, meaning that the trial will be postponed to a later date so that the defense will have time to prepare a case.

In most cases, the prosecution is ready for trial. Prosecutors have all the evidence and basically hold all the cards, and more likely than not, have been preparing a long time. The defense, on the other hand, has not been given the evidence against its client until after the arraignment.

This evidence, including Jencks and Brady documents, can number into hundreds of thousands of pages, even venturing into the millions. Because of the immense amount of evidence to research, it is understandable why the defense usually asks for a continuance, and it is almost certain that a judge will grant the continuance. Keep in mind that, in this case, the prosecution had six years to prepare for this particular trial.

Inculpatory in nature, Jencks documentation is evidence that the government relies on by its witnesses. In other words, it is evidence for the prosecution. It must be given to the defendant after the witness testifies. Exculpatory in nature, Brady documentation is evidence that might be used to prove a defendant's innocence, so this is evidence that exonerates the defendants. Any Brady or Jencks evidence that the prosecution possesses must be given to the defense, according to the laws of the United States of America. Not abiding by the defendant's inalienable rights can lead to a mistrial, a retrial, and many times, a dismissal of the case.

In the EPISD case, the trial was set for August 2016, about four months after the educator's arrest and initial appearance. All six defendants pleaded not guilty and most wanted a continuance in order to prepare for the trial. Over 200,000 documents were provided to the defense two weeks after the initial court appearance. Relatively speaking, that was not much considering the time and attention given to this case. While the defense lawyers were discussing among themselves an almost certain request for a continuance so as to have enough time to review all of the evidence, it was Kanof who asked the judge first. She did so requesting that the court recognize the case as "complex."

Establishing the case as complex circumvented the defendants Sixth Amendment right to a speedy trial. Though it is not uncommon for either the defense or prosecution to request a continuance, the fact that Kanof requested the continuance first after six full years of investigation and two convictions seemed telling. The judge granted the continuance.

The fabricated cheating scandal had been news for at least seven years by this point. Garcia had already pled guilty, served time, and was released by the time of the educator's indictments. All protocol suggested that the government had its case ready, but clearly, it didn't. The judge in the case, David Briones, set the new date for February 2017.

In August 2016, Tanner received a phone call from his attorney, Jim Darnell. Tanner felt fortunate to have Darnell, an attorney of high repute and stature, representing him, especially considering that he was known to successfully challenge Kanof in legal matters over the years. Darnell was also very familiar with the case and he knew that no cheating scandal occurred. Of all the defense lawyers on the case, Darnell possessed the most knowledge about the contrived cheating scandal.

In his characteristic soft and steady voice, Darnell dropped the bomb. "I don't know how to tell you this… but I can no longer represent you. Because of my involvement with other defendants in EPISD, Kanof argued to the judge that my representation of you is a conflict of interest."

Judge Briones agreed with Kanof. Darnell—the most seasoned attorney regarding the case—was dismissed from duty.

However, Darnell offered a suggestion in Elizabeth Rogers, better known to friends and clients as Liz. In the end, Rogers, with a combination of Texas independence and social skills, proved to be as powerful and competent as Darnell had described. But Tanner did not meet Rogers in person until October 2016. El Pasoan Robert Perez was appointed to represent James Anderson. Anderson had already lost a significant amount of money in paying other attorneys, and he could afford no more. Fortunately, Perez was committed to Anderson and quickly saw the lunacy of the case.

Tegmeyer retained the services of Luis Islas, a competent, street smart, bulldog of an attorney with his bachelor's and Juris Doctorate degrees from Stanford and Berkeley, respectively. Thomas was represented by Sheri Bunn, another appointed attorney who completely committed herself to Thomas' cause. Bunn was a graduate of West Point and exemplified the discipline and dedication one expects from that institution.

Finally, Love was represented by Mary Stillinger. Kanof tried to get Stillinger removed from the case but was unsuccessful. Stillinger had a long history with Kanof. Unlike anyone else on the defense team, Stillinger was acutely aware of the unscrupulous actions perpetuated by Kanof over the years. As a member of Compean and Ramos's defense team, Stillinger still felt the sting of Kanof's bullying.

Defendant Damon Murphy had been particularly unlucky in the area of obtaining council. After Murphy had paid $100,000 to retain Sib Abraham, a prominent attorney in the El Paso area, Abraham suddenly and unexpectedly died, leaving Murphy bereft of funds. Murphy's newly appointed attorney must have begun pondering the possibility of a plea bargain with his client.

As the defense attorneys were doing due diligence reviewing the evidence that was turned over at the time, they realized quickly that all the defendants, except for Murphy, supported and believed in each other. Murphy and his attorney were conspicuously absent when the defense was readying the strategy for the February court date. Tanner and Tegmeyer speculated that Murphy was going to make a plea deal, given Murphy's demeanor in the jail cell on the day of the initial appearance. Murphy, like Tegmeyer and Tanner, was troubled by all that had transpired. All spoke about their innocence and wondered how all of this could have ever gotten so out of hand. The conversation was deep. It was hard to believe that Murphy had just met Tegmeyer that day, as they had never worked with each other before.

At one point in their conversation, Murphy looked at Tegmeyer and Tanner and said, "So are you going to make a plea deal?"
Tegmeyer answered by saying that, although he was afraid, he could not see himself ever admitting to doing something when he knew in his heart it wasn't true.

Tanner gave the same sentiments by saying, "I've always said that I would rather serve time than admit to something I didn't do, but this shithole makes me contemplate my words. But no, I won't make a deal. I did nothing wrong."

Murphy had a different sentiment.

"Gentlemen, I wasn't made for this. If I can make a deal and not get jail time, I just might cut my losses and move on," Murphy said.

Ultimately, that is what Murphy did. He made a plea deal where he said he was guilty on one count of fraud. He was led to believe that he was only going to get five years of probation and a $5,000 fine, but that sentencing wasn't going to happen until the trial for the five remaining defendants was completed. The leverage for Murphy was his testimony against the five remaining defendants. Murphy agreed to testify against all of them, including Tegmeyer whom he had not met until he was in a jail cell with him.

146

Once it was established that there would be five defendants, the team of attorneys agreed to ask for another continuance so that the trial could be moved to the summer of 2017. Because Rogers was new to the case and because Murphy had chosen a plea deal, the defense team needed time to organize for the trial. Judge Briones granted the continuance and set the trial for June 12, 2017.

Despite the stress, life continues

The defense attorneys were assuring their clients that they needed to be ready for that court date, as no further continuance was expected. With that, the defendants had to carry on with their lives and find a way to make a living.

Anderson, upon being forced out of his position, had become a successful real estate agent and was quickly becoming prominent in that field before the indictment. After the indictment—complete with his picture and name defamed throughout the city—Anderson's real estate career ended abruptly. With his household now having only one salary, Anderson and his wife sold their home and declared bankruptcy. Anderson was unable to find work until after the mistrial.

Until the indictment, Love had maintained an assistant principal position in EPISD. The indictment forced her to resign. She endeavored on a few careers that included fitness instruction at a local gym, along with beginning a small bakery business from her home.

Tegmeyer had become a middle school assistant principal in the district where he began his career as an educator. Quickly, he was becoming successful and believed that he would soon become a principal. But after the indictment, he was forced to resign. His post-indictment employment forced him to leave his wife for work in Arizona. His brother-in-law gave him work installing blinds and other window treatments for $11 an hour.

By the time of the indictment, Thomas had already lost everything regarding her career. She managed to land a job as an administrative assistant for the Shriners in El Paso. They initially supported Thomas with her situation, but with the indictment, they, too, terminated her employment.

Moving cross country to Washington state's beautiful capital Olympia after his forced resignation in May 2014, Tanner, with guidance from his brother, earned a license in nursing home administration. He was successfully working as an administrator of a skilled nursing facility at the time of the indictment.

"The company I worked with was understanding of my situation and supported me until the time of the trial," Tanner said. "The legal department of the company read everything available regarding the case and ultimately concluded that they could not figure out what crime was alleged to have been committed."

But ultimately, Tanner had resigned his position because he could not be away from his job for as long as the preparation and trial were scheduled to last—which was estimated to be at least a couple of months.

Frye hearings

Curiously, in March 2017, all defendants had to appear in court for a Frye hearing. This type of hearing ensures that the defendants know and understand all that is being offered to them from the prosecution and to make that public. Frye hearings are extremely rare as most of those involved in the legal process assume that defense attorneys are sharing all pertinent information with their clients.

And indeed, in this case, the defense attorneys were most definitely sharing all information. Nonetheless, it was a command performance for all the defendants, whereby they had to take the time to make the appearance in court. For Love, Tegmeyer, Anderson and Thomas that meant reliving the courtroom drama from the previous year. Tanner had the added burden of paying for a round trip ticket from Seattle to El Paso for a hearing that would last less than 10 minutes.

During the hearing, the charges were read out loud again with all the possible consequences including fines and years in prison. Then the prosecution offered a plea for each of them that would effectively end the case and bring everything to a conclusion. Namely, a win for the prosecution.

It was a waste of time for everyone. The defendants had made it clear that they would never make a plea bargain and would never admit guilt to something they didn't do.

Diane Thomas was offered a misprision, which would entail a significant reduction of her felony charge of retaliation. With this lesser charge, Thomas would have to admit that she knew a felony occurred but concealed the truth about it. If she accepted this plea, she would agree to testify against Tanner. A felony would still appear on her record, but there would be no prison time, and possibly no probation.

Arguably, Thomas lost more than any of the other defendants and no one would have blamed her for taking the offer. In fact, most of the defense attorneys thought she would. Defense attorneys often advise their clients to plead guilty even if they know their client is innocent, especially in federal cases. The feds have put many innocents behind bars, not because of overwhelming evidence, but because of their unlimited power to manipulate and silence their opposition. This deal would ensure that Thomas would have her physical freedom.

But Thomas didn't hesitate to decline the offer. She knew that neither she nor anyone else had done anything wrong and she maintained that she would not say she did something she didn't do. As with the rest of the defendants, she would rather endure prison time and maintain her integrity.

Love was offered probation and a fine reduction if she made a plea deal. Like Thomas, Love was not about to admit guilt for something she didn't. She, too, was in this for the long haul.

Anderson, who was taunted with a possibility of 40 years in federal prison, was told that the prosecution was willing to drop two of his three charges and offer probation and a fine as an alternative. Tanner and Tegmeyer, both threatened with 60 years of federal prison, were also given an option of having three of their four charges dropped with a consequence of probation and a fine. Like Thomas and Love, the three men didn't even consider the accepting the offer.

The defendants already knew that the prosecution was lying and that there was no legitimate case. If the prosecution was willing to drop major charges—including the retaliation charge—and give no prison sentences when they were threatening the defendants with what would amount to life in prison, then what real case was there?

Tanner's attorney, Liz Rogers, summed it up best when she discussed the plea bargain with Tanner.

"Why would anyone agree to their deal?," she asked. "It doesn't mean that it's over. For that deal, you'll have to lie about other people so that others will also be coerced into saying they're guilty even if they've done nothing wrong. You and the rest are people of integrity, and I know you can't do that."

So they stuck to their integrity and they stuck together—even when they couldn't speak to each other.

The Frye hearing took place on March 10, 2017, and the deadline to accept the deal was 30 days. All defendants were confident that no one was going to accept any of the "bargains" offered. And no one did. After not refusing the government's proverbial carrot, the innocents were called back to court and given a chance again to accept a plea bargain. Again, no one took the bait. At Anderson's hearing, Briones approached the bench, careful to speak prior to being seated (which would put him on court record), the burly judge told the former associate superintendent, "I'll make sure you get the full sentence if you don't take this plea deal."

The Honorable David Briones

Based on Anderson's experience, it is safe to say that David Briones wanted the defendants to make the plea bargain. He would spend 10 years as a part of this case—from its inception in 2010 to its end in January 2020. In that time, there were many accusations and numerous Grand Jury meetings, but very little success in proving a cheating scandal. The former superintendent had pled guilty, but never went to trial. A former school director agreed to plead guilty before ever being charged with a crime. There was no smoking gun; there were only people falling on their own swords in order to avoid the very real scare tactics of the FBI/DOJ.

David Briones was not the original judge assigned to the case. The original judge was Kathleen Cardone. But Kanof wanted Briones and worked actively to make it happen. Kanof claimed that Briones was the only logical choice for the judge since he was the one assigned to the case against Lorenzo Garcia; in other words, Kanof argued for consistency, since Briones was already familiar with the cheating scandal. It was later learned that Kanof and Briones had an ex parte meeting (done with respect to or in the interests of one side) to discuss the motion. This meeting was filed under seal. Speaking out of both sides of her mouth, however, during the mistrial and on record, Kanof declared that the case against the innocents had nothing to do with Garcia.

Perhaps Kanof didn't want Cardone since Cardone had been the judge during the Compean and Ramos debacle. The national outcry regarding Kanof's corrupt antics in that case may have influenced Cardone to tolerate far less in this case. Or perhaps Cardone was happy not to be involved in another high-profile case where Kanof was the main prosecutor. Either way, Briones was appointed as judge.

Though not advertised publicly, Briones and Kanof had shared interests in the case of Dolores Briones, the sister of the federal judge. Dolores Briones was a county judge in El Paso from 1998-2006. However, she was charged in 2011 and pled guilty to defrauding the county during the time she was a judge. The fraud was in the amount of $550,000 of which she received $24,000 in bribes. Given that she was an elected official, there was speculation that she would receive a sentence of at least five years in federal prison. But because her brother was a federal judge, there was also speculation that she would receive a light sentence, perhaps in the form of probation. Her original judge was Frank Montalvo, a friend of David Briones who also worked in the same building as Briones. Citing a possible conflict, County Judge Dolores Briones was sentenced by a federal judge in New Mexico.[1]

However, there were other co-conspirators in Dolores Briones' defrauding scheme. They, too, were facing substantial sentences. As a rule of thumb, elected officials receive stiffer sentences than defrauders who are not elected officials. But not in this case. In the end, Dolores Briones received a sentence of 30 months in federal prison with three years of supervised release. Her co-conspirator, Ruben "Sonny" Garcia received four years in prison while her other co-conspirator, Cirilo Lara Madrid received 15 years in prison.[2]

Yet, this was not Dolores Briones' only crime. In another related bribery scheme during her tenure as a judge, Dolores steered over $100 million in business to a health insurer. In return, she received unknown amounts of gifts. She admitted to receiving vacations and entertainment tickets as part of the bribes.[3] The prosecuting attorney in this case was Debra Kanof. Kanof publicly acknowledged that Dolores was guilty of the crime, but maintained the status as an "unindicted co-conspirator."

Other conspirators in this case who were indicted received prison sentences and hefty fines. Kanof was questioned by reporters, but failed to answer why Dolores was not indicted. By not being indicted, the public never discovered the extent of the bribes and Dolores never paid a fine or returned the bribe money.

Did having a brother as a federal judge keep Dolores Briones from receiving a stiffer sentence? Was Kanof in the process of a quid pro quo setup with David Briones? It is convenient that Kanof was able to be the prosecutor for David Briones' sister during the same time the fake cheating scandal was brewing. Did Kanof speculate that Briones would grant favors to her in the cheating scandal case because of her leniency with his sister? These are, indeed, fair questions.

Chapter 18: The trial

As the defendants woke up for the first day of trial, they felt the way they had for the past few years: they were in a surreal world where bad was good and good was bad. Still, after years, this overturned world was incomprehensible. The only clarity that hit them in the face was the fact that they stood to serve years in federal prison and judging by the conviction rate of the federal "justice" system, that outcome seemed likely.

Resolved like molten steel to keep their integrity intact, the five defendants were already resolved to keep their integrity intact collectively and individually repeated that they would rather serve time than admit to something they did not do.

Both Anderson and Tanner hoped to get on the stand and finally present the facts of the case. They had never been allowed to tell their side of the story, and this was their opportunity. Yet, Tanner was skeptical.

"James," Tanner said, "They don't want us on the stand. They will find a way to keep us from testifying. I just feel it in my gut. If we are ever allowed to tell our side of the story…."

Anderson, too, was adamant.

"I want to get up there and tell them. They better let us," Anderson said. "If we've had to go through all this, we better be able to give our side. That's our Constitutional right."

Yeah, and so much for that theory! Just like innocent until proven guilty," Tanner said.

Tanner knew that the prosecution never wanted to publicly air what had happened with Cordero and his attempt to run down a student. Nor did they want the public to understand that all the major investigations pointed to the fact that no cheating scandal ever existed. Certainly, Kanof didn't want it known that she used Parra, an individual convicted for possession of child pornography, as her pawn to compel an indictment. Even at the beginning of the trial, Cordero still hadn't made it to the local news.

That was the real conspiracy. The media, the school district, the FBI and the federal prosecutor all conspired to ensure that Cordero's act of child endangerment and the truth about the investigations would never be known. Although the defendants dreaded this day, they were now ready to air the truth and take a chance on "We the People" seeing through the farce that was conceived in corruption.

On the first day—Monday, June 12, 2017—many tasks had to be accomplished. The first were the pre-trial agreements. During this time, Kanof attempted to get the defense attorneys to stipulate (a binding agreement on certain facts of a case meant to save time and simplify matters) to all EPISD business and employee records.

Knowing how Kanof worked, Mary Stillinger counseled the defense team not to accept. Stillinger had amazing instincts because what Kanof actually had included in those documents were all of Ruben Cordero's employee records, including the timeline that proved he lied about his involvement with the FBI to save his job. Had the defense team accepted the stipulation, the discrepancy may never have been discovered. The two-page timeline that exonerated the defendants was not turned over until it was dumped on the defense in an email two weeks into the trial— along with loads of other documents providing a hopeful smoke screen around the exculpatory evidence.

The next major task was selecting a jury. This became controversial. The jury pool was supposed to number 200 from which 12 jurors and three alternates would be selected. Of the 200 jury summons that were mailed, only 100 citizens responded. Of those 100, the defense believed that nearly 60 should have been eliminated based on the jury questionnaire. The judge did not agree. However, after the initial deletions, the attorneys from both sides had a pool of 37 from which to choose a total of 15. The defense attorneys believed this to be too small of a pool from which to sit a jury. It was contrary to their experience, but Judge Briones was intent on starting the trial and he forced a jury to be chosen from the pool of 37.

Choosing the jury was like a sporting event where different sides were choosing their teams. It was revealing. During the questioning of the jury pool, Mary Stillinger asked, "How many of you are familiar with the cheating scandal of EPISD?" Of the 37 that were asked, 35 hands were raised. Then she asked, "How many of you have heard the defense's side of the story?" No hand went up, but many eyebrows did, including many in the jury pool. Of nearly 700 newspaper articles and hundreds of TV newscasts, no one had heard an opposing view of the alleged cheating scandal. By 3:30 p.m., the jury was chosen, and Judge Briones directed the commencement of the opening statements.

Robert Perez began for Anderson and emphasized the fact that the entire case should not have happened in the first place. Perez asserted that the federal government had not only overreached their power into a state issue, but manipulated and intimidated witnesses in a manner that resembled the mafia. By name, he accused Kanof of becoming too involved in the case to the point that she was not only the prosecutor, but one of the main investigators as well. He offered to the jury that the real conspiracy was comprised of the FBI agents, Debra Kanof, El Paso Politicians and the media.

Tom Mills, a Dallas-based attorney with a Texas swagger, presented the opening statement for Tanner. He highlighted Tanner's accomplishments in life and how Tanner's character offered no evidence for the charges levied against him. Luis Islas declined to make an opening statement for Mark Tegmeyer. He elected to reserve his time for closing arguments. Mary Stillinger spoke on behalf of Nancy Love and highlighted the nefarious inclusion of Nancy in this case, given her short tenure at Austin High School.

The highlight of the opening statements belonged to Sheri Bunn, who represented Diane Thomas. She began by looking at the jury and saying, "You are the most powerful people in this room. It is not me nor any attorney in here. It is not the prosecutors. It is not Judge Briones. You in that jury box are the most powerful people in here because you represent a government by the people, for the people and of the people."

Bunn reminded the jury about the important basic rights given by the Constitution and how the government is supposed to follow the will of the people, not the other way around. She went on to explain how Thomas and the rest of the defendants were brave by not caving into the unethical and perhaps illegal tactics of the prosecution and that the jury should realize that the defendants were people of integrity who refused to say they were guilty when they knew they didn't do anything wrong.

She emphasized that the government had been a "steamroller" in the lives of the defendants, taking everything from them before they even had a chance to save what was rightfully theirs.

"But you, the jury of the people, can let the government know when the steamroller has to stop and when it has gone too far. You are more powerful than those who put these defendants in this predicament. It is why the founders of our nation set up this type of system where we don't have kings or dictators that apply the law subjectively," Bunn said. "We have a jury of our peers who decide what is right and what is wrong. Let these defendants know that the steamroller that has crushed their justice ends here."

Upon her conclusion, the prosecution was allowed to begin their case. The main strategy for the prosecution was using witnesses who had already made bargains with the FBI or plea deals with Kanof. Only one witness was an expert witness who had no connection to the case. This chapter highlights the key witnesses of the prosecution.

The prosecution's first step was to assert that it did have jurisdiction over this case. Public education in the United States has been historically and consistently the responsibility of each individual state, not the federal government. The defense had already submitted an appeal to protest the fact that the case was in violation of the 10th Amendment of the Constitution (limits of the federal government). It was a hurdle for Kanof and the FBI to establish this point, and their expert witness, Carlos Martinez, compromised their argument. Martinez was the sole witness without any direct or indirect connection to the case.

Carlos Martinez

Martinez's expertise was established in that he had an extensive background in the knowledge of funding for educational programs designed for English language learners. He had worked with a few federally funded programs at the Department of Education and was knowledgeable regarding how federal funds were funneled to state education systems. But at the conclusion of his testimony, he helped establish a key point for the defense. In sum, his testimony rendered count one of the indictment as null and void. There was no fraud against the US Government.

If count one was invalidated, then inherently, so were counts two and three. Though he stopped short of saying that the federal government didn't have jurisdiction, he established four points:

• Although the states might receive federal monies, it is the state that is responsible for the distribution of funds.
• Although the state uses federal funds, the federal government does not oversee how the funds are used.
• Although the state uses federal funds, the state is the one responsible for the management of the funds and any corrective action necessary because of the misuse of funds.
• The federal government has never been involved in a case against a school district of the state before because it has never been deemed to have this jurisdiction.

Kanof, while questioning Martinez, exposed her strategy of trying to portray the five Anglo defendants as using "soft prejudice of lowered expectations."

"You were talking about extraordinary situations where poor children can be reached out to in an intellectual environment. Give an example of one of those extraordinary situations," Kanof asked of Martinez.

Martinez replied, "I think one that most people know about is Jaime Escalante of Stand and Deliver. By raising expectations and having students follow the rigorous curriculum, he was able to get his students into calculus."

Robert Perez comically pointed out that, the students of the movie, like those of Bowie and Austin high schools, had worked hard and had been accused of cheating, but didn't.

Red faced, the prosecuting attorneys were noticeably frustrated. The defense attorneys were pleasantly surprised with Martinez's testimony as it seemed that he was a witness for the defense.

Martinez was damaging to the prosecution on another point as well. Kanof had argued that the motive for the conspiracy was to manipulate the system in order to receive more federal funding as a result of the district's success. Kanof maintained that those extra funds were diverted into bonuses and stipends for various administrators in the district. Even though that wasn't a charge against any of the defendants, Kanof strived to implicate them in that type of practice. But in fact, Martinez established that the system worked such that when a school was successful, the school—and the district— forfeited substantial amounts of federal funding.

Although the defense team was satisfied with the results of the first day, El Paso's media (online, print, and TV) began a three week-long ritual of reporting the prosecution's case while ignoring the damning cross examination by the defense.

The FBI agents must have believed the media's take that everything was going their way as evidenced from their text messages obtained by the defense after the mistrial. The FBI agents—after the first day of trial—were making post trial plans, advising each other to plan Uber rides to bars in order to celebrate their victory and not worry about getting a DWI.

Perhaps the agents were confident that their power over their witnesses might lead to an easy victory. They had control over Damon

Murphy and possibly did not anticipate that Murphy was vulnerable to questions regarding his intent in the field of education.

Damon Murphy

Anticipated as a star witness for the prosecution, Damon Murphy's testimony drew everyone's complete attention in the courtroom. He had already pled guilty and had agreed to give testimony against the defendants to avoid prison time. Though he himself had done nothing wrong, he was a main target for Kanof and the FBI agents, and by his own admission, he didn't have the financial strength to fight that power. Murphy was a skillful public speaker and he obligated himself to give convincing testimony for the prosecution.

Surely, Murphy must have pondered what had happened to him since arriving in El Paso. He was a close friend and colleague of Garcia, was given an associate superintendent position after Garcia took charge of EPISD in the summer of 2006 and moved his family from the Houston area to El Paso for this promotion. It was a move that proved disastrous in just about every way imaginable.

Before his career fell apart, his marriage failed after his wife left him for a woman in spring 2007. This event devastated Murphy and it was the talk of EPISD. He shared his torment with anyone who would listen. After Tanner heard Murphy's story, he and his wife took compassion on Murphy and offered their home as a place where Murphy could stay and iron out the unplanned changes in his life. Kanof exploited this charitable action when obtaining indictments with the grand jury. She conjured a theory that Murphy and Tanner conspired to manipulate school data while Murphy took residence at Tanner's home.

Eventually, Murphy rebounded from the divorce, got remarried, and then landed the superintendent position with the Canutillo Independent School District (CISD) in spring 2010. By fall 2012, the cheating investigation into EPISD was in full gear and one of its main targets was Murphy. Kanof, Murray and Griego threatened Murphy with "cheating" charges for both EPISD and CISD.

Murphy retained a celebrated El Paso attorney, Sib Abraham, for $100,000. But in step with all the bad luck Murphy had since moving to El Paso, Abraham unexpectedly died with a massive amount of debt. The $100,000 retainer fee Murphy had paid was refunded at 2% of the total. Murphy had no choice but to request a federally appointed defense counsel to whom, given his disposition with Tanner and Tegmeyer in the county lockup, he was more than willing to discuss the possibility of a plea agreement.

On the witness stand, Murphy was questioned by Kanof. Murphy gleefully admitted that he was in the wrong and was a big player in creating a scheme that manipulated the federal mandates of NCLB. He testified that Garcia was frightening to work for and that he did Garcia's bidding out of fear. Then, with pointed and practiced testimony against Anderson, Murphy claimed that Anderson was rogue and allowed all types of cheating to occur in the district.

Murphy then testified that during the time he was transitioning to Canutillo, he became a lame duck associate superintendent at EPISD, and all of his former power was given to Anderson. Even though he was training Anderson to take his position, Murphy claimed that Anderson ignored him and defiantly opposed any and all ethical procedures Murphy recommended to him. Thus, Murphy contradicted himself. He was at first a lead player in the scheme, but then he claimed that Anderson refused to follow his "ethical" practices.

When the questioning focused on Tanner, Murphy claimed they were good friends (and erroneously suggested that they were still friends) and that Tanner was "very good" to him during his time of need. But Murphy also claimed that he was teaching Tanner how to manipulate the system while he was at Tanner's home. He didn't mention that Tanner wasn't principal of Austin during that time. During a court break Tanner commented to the defense table, "No good deed goes unpunished."

Murphy was then asked when Tanner became part of the cheating scandal and Murphy answered that it was on the first day Tanner took over as the principal of Austin. Curiously, no questions were asked about Tegmeyer, Thomas, or Love.

Robert Perez was first to cross examine Murphy. He guided Murphy through his personal journey that had him leave the Houston area and come to El Paso. Perez stressed a timeline regarding Murphy's financial and family setbacks that happened within two years of moving to El Paso. Murphy agreed with the chronology. Perez then asked the critical question of the case, "So, when did you scheme and come up with the plan to commit fraud? Who did you scheme with and where did you scheme?"

Murphy was silent. He finally mumbled, "Can you rephrase the question? I don't think I understand what you are asking?"

"When did you decide to cheat? When did you decide to defraud the US government?"

"Well, there wasn't an exact time. It didn't work like that."

"Then tell us how it worked."

Murphy paused again and then Perez asked, "Was it your intent to come to El Paso and cheat students out of an education?"

"No."

"Did you think you were doing good things here?"

"Yes, at the time I thought we were doing the right thing for kids."

"When did you realize you were not?"

"The FBI agents educated me on what was wrong. I did not know until then."

"Until the FBI told you that you were doing something wrong, did you think you were breaking the law?"

There was a long pause and Murphy finally answered, "No, not at the time." Murphy's bravado disappeared and Perez passed the witness to Tom Mills.

Mills questioned Murphy regarding his working relationship with Lorenzo Garcia. At one point, Murphy compared Garcia to Darth Vader. He elaborated on how Garcia would call him late at night and cuss him out while calling him all types of vile names. With that sentiment, Mills asked Murphy, "So, while you were working as Garcia's right-hand man, you were really a puppet on his string and you couldn't really make your own decisions or be your own person. Am I getting that right?"

"That is completely right. I was a puppet on a string."

"And now that you are no longer Garcia's puppet, it seems that you have transferred control to the prosecuting attorney, isn't that right?"

"I don't follow. What do you mean?"

"Well, isn't it true that you made a plea bargain with the government?"

"Yes."

"Isn't part of that bargain based on your testimony here?"

"Yes, but I am telling the truth."

"And if you don't testify as you were told, then your plea bargain can be pulled, isn't that right?"

"Yes."

"So, now instead of being on Garcia's string, you are now on the puppet string of the prosecutor based on your testimony here, isn't that right?"

Murphy was at a loss for words and was not answering the question. After a pause, Mills asked his last question, "You testified that before you spoke to the FBI agents, you didn't feel you were doing anything wrong. In fact, you believed you were doing many good things for students. Is that correct?"

"Yes, that is what I said." By this point, Murphy was meek, and his voice began to quiver as he began to cry.

"I pass the witness."

Both Mary Stillinger and Sherilyn Bunn elicited a definitive response from Murphy that neither of their clients had anything to do with the cheating scandal. Stillinger asked if Murphy ever meant to include her client, Nancy Love, as part of the alleged "conspiracy" when he talked about it. He responded, "Absolutely not." He had the same response for Thomas. By this point, Murphy was not just crying; he was sobbing and needed tissue to dry his eyes and blow his nose.

At this point, Judge Briones signified a need for a 15-minute recess. During that recess, Kanof approached Murphy. The defendants did not know what she was scream-whispering to him, but those in the courtroom could hear her sounds of frustration as she was pointing her finger in Murphy's face. Murphy was visibly shaken. By the end of the recess he had effectively composed himself.

When court was back in session, Kanof questioned Murphy on her redirect. Using a voice like a teacher admonishing a misbehaving student, Kanof asked, "Mr. Murphy, would you like to take back your plea?"

"No ma'am!" Murphy said loudly and emphatically.

"Am I controlling you? Am I telling you what to do? Are you my puppet?"

"No MA'AM!" Murphy said, as he twitched in his chair.

It was clear who was controlling whom. Kanof did her best to manage damage control, but it was too late. She passed the witness.

With Murphy visibly shaken, Robert Perez took the non-verbal cue from the other defense attorneys. "No further questions," he said, and the rest of the defense attorneys responded in kind.

Damon Murphy was dismissed. His exit the court room was much different than his entrance. Head down, his crying had not stopped. In vain, he tried to make eye contact with the defendants. As Murphy left the court room, Liz Rogers whispered to Tanner, "I hope he still gets to keep his plea deal."

Jesus Chavez

Jesus Chavez, one of the central figures of the fabricated cheating scandal of EPISD, followed Murphy on the stand. He had been the principal of Bowie High School, the school at the epicenter of the accusations. Conventional wisdom would have predicted Chavez's indictment given all the press and attention he received from the media and from Eliot Shapleigh. The Department of Education had distinctly mentioned Bowie and Chavez in their report regarding policies and procedures that needed to be amended immediately. TEA concurred, also mentioning Chavez by name.

Interestingly though, it was discovered after the mistrial that Chavez had secretly been working with TEA and the FBI to set up the defendants in exchange for favorable actions toward him. Needless to say, he kept his teaching certification and was never indicted. While Chavez was questionable in his ethics regarding his policies and procedures at Bowie, no crime was alleged personally against him.

Chavez was candid about his approach to improving a school. He did not see himself as someone who was doing something for the students. He saw the students as being able to do something for him. When it came to the state exams results, Chavez viewed them as numbers to advance his career. It was clear that his primary motivation in education was not the students; he wanted them to succeed because that success enhanced his career. Chavez informed his faculty and staff frequently that he was not a "long-timer" at Bowie. He verbalized that he was going to advance to bigger and better things— he wanted to become a superintendent as quickly as possible.

But that would not happen. Shapleigh's baseless accusations and the FBI agents' desire to have prestige with a big case became the wrench that ended any hope of Chavez's personal plans in the field of education.

Open with his colleagues about his compliance with the FBI, Chavez shared that he had notebooks of policies, emails, and documentation of correspondence between himself, TEA, Garcia, Murphy and Anderson showing that he was acting legally. After he was removed by Interim Terri Jordan, Chavez attempted to use this same documentation to take down his perceived adversaries, which included Anderson. Working with his attorney, Chavez reached out to the FBI and Kanof and offered his assistance in any way he could. It appears he became friends with the FBI agents, and Kanof spoke of Chavez as one who cooperated fully with their investigation.

It is difficult to ascertain what information Chavez gave to Kanof and her crew, but he managed to make a deal with them whereby he was not indicted. Through a deal with TEA, he was allowed to keep his teaching credentials after a five-year suspension, but he knew that his educational career would be over before that. To move on with his life, Chavez chose a career in health care and became a pediatric registered nurse.

When he entered the witness box, it was assumed that Chavez was an unindicted co-conspirator of the EPISD Cheating Scandal. He did not deny any involvement as he was a cooperative witness for the prosecution.

Robert Perez began cross examination by questioning Chavez about Shapleigh's allegations of disappearing students. Kanof objected by saying that the case had nothing to do with Shapleigh's original claim, emphasizing once more that the original accusation was unfounded. Despite this, the local media in the court room still refused to report that Shapleigh's original allegations had been debunked.

Perez then focused on Chavez's testimony against Anderson. Chavez didn't attack Anderson. Instead, Chavez verified that he and Anderson argued about the proper placement of students in and out of the 10th grade.

Chavez testified that he felt targeted by Anderson and believed that he did not receive proper due process regarding the allegations Anderson had against him. Chavez further testified that any impropriety that he committed while at Bowie was a result of following the directives of his superiors, including Anderson.

Key in Chavez's cross examination—as it was for almost all of the prosecutions' witness with regard to the fraud charges—was when Robert Perez asked him essentially the same question that had stumped Murphy, "When did you know you were in a conspiracy to defraud the US government?"

Like Murphy, Chavez was silent and then asked for the question to be repeated. Perez repeated the question, "When did you know you were in a conspiracy to defraud the US government?"

"I don't think there was a time. I just knew it. It was something that happened over time."

"So, over that time, when did you know that it was a conspiracy to defraud? When did you know you were committing a felony?"

"I never thought I was until the FBI agents let me know."

"Did you think you were doing good things for students?"

"Yes, I did."

"Then can you tell me or the members of the jury why you are not indicted with the rest of the defendants here? It appears that your school did far more activities than Austin, but you are a witness for the government while they are indicted."

"I am not aware as to the specifics of their case."

"I pass the witness."

Briones called for a recess after Perez's questioning. During the break, Chavez's chummy relationship with the FBI agents and prosecutors was noted by the other defense attorneys.

Tegmeyer's attorney, Luis Islas, questioned Chavez after the break. Islas demonstrated his junkyard dog style with a question he had for Chavez. Islas really had no dog in the fight as Chavez and Tegmeyer had no contact whatsoever, but Islas was irritated at Chavez's smugness and wanted to expose what he had observed. Islas began, "So, Mr. Chavez, are you getting paid for your testimony? Remember, you are under oath."

"No, I am not getting paid," responded Chavez with an element of surprise in his voice.

"Did you practice your testimony either with the prosecuting attorneys or with the FBI agents?"

"No."

"No, you didn't? Then how do you know them so well? During the break I noticed that you are good friends with the FBI agents. You were with them in a corner and you all were laughing, and you're obviously on a first name basis with them."

"Well, I haven't denied that I have worked with them. We do get along, but I wouldn't call it a friendship."

"I am just observing that it looked like a friendship. With you working with them, you didn't practice your testimony? You didn't know the questions that were going to be asked?"

"Well, while working with them, we discussed many things. I wasn't surprised by the questions, but I wouldn't say that I rehearsed them."

"So, you weren't surprised at the questions because, as you said, this was the topic you discussed with them. Those agents over there who you get along with, but are not your friends?"

"That is correct."

"Thank you. I pass the witness."

Again, it appeared that the prosecution had another witness designed to bring down the defense, but instead it exposed their motivation. Chavez had been pointed out as one of the biggest orchestrators of the alleged scandal, yet, he was not on trial.

Mark Mendoza

Enter Mark Mendoza, the next star witness for the prosecution. Prior to December 2010, Mendoza was the director of pupil services. He applied for that position in the nick of time to save his own career as an administrator in EPISD. He had been a principal of an elementary school located on a military base, but during his tenure there, it was known by other school principals that he managed the perfect trifecta of alienating parents, teachers and students alike. The school was low-performing academically as a result of Mendoza's poor leadership, but there were personnel issues with him as well.

Had Mendoza not found an alternative to being a campus principal, most likely he would have been demoted to an assistant principal with the likelihood of finishing his career in that position. Using the legacy of his father, a respected principal in the district, Mendoza was able to escape the elementary school setting and continue his administration climb at central office.

During his questioning by the prosecution, Mendoza attempted to bill himself as the moral conscience of EPISD. He revealed that he had made himself an informant for the FBI as soon as they began investigating EPISD in December 2010. He testified that he went to the FBI because of his altruistic nature and his love for El Paso and EPISD. There was another motive, however.

Mendoza was proficient, but not spectacular, in his position as director, and he wasn't advancing in his career. In order to advance, Mendoza was intent on impressing his superiors, namely Lorenzo Garcia. To ingratiate himself to Garcia, in January 2008, Mendoza came up with an idea that he later blamed on Garcia. As a school located right next to the Mexican border, Mendoza believed that many of Bowie's students lived in Juarez. To assist Bowie with its challenging situation of educating students who were not fluent in English, Mendoza implemented a plan whereby he would stand at the border and take the pictures of individuals he believed to be students at Bowie, but living in Mexico. Mendoza planned to reference the pictures, along with Bowie student rosters to determine if the students were eligible to attend the American school.

The plan was a bust. The pictures were not clear and it was difficult, if not impossible, to determine if those in the photographs were students at all. In no time, the plan was scratched. That would have been the end except that Shapleigh had heard about it and exploited the action to "prove" the cheating scandal. While taking pictures of people as they cross the border isn't illegal, Shapleigh tied it to a denial of civil rights, the language which the FBI used as part of their fodder against Garcia.

By December 2010, it was no secret that the district had taken these pictures. Public comments from articles in the *Times* indicated that the citizens of El Paso were split on the practice. Mendoza, however, was savvy enough to conclude that Shapleigh's accusations of wrongdoing at EPISD were going to stick once Shapleigh was able to get the FBI on board. To cover his actions, Mendoza's self-preserving strategy was to go to the FBI at the outset to offer himself as an informant before being discovered as the brainchild behind the student photographs. His new narrative was that he was forced against his will to take those pictures.

Mendoza, like Chavez, is a survivor, but a "survivor" who cowardly twisted the truth in a manner that made him look like Garcia's victim. Under cross examination, Mendoza was able to talk incessantly without ever answering a question. The defense attorneys intended to call Mendoza back to the stand when it was their turn to present the defense's side. But of course, that never happened. After the mistrial was declared, the jury was questioned about the case. Regarding Mendoza, the consensus among jurors was that Mendoza was not credible.

Additionally, it was exposed during the trial that even though Mendoza was in charge of tracking down all dropout students and helping them to re-enroll, he was violating federal law (FERPA) by taking files he generated to Shapleigh's office to bolster the senator's accusations. Therefore, rather than doing his job and actually helping those students, it appears that he was purposely failing at it in order to assist the FBI and Shapleigh in their accusations.

Vanessa Foreman

As she had made a plea deal and part of her deal was to testify against the defendants in the trial, Vanessa Foreman's testimony was tainted before she ever was asked a question. Like the other defendants, Foreman, too, was innocent, but the FBI did not appear to like her and she was, consequently, implicated in the "scandal."

When Foreman first became an administrator in EPISD her mentor was Mark Mendoza's father, the principal who hired her as his assistant. A bond developed between Foreman and the Mendozas and they were quite close, with Foreman attending Mendoza family gatherings. Foreman says that she viewed Mark Mendoza like a brother.

Foreman's experience with the FBI was nightmarish. By the time the FBI agents asked for an interview with her, they had already spoken to a few disgruntled employees who implicated Foreman as difficult, but not a criminal. She'd been a director at a troubled high school where she was working to establish a functional system that would benefit the students, but her work was met with resistance by some of the faculty and staff. Believing she had nothing to worry about, Foreman, like so many, had freely agreed to the meeting with the FBI agents. She was wrong. True to form, the agents were aggressive, bullying and threatening prison time. After three hours of being the recipient of yelling from the FBI agents, Foreman exercised her right as an American citizen and left the Gestapo-like interrogation.

After her horrific experience, she sought comfort with Mark Mendoza. Seeking his friendship and support, Foreman went to Mendoza to decompress. To her face, he gave her that friendship. Behind her back, it is speculated that he went to FBI agents and embellished what she said about them and provided baseless innuendo implying that Foreman was complicit with unorthodox practices at Jefferson High, her assigned school.

As a single mother who had lost her career, Foreman believed the only way to remain free was to make a plea bargain with the prosecution. Her admission of guilt was a feather in the prosecution's cap, and the agents and Kanof seemed to believe it would add credibility to the charges against the defendants, namely Anderson, Tanner and Thomas. Like the previous witnesses, however, her testimony exposed enormous questions about every indictment in the case.

Kanof wanted to establish a connection between Foreman and Thomas. But it was revealed that Foreman didn't work with Thomas at Austin High School. Foreman was at Austin before Thomas ever became an assistant principal. In a flip turn to establish solid ground again, Kanof quickly turned to Foreman's time at Jefferson High School to prove Anderson's guilt. But that effort, too, was futile. Through Kanof's questioning, it was established that Foreman and Anderson worked together to help Jefferson High School and there were no indications of illegal behavior.

Trying to salvage the testimony, Kanof transitioned back to focus on Tanner. She had Foreman testify about an audit conducted at Austin regarding the class of 2012. However, the audit in question did not exist. The prosecution did not have the evidence of the audit and EPISD claimed that they did not have any record of such an audit. Nonetheless, Foreman testified that the nonexistent audit concluded that ultimately nothing wrong happened at Austin with the class of 2012. After inadvertently demonstrating that she did not understand her own case, Kanof then passed the witness to the defense.

Anderson's defense attorney Robert Perez questioned Foreman about her first meeting with the FBI. She revealed that it had turned into a three-hour marathon that began with what looked like a mug shot of Jefferson High School Assistant Principal, Maribel Guillen, placed on a table, insinuating that Guillen had been arrested. Guillen hadn't been arrested; the whole ordeal was set up for intimidation. Foreman testified that Agent Murray yelled at her and bullied her to the point where she walked out and she sought an attorney. With the attorney, Foreman wrote and signed an affidavit of her experience and the tactics used by Murray and Griego. This affidavit was essential to disproving the narrative of these allegedly ethical agents.

Perez then ventured into a sensitive area: the FBI had alleged that Foreman and Garcia had an extramarital affair. When Perez began this line of questioning, Foreman displayed anger and deep sadness simultaneously.

"You actually had to stop people from spreading rumors about you and Dr. Garcia; isn't that right?" asked Perez.

"Yes, sir," she replied.

"What kind of rumors?"

"That people were saying that I got my job because I supposedly slept with him." Foreman said, holding back tears. She gained the sympathy of every person in the courtroom, especially the women.

Perez continued, "Who did you confront with respect to those rumors?"

Foreman replied that she confronted many individuals including Garcia himself and Damon Murphy. Though the line of questioning was ended due to an objection of relevance, Perez shed light on the lengths to which the FBI went to pressure people.

Foreman was next cross-examined by Sheri Bunn, attorney for Diane Thomas. Under questioning, Foreman admitted that, like Damon Murphy, she never thought she was doing anything illegal. Like Murphy and every other defendant who pled, it was the FBI who finally convinced her that she had done something wrong.

"So, you need to give a truthful testimony," Bunn told her. "You already admitted that you didn't believe you had committed a felony until the FBI agents informed you. But you are a witness for the prosecution, and you are testifying as part of your plea so that you do not serve time.

But you are under oath and have promised to tell the truth. After everything that has happened, do you believe you did anything wrong?"

This was a moment when one understands that silence can be deafening. After a long, pregnant pause, Foreman answered clearly, "No, I don't."

From the back of the room where the observers were sitting, a collective gasp could be heard. If the jury was picking up on the theme of the case so far, Foreman verified that this cheating scandal was contrived, and the prosecution was only getting people to plead guilty using fear tactics. Every star witness thus far had testified that they thought they were doing right by students and never believed they were doing anything illegal. Foreman admitted after her charges were dropped that the FBI and Kanof had stated to her that the case would never go to trial. Even after the Frye hearings, agent Murray told her that the educators would plead at the "midnight hour."

Clearly, the prosecution was having a difficult time with their witnesses and their case. When Kanof and company called Don Southerland, the lead investigator for the Weaver Group and a former FBI agent who had interviewed dozens of EPISD employees including Tanner, Anderson and Tegmeyer, they must have believed he would change the course of the case. He didn't.

Don Southerland

Paid over a million dollars to perform a forensic investigation, the Weaver Group was a private company contracted by EPISD. As an investigator for Weaver, Don Southerland's purpose was to corroborate that he found evidence of wrongdoing in EPISD at the hands of the defendants, namely Anderson and Tanner. Like so many of the prosecution's witnesses, however, Southerland seemed to bolster the case of the defense. While the prosecutors questioned him, Southerland alleged that there was a special concern with the LEP (limited English proficiency) population especially as it related to Bowie and Jefferson high schools. He also testified that Tanner illegally restored grades to students who had not qualified for a restoration of credits.

Upon cross examination by defense attorney Robert Perez, Southerland admitted that he discussed his EPISD interviews with the FBI agents investigating the district. For a forensic and independent investigation, Southerland should not have been talking to any FBI investigators for any reason as it inherently tainted his audit.

Perez continued the cross examination by targeting information that the Weaver group had not correctly documented during their investigation. This exchange is directly from the trial transcript.

Perez: And when Anderson comes on board, Bowie's numbers jump by 40, correct?

Southerland: Correct.

Perez: So Anderson should get credit for that, should he not?

Southerland: There again, Mr. Kehrwald told us that it was as a result of his internal audit. When he went into Bowie, he looked at the LEP population and realized that it was unrealistic, that it couldn't possibly be 49, and he was the one that readjusted it up to 89.

Perez: Are you aware that Craig Kehrwald was actually hired by James Anderson?

Southerland: don't know that to be a fact. I know that Kehrwald did some work out at one of the high schools.

Perez: And that he worked directly under James Anderson?

Southerland: I don't know that either. Perez: Did you question Mr. Kehrwald as to who sent him to Bowie High School and told him to look and put them under a microscope?

Newaz (prosecutor): Objection, hearsay.

Judge Briones: Overruled.

This testimony exposed that the Weaver investigation actively withheld information that directly exonerated the defendants long before they had been indicted.

Tanner's attorney Liz Rogers continued to question Southerland about his interview with her client. Rogers asked Southerland why he was interested in Foreman's sex life and why he would ask Tanner about that. "What interest did you have in Tanner knowing anything about the affairs of Lorenzo Garcia?" Rogers asked.

"Credibility. We were looking for specific people without asking about specific people."

"But your partner, Mr. Manson, asked Tanner specifically about Foreman and Garcia, right?" "I don't remember."

"But if that is what your transcript alleges, then that is what was asked, right?"

"If that's what the transcript has, then I guess so."

"You claim that you didn't discuss the investigation with the FBI, but both you and the FBI were curious about Foreman's alleged affair with Garcia? Is that a coincidence?"

Southerland didn't answer affirmatively or negatively. Instead, he blamed a faulty memory. But Rogers established that the Weaver Group was collaborating with the FBI agents.

Rogers continued to question Southerland about an accusation that came from the Weaver Report. The report concluded that Tanner did not follow TEA's guidelines of implementing a "principal's plan" for students who were seeking to recover lost credits due to attendance.

"A principal has to develop a written plan for a student who is seeking credit recovery," testified Southerland.

"Can you show me exactly where it says in the law that it has to be written?" asked Rogers.

"With chapter four of Texas state law that addresses public education."

"I am aware that the law says there needs to be a principal's plan, but I don't see where it states it needs to be written or even documented. Am I missing something?"

"Well, I thought it said written. I guess it doesn't. I am not an educator. I was just investigating a school district."

"So, a principal's plan could be a verbal agreement between the principal and a student?"

"I guess so."

Rogers managed to make it clear that the Weaver Group found that Austin High, under Tanner, utilized credit recovery correctly and that there were no concerns with the limited English proficiency (LEP) population. Rogers continued the cross-examination about his accusation that Tanner allegedly used an illegal form to grant credit to students. It wasn't that the credits were in error; they were merely documented on a form that Southerland determined was illegal.

"What was illegal about it?" asked Rogers. Sutherland responded,

"It was not the form designated by the district."

"Where does it specify that the district must have an authorized form?"

"Chapter four of the state code."

"Where in the chapter does it state that?"

"Well, I thought it was there."

"What other schools used this 'wrong' form?"

"Only Austin."

At that point, Rogers displayed evidence showing that the form Austin used was exactly like the one used at most of the high schools in the district. She then asked, "Mr. Southerland, did you look for other forms at other schools?"

"No, I did not," was the response.

"So, you only gave this finding on Austin without verifying if any other school was using the same form or was in violation. Is that correct?"

"That is correct."

With a few questions, Southerland, Weaver's main investigator, discredited a major portion of the Weaver Report. He showed that this report used rumor and innuendo as fact against dozens of good people and it was used to terminate good educators. The defendants and their attorneys had to wait over four years to find out that the investigator had no working knowledge of education law in Texas. He made it up. One huge question is left to ask: Who instructed him to do this?

The prosecution's next witness was Emi Johnson. Johnson's purpose was to provide evidence against Anderson. Johnson did not want to be a witness and her demeanor on the witness stand indicated that she was uncomfortable.

Emi Johnson

It was amazing that the prosecution even called Emi Johnson to be a witness against Anderson. Working with TEA as a special investigator, Johnson oversaw the EPISD investigation and was the one who cleared EPISD—twice—of any wrongdoing in 2010. Her superiors were Adam Jones and Robert Scott. Jones was serving as Deputy Commissioner of Finance and Administration of TEA and Scott was the acting Commissioner of Education of the Texas Education Agency at the time. It should be noted clearly that Adam Jones was the Deputy Commissioner of TEA when EPISD was cleared twice of misconduct. Yet, just about two years after those findings, he was hired by the Weaver Group and worked directly with Emi Johnson to secure the contract for Weaver from EPISD with a mandate of finding misconduct, in what was clearly a conflict of interest.

This was not the first time that Jones and Scott, longtime friends before they arrived at the Texas Education Agency, had been known to work in this manner. A 2007 Dallas Morning News article reported on the manipulation of contracts under Jones and Scott as early as June of that year.

"The investigation began in February, after Dr. Neeley received a complaint about a grant program that trained principals. According to the report, 'the original complainant expressed the belief that the Education Initiatives Division [of TEA] regularly and systemically manipulated the contract and grant process."[1]

Johnson, in her testimony, claimed that she was not aware of the federal laws for academic accountability and that she had no significant information regarding audits of EPISD, other than the ones she conducted. But given that knowledge of the federal system was tantamount to her position with TEA, her claims are dubious. In addition, Johnson worked with colleagues who understood the federal system completely, Jones and Scott included. Again, the discovery disclosed after the mistrial showed that Johnson was working directly with the FBI and the USDE as early as January 2012.

Johnson work at TEA included collaboration with an established division called the Student Improvement Resource Center (SIRC). This division worked primarily with schools who were in academic trouble because of federal accountability standards to monitor how the state was spending NCLB Title I funds for school improvement. Part of SIRC's responsibilities was to place monitors in troubled schools and districts. The monitor's role was advisory on paper, but any stage five school who acted without the approval of the assigned SIRC would go on report. This report went to the district superintendent, the Texas Education Agency and could result in loss of funding or disciplinary action against the principal. Johnson knew that no school could implement any action without the approval of a SIRC monitor. The SIRC monitored how funds were allocated and how plans were implemented. Any actions not approved by the monitor was to be reported to TEA.

As Shapleigh increased his attacks on EPISD and Garcia, Anderson called Johnson at TEA to ask for an audit of the district in June 2010. At that time, Johnson denied his request saying that the district had to perform its own audit. This was a phone call that Johnson had previously told the FBI never happened until phone records proved that it did. Further, while she was denying Anderson's request for an audit, she never revealed to him that she had already authorized one on Bowie High School at the request of Lorenzo Garcia.

In addition, she and TEA had repeatedly stated that hiring onsite auditors was out of the question. However, as early as 2006, TEA had hired 10 new auditors to investigate cheating on the TAKS test throughout the state, including San Antonio ISD, the district where Jesus Chavez was employed as a high school principal at the time of that investigation. This demonstrates once again that Johnson misrepresented the truth to Shapleigh, the USDE, the state auditors and FBI investigators when stating that the desk audit was the only option in the EPISD investigation. The results of the audit that began under Johnson in May 2010 were revealed in October 2010 and they cleared EPISD of impropriety. However, that audit cited some administrators for questionable practices; Anderson gave written reprimands to those cited.

When Shapleigh publicly challenged the results of the audit, Johnson reviewed her work and cleared EPISD for a second time. Johnson maintained her stance as she participated in the federal investigation conducted by the Department of Education. Following Adam Jones' direct reports, she was present at the exit meeting of the U.S. Department of Education as EPISD was again cleared. At this meeting, the USDE was clear-cut that EPISD was following the laws and procedures put out by TEA and that changes needed to be made at the state level.

Johnson's story changed in fall 2012 when Shapleigh, Escobar and the FBI continued to insist that a scandal occurred. Bob Moore, the editor of the *Times* was part of the pressure team along with Byrd and her questionable PAC. Under this enormous and unprecedented stress, Johnson changed her story in lieu of exposing her misrepresentations. In sum, Johnson's version of events changed when her former boss, Adam Jones, secured a contract for the Weaver Group.

From that point Johnson categorically denied—to the FBI—that she had ever spoken to Anderson. This was her stance until the phone records were presented at trial that proved that Anderson had called her on several occasions.

Confronted on the witness stand with this discrepancy, she had no choice but to admit the truth. She admitted that she knew of Anderson's initial request for the audit. She then claimed that she denied it because it was protocol for a district to conduct its own audit first. With further questioning, however, she admitted that she had already embarked on the audit—for Garcia—that she had denied to Anderson.

This admission exonerated Anderson of the main accusation from the FBI; namely, his alleged dereliction of duty by allowing a cheating scandal to exist and not doing anything about it. Johnson proved that Anderson did not ignore the allegations. In fact, he wanted to get to the truth of Shapleigh's claims.

Further questions for Johnson focused on her knowledge of the district in terms of its history with the "cheating scandal." Johnson said she took the Shapleigh's accusations seriously. In regard to the main accusation whereby Shapleigh accused Bowie of "disappearing" students, Johnson testified that she obtained a list from EPISD and from Shapleigh of 381 students who were allegedly compromised. The result of her investigation, however, concluded that all 381 were never lost or "disappeared." One hundred percent of these students were accounted for.

This was yet another bombshell exploding the government's case. Even more interesting was that this finding of the investigation came out in 2010. The reporting of the "disappeared" students was a mainstay of Shapleigh's allegations repeated over and over in the El Paso news media all the way up to the trial in June 2017. Yet the truth had been found early on and the media had never reported it. Not even after the trial.

In the end, Johnson was yet another witness for the prosecution who ended up giving exonerating testimony for the defense. She was the final significant witness in the prosecution's case regarding Anderson.

The information discovered about Johnson after the trial points to even more corruption as it was discovered that she and the FBI had been working jointly on the "cheating scandal" despite her denial of that allegation. In the hundreds of thousands of documents that were kept from the defense for the trial, emails and documented communications were discovered between the FBI agents and Johnson. Seemingly, one of her main motives was to keep the FBI focused on EPISD rather than TEA.[2]

In order to accomplish this, she implicated EPISD in the manner that the FBI dictated. Her own personal hand-written notes indicated her anxiety due to the FBI's intimidation. To prevent herself from becoming an FBI target, she scapegoated EPISD as evidenced by the manner she screened and filtered data from TEA to the FBI.

The remaining witnesses for the prosecution were targeted towards Tanner, Thomas, Tegmeyer and Love. The prosecution was attempting to prove that there were practices happening at Austin that were in line with the fake cheating scandal whereby two teachers were alleged victims of retaliation as a result. Interestingly, the prosecution spent an inordinate amount of time trying to prove retaliation even though this was a charge they were willing to drop during the Frye hearings.

At this point, the prosecution attempted to bring up the "illegal attendance" issue they invented. Attendance issues at Austin were never a part of the original allegations of the fabricated cheating scandal. But when the prosecution could not prove its case, it used speech teacher Jeanette Halliday's allegations to try and substantiate a scandal through improper attendance procedures. The "evidence" for this allegation was gathered over a year after Tanner had left the district. Tanner wasn't informed about this allegation and was never allowed to view the "evidence" until it was presented at the trial. This was yet another example of a defendant being denied due process.

Nonetheless, to prove the attendance component of the cheating scandal, the prosecution called Guadalupe Montelongo to the stand. Montelongo was the lead attendance clerk at Austin and was a compliant witness for the FBI. She continuously tried to persuade the assistant attendance clerk, Lupe Lucero, to comply with the FBI's wishes. Lucero, who refused to lie about people she knew were innocent, was another individual who was tormented by the FBI.

Guadalupe Montelongo

The FBI spoke to Montelongo in the summer of 2013. Montelongo was cooperative and seemingly protected by the FBI. Allegedly, Montelongo was rather smug as she offered advice to Austin personnel suggesting that they better not support Tanner in any manner, or they would lose their jobs. Sadly, Montelongo had no idea of the lengths that the FBI/DOJ would go to prove a fake cheating scandal. She would learn this at the end of her testimony.

Montelongo claimed that Tanner was instructing an assistant principal to falsely manipulate the attendance of students. The only evidence used for this manipulation was one teacher, Jeanette Halliday, who purportedly kept meticulous attendance records for a month during the fall of the 2009-2010 school year. However, when Halliday testified, it was discovered that her record-keeping wasn't that meticulous. (In fact, she became confused by her own hand-written notes and charts during cross-examination.)

The tampering with attendance accusation was ludicrous. If Tanner was cheating with attendance, then he was inept considering that Austin's attendance rate did not improve while Tanner was principal. The prosecution helped the defense establish this fact while they questioned Montelongo. Robert Perez was the first to cross examine Montelongo.

"Ms. Montelongo, you testified that the attendance rate went down. But the school was improving under Dr. Tanner's leadership, wasn't it?"

"Yes, it really was," Montelongo answered.

"From what I hear, discipline was better, there were fewer tardies, and grades increased. Is that a fair assessment?"

"Yes, the school really improved with Dr. Tanner."

"So, explain to me what is done for students who go on a school sponsored trip?"

"They are counted absent."

"But they went to school and they are on a school sponsored trip with district approval. Don't you have a code that shows they are present?"

"No. They are absent."

By asking these questions Perez was uncovering Montelongo's incompetence. Intended to be a credible witness for the prosecution, Montelongo became confused and Perez seemed to try and help her answer correctly.

"Wait. Maybe you are not understanding. Let's say I am running track and I must go to a meet in the afternoon and I am going to miss my afternoon classes. Do you get a notice about those students not being in school?"

"Yes, the coaches will give me a list of the students participating."

"So, those students will be considered present for the day even though they are missing their classes, right?"

"No, they are absent and counted absent."

Her responses were completely incorrect for obvious reasons. Anderson turned to Tanner at the defense table and whispered, "Austin's problem with attendance had nothing to do with the students. It was your attendance clerk!"

Rogers then took over the questioning. During this time, Montelongo admitted that Tanner had never told her to do anything wrong. She admitted that Tanner's name was only used when the assistant principal in charge of attendance used it. Montelongo also admitted that she never approached Tanner regarding attendance.

"You testified that Halliday is meticulous with her attendance, correct?"

"Yes. She is very meticulous and by the book."

"How many teachers are at Austin?"

"Oh, let's see. About 90. No, maybe more. Maybe 94."

"Out of all of those teachers, how many others came to you because of attendance?"

"No other teacher complained to me."

"So, out of almost 100 teachers, only Halliday complained? Is she the only one out of almost 100 who keep meticulous records?"

"No. We have many good teachers at Austin."

Just as Rogers was about to pass the witness, she addressed Montelongo again. "You know that you're an unindicted co-conspirator of the EPISD cheating scandal?"

"No, I'm not," Montelongo responded, but her nervous response indicated that she was blindsided by Rogers' statement.

"Actually, you are. Didn't the US attorneys tell you that you were an unindicted co-conspirator?"

"Not to my knowledge," Montelongo responded, again with a confused look on her face.

In fact she was. When Debra Kanof first took this case, she fed the media an enticing piece of information. She claimed that the cheating scandal was a conspiracy concocted by Lorenzo Garcia along with six other co-conspirators. The public speculated on who those co-conspirators could be. Most people guessed individuals such as Damon Murphy, Jesus Chavez, or other high level administrators of EPISD's leadership team. However, Kanof never disclosed the identities of those "unindicted co-conspirators." Yet, right before Montelongo took the stand, Kanof informed the defense lawyers that she was one of them.

The revelation lay somewhere on a continuum between desperate and comical. To think that an hourly attendance clerk making little more than minimum wage was part of the huge scheme to allegedly cheat the students of EPISD was absurd. The prosecution's desperation was fully transparent. Continuing with the desperation, the prosecution called Elizabeth Saucedo as another one of their valuable witnesses.

Elizabeth Saucedo

Elizabeth Saucedo was the lead counselor at Austin High School; her initial involvement with the FBI centered on her intent to get Diane Thomas fired. Thomas was Saucedo's direct supervisor and Saucedo believed that Thomas was too demanding of her and her colleagues. Saucedo had complained to Tanner, but he had supported Thomas. Taking her complaints against Thomas higher, Saucedo went to superiors at EPISD's Central Office, and this complaint led to Saucedo becoming a witness for the FBI and a close friend of FBI Agent Griego.

Saucedo was an informant for the FBI and during her cooperation, she had worn a hidden recording device to try and get a confession from

Tanner regarding the charges alleged. Tanner knew he hadn't said anything to support the charges, but he was concerned about one thing in the recording: his language.

But, like the others, Saucedo proved to be an ineffective witness for the prosecution. She couldn't answer simple questions regarding her employment history in EPISD. Her knowledge of timelines and dates was practically non-existent. Overall, her testimony was scant, so Kanof's strategy was to let the tape recording of the conversation with Saucedo be the smoking gun with the intent to disparage Tanner's character.

Kanof announced to the courtroom, "Elizabeth Saucedo became an informant for the FBI and then agreed to use a recording device that looked like a car key fob for a meeting that she set up with Dr. Tanner and Ms. Diane Thomas. The purpose of the meeting was to solicit evidence of the retaliation against the two teachers, Mr. Cordero and Ms. Halliday."

At that point, Kanof pushed a button and the recording began. But it wasn't the smoking gun that Kanof expected. The recording revealed the stress in Tanner's voice during the time of the investigation, yet it also codified his commitment to the school and the students.

When explaining the constant harassment he was suffering under the weight of the investigation at the hands of the oligarchy and the FBI, Tanner uttered the words that Kanof hoped would bring him down.

"Bring it on, motherfuckers!" Tanner said in a moment of defiant exasperation. He was exasperated, yes, but he was going to keep the good fight going.

Those present in the courtroom did not seem phased; in fact, many spectators and jurors reacted with laughter. The tape further proved that Tanner and Thomas did not retaliate against either Cordero or Halliday. Yes, Tanner's language was salty in some parts, but that wasn't illegal. In fact, given the constant torment he had experienced, it was understandable.

When the recording ended, Kanof seemed visibly surprised by the reactions in the courtroom. It wasn't tense and there were smiles exchanged between people across the room. Kanof then said she had no more questions for Saucedo and passed the witness to the defense. The smoking gun that Kanof had hoped for backfired.

Judge Briones took this break as an opportunity to adjourn court for the day. It was noon on Friday, June 23 and the defense attorneys were going to use the weekend to prepare for the third week of the trial.

As the court room stood for the judge and jury to leave the room, Tanner leaned to Liz Rogers and asked, "So, how bad was that for me?" She answered with a gleeful smile, "That wasn't bad. Quite the opposite."

Tanner then turned to Tom Mills and asked, "How much is that going to hurt us?" He answered, "Hurt us? Not at all. Didn't she hear it before she played it? That is only going to help us."

That opinion was echoed by the observers in the court room. Most were bewildered as to why the prosecution used it as evidence against Tanner. One observer came up to the defendants and uttered, "That exonerated you of all retaliation charges. That was awesome!"

The weekend was underway, and information continued to unfold. First, the prosecution handed over a piece of evidence to the defense, wanting to ensure "out of an abundance of caution" that they had given it. The first of many pieces of evidence discovered to have been withheld, it was a timeline of events for Ruben Cordero, produced by Chere Williams, an investigator in EPISD. The timeline showed that Cordero was set to be terminated by the school board on June 26, 2012. The matter had already been approved by EPISD's legal department. It was a done deal. But then it didn't happen, and no explanation was given.

On the timeline, August 21, 2012 was noted as the date that Cordero had told EPISD's Human Resources that Tanner was retaliating against him because allegedly Tanner knew Cordero was working with the FBI. However, it wasn't until eight days later, on August 29, 2012, that Cordero spoke to the FBI for the first time. Tanner couldn't have retaliated against him for being an informant for the FBI a week before he even spoke to the agents. In legal terms, this information is considered exculpatory, or Brady evidence, because it complete exonerates the defendant. By law, the prosecution must turn over such evidence far in advance of the trial. It was only at the end of the second week of trial that Kanof and her crew turned this over to the defense. In fact, she kept this piece of evidence in her office for years and had removed it from a stack of evidence that had been given to the defense. Surely, Kanof was aware of her misconduct.

In addition to the timeline, there was a second incident after Saucedo's testimony where the prosecution team met with Myrna Gamboa and her husband at about 3:00 p.m. on Friday, June 23. As the prosecution's case began going south—and quickly—Kanof and her cronies decided that they needed Gamboa as a witness. Gamboa, however, vehemently refused to comply. Mentally, she was fragile. In addition, she told the prosecution that she did not believe she had done anything wrong. Allegedly, she was close to saying that her confession to the FBI was coerced and not her words. The rumors were that she felt she was tricked into her plea agreement.

As soon as the prosecuting team learned about this concern, they were obligated to tell this to the defense team immediately. Instead, they waited 48 hours. There was a meeting of the defense attorneys on Sunday night, June 25, to discuss how they should proceed. Given the nature of the evidence withheld and the visit to Gamboa, the defense team naturally wondered what other evidence had not been given. They decided to write a motion for Judge Briones to consider dismissing the case and/or calling a mistrial due to prosecutorial misconduct.

Monday, June 26, 2017

On Monday morning, June 26, the trial did not begin as normal. Without the jury in the room, Judge Briones listened to the defense regarding the allegations of misconduct toward the prosecution. The prosecution could not deny that they had failed to give pertinent information to the defense, but Kanof tried to pass it off as inconsequential.

Kanof addressed the court, "It was just one cover sheet in an email that had timeline on it, and I didn't read it because I didn't think it was relevant."

What she didn't mention was that the "email" that was sent was a huge document where the only missing pages were the ones that exonerated the defendants. This was the very evidence that was the subject of the email chain between Kanof and Bruce Koehler presented in chapter 11. It was inconceivable that she was unaware of two small documents being deliberately removed from a much larger one and those emails proved that she was completely aware of that fact.

Briones was visibly furious with the prosecution. He instructed Kanof and the crew to give their explanation in writing as to why this happened. Kanof said she only needed about two hours and asked to be excused so that she could write up her explanation. Briones refused her request and told her that it was due on Thursday morning. He then addressed the prosecution directly.

"What do you mean that you didn't give over all the information to the defense? You have had this case for years now. I find this very disturbing. This case is important to our community. These defendants have their liberty on the line…. This is unacceptable." With that, Kanof feigned regret and the trial was set to resume on Tuesday morning. Judge Briones allowed the defense attorneys to use the rest of Monday to go through the evidence that had just been given to them.

On Tuesday morning, the trial continued as Liz Saucedo was brought back to the stand for cross examination. Liz Rogers was the first to ask Saucedo questions. Surprisingly, Saucedo only said good things about Tanner. She said Tanner was a good principal who cared about the students. She continued to say that Tanner had gotten many students into college and had created a good atmosphere on the campus. She also admitted that Tanner had never given her a directive to do anything wrong.

In a surprise turn, Rogers played the rest of the recorded tape that Saucedo had turned into the FBI. Unaware of what she had done, Saucedo had accidently left the recording device on for almost four consecutive hours. In the midst of that recording was a conversation between her and Special Agent James Griego. On the recording, her comments indicate more than just an investigator-informant relationship between the two, and Saucedo referred to Vanessa Foreman as a "bitch."

Sherilyn Bunn took over the questioning of Saucedo. Bunn focused on pertinent dates and timelines and she would not allow Saucedo to guess at the dates. Instead, Bunn was ready with actual events with definitive dates. She finished with a few more questions that established Saucedo's extreme dislike for Thomas. Saucedo was dismissed and left the courtroom. As she left, Griego followed her. They were last seen going into the elevator down to the first floor. Griego did not return for the rest of the day.

The last witness of note was a colleague of Saucedo's, Maria del Rosario Parsley. Parsley was an interesting choice for the prosecution to have on its list. Parsley genuinely hated Diane Thomas and would do anything to get rid of her. Thomas was not the first colleague to have issues with Parsley. Everyone who worked with her soon discovered Parsley's incompetence.

Rosario Parsley

Parsley wanted to do a good job and was willing to dedicate the time to the position, but she didn't possess the skillset necessary to be a high school counselor. To her credit, she laboriously tried to perform well and would work extra hours to try and get her work completed, but there were always mistakes. Huge, gigantic, monstrous mistakes.

Top performing students who were assigned to Parsley as a counselor found avenues to ensure that they were assigned to someone else. Parents made appointments with the principal for the purpose of getting their child switched from Parsley's roster. She kept some students from graduating on time, missed deadlines for students to get scholarships or even entrance into top US schools, and gave students classes on their schedule that they had already taken. When the mistakes were pointed out Parsley refused to correct them or admit that an error occurred.

Thomas was not the only person who would get frustrated and upset with Parsley. Just about everyone—administrator or colleague—who had worked with Parsley experienced that frustration. Liz Saucedo would often verbalize her frustration with Parsley and often used "incompetent" to describe her work.

As the prosecution asked her questions, Parsley would not answer with a simple yes or no; instead, she went off on tangents. If the defense attorneys were not objecting to her narratives, the prosecution was cutting her off. At one point, after Judge Briones had cautioned Parsley many times to "just answer the question," he finally lost his temper and civility. With a loud and condescending tone that a parent uses when disciplining a child, Briones admonished her, "Just answer the question. You have been told numerous times. You are wasting the court's time and patience. Just answer the question. What don't you understand about that?"

When the defense began cross examination, Rogers was the first to question Parsley. Like Saucedo before her, Parsley did not say anything against Tanner or accuse Tanner of doing anything wrong. She even admitted that the students loved Tanner and that Tanner cared for the students. Her only complaint regarding Tanner was that he would not side with her when she complained about Thomas.

Rogers did not spend much time with Parsley before she passed her to Bunn. As Bunn began questioning, no one was prepared for what was revealed. Bunn's questions focused on a student who caused many headaches. This was a student who wanted to graduate on time but did not have all the required credits. Part of the reason for the student's dilemma was the student herself, but Parsley was also part of the problem. Parsley had the student repeat courses she had already passed and did not have her take courses she needed for graduation. Since this student was coded as a high risk for not graduating, it was imperative for the school to try and figure out a way for this student to graduate legitimately and as quickly as possible, as per the mandates of TEA.

Thomas and Parsley argued about this student intensely. The student's parent was upset; eventually, the executive director of counselors for EPISD became involved and concurred that Parsley had made many errors regarding this student. When the FBI discovered this issue, they inserted themselves in the matter and tried to use it as evidence for the alleged cheating scandal. Bunn began her questioning with an emphasis on this student.

"When you went to the FBI, you spoke about how you thought Ms. Thomas was trying to force you to graduate a student who didn't have enough credits."

"That is right. Ms. Thomas would get all over me and would sometimes even call me names...."

"Thank you, Ms. Parsley. Just answer the question. Did you provide information to the FBI?"

"Yes. I brought them the information on this student and then gave them all types of information."

"Was this just on one occasion?"

"No, I went several times to see them."

That little slip up was the sentence that changed the entire course of the case. With the evidence that was given to the defense by the prosecution, there was only one record of Parsley ever speaking to the FBI. As per FBI requirements, any time there is a conversation with a witness, no matter how slight or trivial, documentation of that conversation must be produced. Bunn used this knowledge to continue her questioning.

"Let's talk about the first time you went to visit them. It was at the beginning of May 2013."

"Yes, that sounds about right." "Did anyone go with you to the meeting?"

"Let me think... Yes. Liz Saucedo was with me at that meeting."

"Was she with you when you spoke to the FBI agents?"

"Yes, she was sitting in the room." (This was a direct contradiction to what Saucedo testified. Saucedo was adamant that she had not been at Parsley's FBI interview. By being in that interview, it contaminated the process, according to the FBI's own protocol.)

"You also said that you gave the FBI several pieces of material on several occasions."

"That is right."

"About how many times do you believe you met with them?"

"At least three or four times."

"Thank you, Ms. Parsley."

"Your honor," Bunn said, as she began to address Briones, "We do not have the documentation of the meetings that Ms. Parsley had with the FBI. We only have one document. Where are those documents and why don't we have them?"

The prosecution, after looking for the evidence had to admit that they did not possess the documented interviews that Parsley had with the FBI. Parsley was excused from the witness stand. Court was adjourned, but no attorney took a break that night.

The defense attorneys were just beginning to understand how much evidence had been withheld from them. The more they discussed it, the more they realized that the prosecution had most likely withheld copious amounts of exculpatory evidence. Their concern attracted the attention of Judge Briones.

Wednesday, June 28, 2017

This day did not begin like the others. A special hearing had been called in the courtroom and the jury was not allowed to attend. Because of the previous day's events, the defense attorneys agreed that it was necessary to move again for a dismissal and/or mistrial due to a large sum of evidence that had not been given to the defense. Judge Briones agreed to hear the concerns before continuing with the day's trial proceedings.

A few minutes before the hearing began, a prosecutor handed Bunn a stack of 295 pages of evidence that they had not yet submitted to the defense. This only added to the defense's fuel. After that handoff, the rest of the prosecution team, along with the FBI agents, entered the courtroom. There seemed to be tension between all of them as they were not smiling nor speaking much to each other, unlike every other day of the trial when they were friendly and rather talkative. Kanof, especially, seemed haggard as she was curt with her colleagues.

Briones walked in the courtroom and began the proceeding. Bunn was the first to speak. She reviewed how the prosecution had not submitted the required documentation to the defense as required by law. Further, she emphasized how some of the information was exculpatory evidence. She then held up the stack of evidence that had just been given to her just minutes before Briones walked in the room.

Bunn implored, "Your honor, why are we getting this now? The prosecution has almost completed its case and now they are giving us evidence that we should have had before the trial ever began. They have had this in their possession for years. They have tainted the entire judicial process and have put you into a terrible situation. But I see no other justifiable alternative and seriously ask you to declare a mistrial."

All the defense attorneys addressed Briones and asked for the same as Bunn. In response, the prosecution asked to place James Griego on the stand in order to answer questions pertaining to the withheld evidence.

Griego took the stand and shocked the courtroom with his calm demeanor as he admitted that the FBI had "many boxes of evidence" that had not been given to the defense. He tried to claim that his team didn't think it was important to the case. But then Tom Mills asked a question, "Do you think there might be any evidence that would help my client with his defense?"

Without hesitation, Griego answered, "Yes, there might be."

"Do you think by not giving this evidence you have created a situation where this is not a fair trial?"

"It is not fair that you did not have the evidence," Griego conceded.

It was a shocking admission. Why was Griego was so forthcoming with the malfeasance at his own hands? There was no indication that he wanted to defend his actions.

Following his lead, Kanof addressed the court as she feigned tears. "Your Honor, I am so embarrassed. Nothing like this has ever happened to me before in all my years. I really do not know what to say or how to explain what happened…"

Briones was visibly upset. He reiterated how important this case was to the community and how long the defendants had waited for a trial. But given the circumstances, he said, "I have no other choice but to declare a mistrial."

It was a mistrial based on prosecutorial misconduct. Kanof clearly invited a mistrial. This was demonstrated even more forcefully right after his ruling when Judge Briones turned to the defense and stated, "I have already reviewed the law and there will be another trial." Once he left the courtroom and the door to his office had barely closed behind him, Kanof went from tears to a gleeful smile and celebratory high fives with her prosecutorial team. Anderson and his defense attorney, Robert Perez, watched this in stunned silence.

The defendants did not understand the full implication of a mistrial at the time. From the bench, Briones explained that just because it was a mistrial didn't mean that the defendants wouldn't be tried again. In fact, he said there would be another trial. But the defense attorneys gave their clients caution by saying that no one knew for sure what was going to happen. In any event, the defendants were told by their attorneys that it was good news.

Before leaving the courthouse, the attorneys went to speak to the jury to ascertain their perspective on the case. This proved to be valuable information. As a reminder, they had only heard the prosecution's case. Typically, after a prosecution team has presented the case, the defense feels the heat and wonders how they are going to create an argument to get the jury to see another side of the story. But in this case, no defense attorney felt that way.

All the defense attorneys believed the jury was hung even before they presented their side of the case. When they polled the jury to where they were leaning, that is exactly where it was. Of the six women on the jury, all but one was already leaning toward acquittal. One was not giving an opinion as she was wanting to hear the defense's case. Of the six men, one was leaning for acquittal, one was leaning toward guilt and the rest were wanting to hear the rest of the case before making a judgment.

When the jury spoke specifically about the witnesses, they were all in agreement on three of them. They did not like or believe Montelongo, Saucedo and Parsley. Some mentioned that this case was being tried over office politics that had nothing to do with the law.

With so many years of stress and frustration, it was comforting to know that "We the People" were seeing the injustice of the entire case. But the frustration and stress were going to continue because the case was not over. Nonetheless, a celebration was in order and the defendants and their loved ones indulged with an impromptu celebration. This weekend began on a Wednesday afternoon.

Chapter 19: The Aftermath

After the bombshell of the mistrial, the media predictably downplayed the lack of evidence, claiming that it stemmed from procedural errors from the prosecution. Kanof was filmed saying that she made mistakes, but that she and her team would be ready to try it again. She apologized to the public for not convicting the defendants. There was no mention of Cordero, the exculpatory documents that were withheld or any other details of the outrageous misconduct.

A few of the defense attorneys gave some statements to the media. Only sound bites of those interviews made it to the airwaves. In the online edition of the *El Paso Times*, the story ran with the pictures of the defendants during their perp walk on the day of the indictments, along with photos of them leaving the courthouse en masse, delightfully stunned.

But the media's rendition was clear: they wanted the public to believe that the defendants found a loophole and got away with a crime. This consistent portrayal of the defendants explains why they have never given an interview to the El Paso media and why they probably never will. But the media's influence in this case has diminished substantially. A mistrial because of misconduct was now public information. The event of a mistrial is an interesting phenomenon as it can be declared for various reasons including the following:

• A hung jury
• The defense requests it due to procedural anomalies
• Prosecutorial misconduct as determined by the judge at the trial

With a hung jury, the prosecution has the discretion to decide to dismiss the case or to retry it. If the defense requests a mistrial, and it is granted, then the prosecution has the right to retry the case. However, if there is prosecutorial misconduct that led to a defendant's rights being denied due to exonerating evidence being withheld, then the case should be dismissed since a retrial would constitute double-jeopardy.

This case was a combination of the latter two. The defense team requested a mistrial, based on prosecutorial misconduct. That left the defendants in a legal limbo where they had to wait on the judge to decide. Briones had stated at the end of the mistrial that he wanted a new trial before the end of the 2017 calendar year.

The team of defense attorneys believed they had another venue to argue for the dismissal of the case. There is a precedent in US court proceedings whereby double jeopardy is considered when the prosecution "goads" the defense to request a mistrial and in their motion to dismiss, they cited evidence to that effect. The motion pointed out that the prosecution was aware that the case was not going well, a fact that was confirmed when the jurors were polled afterward.

The motion went on to argue that, in order to save their case and get a "do over," the prosecution purposely caused a mistrial to happen. These were seasoned prosecutors who knew that the withholding of evidence would cause considerable doubt regarding the fairness of the case. The day they gave almost 300 pages of new evidence that had been withheld, they gift wrapped sufficient cause for the defense to request the mistrial. Moreover, instead of arguing for the trial to continue, they conceded that they were in the wrong. Kanof theatrically managed a tearful apology to the court.

Judge Briones, as the presiding judge in the case, had decision-making power regarding the motion to dismiss. If he decided to dismiss, the case would be completely over. If he decided not to dismiss, then the case was set to go to the Fifth Circuit Court of Appeals. Even though the trial strongly suggested corruption on the part of the FBI and Kanof, no one on the defense team believed that Briones would dismiss the case, even with outrageous prosecutorial misconduct. The motion to dismiss was based on prosecutorial misconduct not only for the trial, but also going all the way back to the indictments. The plethora of information acquired by the defense just before and since the mistrial substantiates the misconduct and corruption of the fake cheating scandal from its inception. The following is a list of items and incidents that bolstered the argument of misconduct by the AUSA and FBI for the purpose of a dismissal.

- Intimidation of witnesses
- Suppression of evidence with the grand jury
- Denial of due process
- Intentional suppression of evidence that
exonerated the defendants
- Co-conspirators who pled guilty were unable to express or
articulate their guilt.
- A conspiracy had not been proven with testimony coming from
alleged co-conspirators (both indicted and unindicted) all of whom

testified that they never believed they were engaging in illegal activity.

• Debra Kanof did not argue against the mistrial; in fact, she hinted that it was warranted as the result of her actions and those of the FBI agents.

• Disclosures of evidence whereby a critical timeline was deliberately pulled from documentation that proved retaliation didn't happen.

• Proof that Cordero lied when he claimed he was an informant for the FBI a week before he ever spoke to them.

• Agent Griego testified that he witnessed Tanner's testimony at Diane Thomas' TEA hearing. Tanner did not attend that hearing.

• Kanof and Griego possessed documented information confirming Cordero's incidents of choking one student and trying to run over another; however, both Kanof and Griego denied knowing about the choking incident.

• Griego testified to the Grand Jury that Cordero testified about attendance issues prior to the September 2011 car incident when in fact Cordero did not testify until August 2012.

• Failing to instruct the grand jury properly. Kanof told the members of the jury that the Austin defendants were co-conspirators without offering an explanation as to how they were co-conspirators.

The motion to dismiss was submitted in mid July 2017. The prosecution was granted an extension of time to respond and finally gave its response on September 8, 2017. With the response, Kanof and the agents also turned over several computer disks of information along with 51 boxes of evidence and a computer. It is worth noting that the evidence they turned over was more than the amount of evidence they originally submitted for the trial.

In addition to this motion, there was already a motion to dismiss based on the 10th Amendment whereby the defense argued that the federal government does not have jurisdiction in a state matter and the state of Texas had already rejected the case. Further, that motion also described that No Child Left Behind (NCLB) protected educators from criminal charges stemming from practices designed to comply with the law.

As both sides were arguing via motions regarding the dismissal, the defense attorneys jointly reported Debra Kanof to the Department of Justice and to the Texas State Bar for her gross misconduct. The federal entity responded that they would not consider any discipline on Kanof while the case was still pending.

Everything is up in the air

The Texas Bar Association, for its part, agreed to consider the allegations against Kanof. Originally, the Texas Bar was going to decide on Kanof's conduct in December 2017, but because of repeated requests for continuances from Kanof, her fate wasn't decided until August 2019.

The defense attorneys discouraged the defendants from believing that Kanof would receive any type of discipline, no matter how warranted. The truth of the matter is that in the United States, federal prosecutors are protected. It is extremely rare—less than 1% of the time—for a federal prosecutor to get reprimanded, much less disbarred. It speaks to the gravity of her behavior that the State Bar of Texas was going to make Kanof defend herself.

By the end of 2017, Judge Briones had not made a decision regarding the case. Originally, he claimed that he wanted the trial to occur before the end of the calendar year, but that did not happen. Instead, Briones called for a status hearing in January 2018. With all the attorneys present for both sides, Robert Perez suggested to the court that Briones did not have jurisdiction in the case given that the original motion to dismiss based on the 10th Amendment had not yet been decided by the Fifth Circuit Court of Appeals.

Briones admitted that he did not know if he had jurisdiction or not. Nonetheless, Briones charged the attorneys to be ready for a trial in June 2018, a full year after the mistrial. He then informed them that he would conduct another status hearing soon to discover if he had jurisdiction or not.

The defense attorneys began planning for the summer while discussing their disbelief of the injustice in the case. Whereas Briones had not made a judgment on the dismissal, there was hope from the defendants that the decision would be taken from his jurisdiction.

In late February 2018, Briones called for another status meeting where he declared himself as having the legal jurisdiction in the case. Thus, he denied the motion to dismiss the case, but agreed that before a trial could happen, there needed to be an evidentiary hearing to address the reasons that led to the mistrial.

Trust in the system was difficult to maintain especially considering Kanof's blatantly corrupt actions. Yet, because of a federal judge's power and his quid pro quo relationship with Kanof, no one believed justice would occur without some type of intervention. With that in mind, Liz Rogers reached out to John Bash, the new US Attorney of the Western District of Texas.

Bash replaced Richard Durbin in December 2017. Although some of the defense attorneys reached out to Durbin during this case, he declined to meet with any of them. Bash proved to be different. He agreed to meet with Rogers at his office in Austin at the beginning of April 2018. Rogers took Stillinger and Bunn with her.

At the meeting, the defense attorneys voiced their concerns regarding the conduct of the prosecution. Bash listened and asked questions. Without sharing his perspective on this issue, he thanked the attorneys for their time and said he would study the case and contact them later. On May 16, 2018, Bash removed Debra Kanof from the case.

In the legal world, this was monumental. Federal prosecutors have enormous powers and privileges. To be removed from a case indicates that Bash found significant merit to what the defense attorneys had presented to him. Briones was not part of the decision-making process for her removal.

The evidentiary hearing to discuss the mistrial occurred on June 14, 2018 and the time came for Briones to determine if the misconduct was intentional or merely negligent. Of course, the defendants were hoping that Briones would honor his duty to justice and dismiss the case, but the defense attorneys cautioned that this was a federal case and rarely do federal prosecutors or judges admit to widespread errors that might hint at corruption.

The attorneys' caution was soon justified. As Briones entered the court room, and before he made it to his chair at his bench, he audibly whispered, "There's not going to be a dismissal, if that's what they think is going to happen. There will not be a dismissal." He made it clear that his decision had been made before hearing the evidence.

The defense wanted the FBI agents to take the stand. However, Briones did not allow that to happen. Instead, he only permitted Kanof to take the stand as the defense attorneys asked her questions related to the misconduct. Kanof danced around, asked for clarifications and dodged questions for almost five hours, only admitting that she did not mean to be so disorganized with this case.

At one point, she went so far as to explain that she withheld the exculpatory evidence on Cordero because it made the defendants look "too guilty." Jaws hit the floor with this declaration. What prosecuting attorney would do this? In truth, the real reason was quite the opposite, as the withheld evidence cleared the educators of the retaliation charge. Sheri Bunn, Diane Thomas' defense attorney, asked Kanof point blank if she really meant what she said about this evidence making the defendants look "too guilty"? Kanof repeated that she did and the thud of jaws hitting the floor once again echoed around the courtroom.

Briones ended the hearing abruptly and voiced his decision. Not surprisingly, he declared that the prosecution was negligent, but not intentionally negligent. Yet, he dismissed Count 4, the charge of retaliation against Cordero and Halliday, with prejudice. He declared that the rest of the charges still stood and that he hoped for a trial before the end of the 2018 calendar year.

The linchpin had been pulled. Retaliation, the charge that most powerfully led to the indictments, had been dismissed by a judge, who clearly, favored the prosecution. Further, Judge Briones dismissed the charge with prejudice, and that is significant. By legal definition, that means that the charge was "vexatious and brought in bad faith." In layman's terms, it means that the FBI and Kanof knew that the charge was false from the beginning, but they went for it anyway.

For Diane Thomas, the case was now over, as retaliation was the only charge against her. She was free from the ordeal, but the harm done to her was irreparable. Her reward for not lying and maintaining her integrity was having her freedom back, but it did not mean that she retrieved her teacher's certification. That had been revoked by TEA after Thomas refused to endure any more of their kangaroo court proceedings.

Nancy Love still had to endure the charge of perjury, even though it was related to the charge that was dropped. Tanner, Anderson and Tegmeyer still had three charges against them, all of which claimed fraud against the US government. Almost immediately after the hearing, the defense attorneys predicted that the prosecution would find a way to allow Love and Tegmeyer to walk while focusing their attention on Anderson and Tanner.

Kanof's fate was still undetermined. Though officially taken off the case, she was still dodging her hearing for misconduct in front of the Texas Bar. She was able to postpone her meeting with the Bar five times over a period of two years.

By December 2018, the prosecuting attorneys called the attorneys for Love and Tegmeyer. As predicted at the time of the evidentiary hearing, Love and Tegmeyer were offered Pre-Trial Diversion (PTD) without admitting guilt. PTD allows a defendant to remain on a probationary period while complying with all laws of the United States. If successful, then she or he will have all charges dismissed with no convictions. It was highly significant that the PTD came with no admission of guilt.

It was an offer that was impossible to refuse especially since no admission of guilt was required. As far as the defense attorneys know, this offer is unprecedented for a federal case in West Texas District of The United States. By not accepting, Love's and Tegmeyer's waiting period for a new trial could have taken years, and it was more than just waiting. Waiting meant that those charges would still show up on any background investigation for employment, and it is near impossible to attain a professional position with federal felony charges pending. Both accepted the offer in order to cut their losses and try and begin anew in the professional world.

Though Tegmeyer and Love were no longer a part of the case, that didn't mean that the feds had let up. Tanner and Anderson were ordered to appear in court on January 3, 2019. It was a status hearing to discuss the case and to set a new trial. The prosecutors still offered a plea deal that would include admitting guilt to one felony charge with five years of probation. Ready for trial, and not about to admit to something they had not done, Tanner and Anderson both denied the offer loudly and clearly.

Working out all the details resulted in another status hearing in February, where a practical question was proposed. With her disarming Texas charm, Rogers reminded Briones that any prosecutor associated with the case was disqualified because they had been privy to documents that the defense attorneys were required to provide to Kanof for her defense in front of the Texas Bar. Briones listened, and he directed Rogers to write her motion. His facial expression indicated that he followed her logic.

Nonetheless, a trial date for August 19, 2019 was determined. No one believed that the trial would take place at that time, given that one of the two remaining original attorneys left his government job and moved to another city. The incoming attorney slated to take the case knew nothing about it and probably didn't want to touch it, given what had happened to Kanof. Ironically, Kanof's Texas Bar hearing was rescheduled for August 21, 2019, two days after the trial was set for Anderson and Tanner.

Another small, but significant breakthrough took place at the hearing. It was established that Tanner and Anderson could now speak to each other. This allowed them to work together on all the information that had been withheld by the prosecution for what now amounted to eight years. As they worked together, they discovered that there was even more information withheld than what was in the 51 boxes.

In fact, there were two conference rooms filled with boxes containing files, blue ray DVD's, CD's and audio recordings that the prosecution had not handed over. The sheer volume probably meant that the prosecution hadn't reviewed most of that material either. James Anderson spent three eight to ten hour days scanning these documents while an armed FBI guard watched over him. In total, the additional material amounted to another two million or more pages of documents that had not been given to the defense, filled with exculpatory evidence.

Key examples of withheld information within these boxes were two large binders labeled "Summary of EPISD District Argument" from the Safi group (EPISD attorneys) that had not been given over: A single page documenting several government files, including 1A files used to document how and when the FBI received their evidence with names and dates missing of who was interviewed and which agent received it; exculpatory evidence that was undated and not reviewed until after the mistrial; finally, two thumb drives with over 90,000 emails of high level EPISD administrators including James Anderson. Federal law demands any defendant's correspondence, exculpatory or not, must be handed over to the defendant to whom it belongs. Federal discovery laws were broken by the prosecution on each of these individual examples.

Most disturbingly, the evidence in these boxes showed FBI 302 witness statements that had been written *five years after the interview and three months after the mistrial*. As a result, more motions were filed and the prosecution was most likely becoming fatigued. That assumption was fortified with the information that the last remaining prosecutor of the original case was moving to another city and was purported to have said that he no longer wanted to jeopardize his career by remaining involved.

Knowing that information, Tanner and Anderson were still ready to fight and figured that the federal prosecutors would keep this case going for another three to five years. As much as they did not want to wait that long, they were committed to defending their integrity.

On April 16, 2019, however, Tanner and Anderson received word that they were being offered PTD with no admission of guilt. Tanner immediately wanted to reject the offer, but Anderson believed it was something to seriously consider. There was a catch to the offer. Both Anderson and Tanner had to accept it jointly or neither one could get it separately.

Defense attorneys generally view PTD as a win because there is no conviction and the government, officially, failed to prove its case. It is the way that the feds give up. Something unforeseen must have happened for this case to have cratered so spectacularly in the early months of 2019. Not only did the government offer PTD to Tanner and Anderson (without either one requesting it), but they also allowed three individuals who had already pled guilty—Vanessa Foreman, Maria Flores, and Damon Murphy—to withdraw their pleas and enter deferred adjudication. This offer surprised the three and their attorneys. This is completely unprecedented for a federal case in the state of Texas, if not in the entire United States. None of the defense attorneys had ever heard of such an action.

Knowing all of that, Tanner was still hesitant to accept because he felt the case should have been dismissed by either Briones and/or Bash. But Tanner also learned over the past years that justice for defendants is not the top priority for the federal Department of Justice. Like most major institutions, the US Department of Justice and the FBI do not want the public to believe that they make mistakes. Their first priority is to save face.

However, Tanner didn't want to interfere with Anderson's life goals, as Anderson who was in his early 40s, had a family to support. Frankly, Tanner also needed to work again. There were many bills to pay and a retirement to rebuild from scratch at the age of 56. While waiting another two to five more years for a trial is great for a legendary tale, paying bills and earning a salary are the necessities of life.

Therefore, for the same reasons as Love and Tegmeyer, Anderson and Tanner agreed to the offer of PTD. That is, until they were told that the offer required them to spend 18 months in the program before the charges would be dropped. They denied that offer, and as their attorneys said they would try to get the feds to agree to a year, they denied that one as well.

Allegedly, PTD must be served for a minimum of six months. Anderson and Tanner insisted on the minimum or a return to trial. It took from April 16 to July 1, 2019 for all sides to agree that they would comply with the minimum. Anderson and Tanner began PTD on July 1, 2019 with an end date of December 31. It was beneficial for them to be able to move on with their lives without waiting years for a new trial. Regrettably, they were also doing the government a favor.

Acquiescing to accept PTD was not the desired outcome. But it was a victory for the defense and a colossal loss for Kanof, Murray and Griego. There was no admission of guilt and all charges were dismissed. Their names and reputations had already been destroyed, so they had nothing more they could really lose. But they now could move on with their lives and expect a clear background check.

As Anderson and Tanner were beginning their PTD, Love and Tegmeyer were ending theirs. When Love was completely free, she was rewarded with a full news story complete with tabloid innuendo of her "getting away" with something. As usual, the pictures which accompanied the story displayed the perp walk. Surprisingly, there was no report whatsoever when Tegmeyer completed his PTD at the end of July.

The last remaining knot of the entire sham was Debra Kanof's future. For the fifth time, she had her Texas Bar hearing postponed to August 21, 2019. A panel of attorneys on the Bar were ready to hear her case and decide her status as an attorney in the state of Texas. Hiring an attorney from Washington, D.C. to represent her, Kanof was now on the other side. It seemed fitting that, at least for a little while, she would experience what she had put so many through during the course of her ruthless career. She had been reassigned in her position and was the talk of the El Paso legal community. It was certainly not the way she wanted her career to end.

The defense attorneys emphasized to their clients that they should be satisfied merely by Kanof having to answer for what the real world considers crimes. The attorneys did not offer hope of any discipline. The possible outcomes for Kanof were:
1. No consequence at all
2. Private reprimand
3. Public reprimand
4. Suspension
5. Disbarment

In early August 2019, the local grievance panel that was to hear the case against Kanof was notified by the Texas Bar counsel that the case had been settled and that the State Bar Commission agreed to a private reprimand. The defendants were initially disappointed that a *deux ex machina* had seemingly swung down out of the sky, ending Kanof's reprimand without explanation.

But then a realization hit. It is most extraordinary, almost unheard of, for a federal AUSA to have to answer for misconduct, much less receive any type of discipline. It just doesn't happen.

A private reprimand means that a disciplinary mark doesn't go on her record and it is not supposed to be public information. But it has been the worst kept secret in the El Paso legal community. Kanof had been brought down and everyone was talking about it. For the first time in a long career that had terrorized, denigrated and ruined so many lives unnecessarily, a bit of karmic justice finally allowed Debra Kanof to be exposed as a formal disgrace.

The legal aspect of the fabricated cheating scandal of EPISD is over. But the fallout will continue for years. For the innocent victims—the defendants—much of the damage is irreparable. As strong people of integrity, they vowed to not only survive, but to thrive, and each has gone on to a career that is ontologically different. They have joined the members of the club known as "You Think It Won't Happen to You."

As for the downtown redevelopment plan, there have been many challenges to the unethical practices of the land developers and the El Paso City Council. Yet, that oligarchical regime marches on with their goal of erasing the history of south El Paso for the development of strip malls, parking lots and a sports arena.

Using old EPISD schools that are becoming charters, money that was earmarked for education is being funneled to buildings such as condos and tax credits for new businesses. Since the EPISD superintendent is in favor of charter schools while the district's attendance drops dramatically, he will continue to receive praise and support from those who placed him into power.

In fact, in an *El Paso Times* article from November 11, 2019 entitled "EPISD board to consider adopting tax incentive policy to bring businesses and families to the district," it is suggested that this is a good incentive for the district. However, when reading the article, one learns that the incentive is for business owners. For-profit business owners will benefit from tax revenue that was originally meant for students.

Lauded in the article for bringing this "opportunity" to EPISD is the Borderplex Alliance, the same group associated with the PDNG, with Mayor Dee Margo and with the superintendent's brother, Rick Cabrera, who's an account executive for a firm associated with Margo. Not surprisingly, no journalistic outlet is challenging this affront to the students of EPISD. Surely, no one from EPISD will challenge what is happening. If they did, they might be accused of cheating.

Once Anderson and Tanner were finally cleared of the federal indictment, the Texas Education Agency began attempts to clean up their part of the mess. TEA did not want to admit defeat, but were even less inclined to have hearings for those whose charges had at long last been dismissed by the DOJ. In an apparent attempt to intimidate the remaining four (Anderson, Love, Tanner and Tegmeyer) into giving up the fight, the new crop of TEA attorneys came out in true Kanof style with petitions to the State Office of Administrative Hearings accusing this battle hardened group of everything from violating Texas education law and "hindering the reporting of child abuse" to being "unworthy to instruct or supervise the youth of this state" and "violating the Educator's Code of Ethics."

After filing the petition in February 2020, TEA offered the four a deal for their certifications on a tarnished platter without having to go through the legal process of a formal hearing. The catch was that they would have to accept a worse reprimand than Kanof's on their Texas educator certifications. It would allow them to work for Texas public schools and it would mirror the reprimands given to dozens of other EPISD educators who accepted the condition in order to maintain their employment.

But with a mark on their certificate and not having been able to work in education since their indictment, finding employment with that flag on it would be practically impossible. More importantly, they hadn't buckled to the enormous pressure of the FBI/DOJ. Why would they ever entertain the idea of a deal from an agency that, at this point, held absolutely no power over their lives? They refused the deal.

The defendants correctly saw this as simply a continuation of the injustice that they had already been forced to endure. All four decided to push forward toward a showdown with TEA and were still committed to the principle that they would not admit to something that they did not do. Their tenacity and stubbornness ultimately paid off.

Just before noon on Friday, May 8, 2020, the day after a seventh petition with new charges was filed against James Anderson and as this book was in the final stages of editing, the call came to the counsel of each defendant that the Texas Education Agency was dismissing the case against all of them and that their educator certifications would be cleared.

The motions for all four defendants stated that the requests for dismissal were due to the Covid-19 pandemic and the reallocation of TEA resources "that prevents the Petitioner [TEA] from being able to continue this litigation." Given modern audio and visual technology and the fact that the language of the petitions portrayed the character of these individuals as somewhere just short of a mafia crime family with regard to public education, the idea of Covid-19 derailing this process is completely absurd.

As with the PTD agreements which manufactured a way for the FBI/DOJ to avoid responsibility and save face, Covid-19 became the manner chosen by TEA to avoid taking responsibility for their role and for what surely would have been some rather embarrassingly informative hearings.

After everything was said and done, the final result was the same for the four. Ultimately, all charges against James Anderson, John Tanner, Mark Tegmeyer and Nancy Love were dismissed. They were completely innocent at all levels and against all accusations, state and federal, civil and criminal. Diane Thomas was equally innocent, but made the unfortunate mistake of believing she would get a fair hearing from TEA at the height of the scandal. Though their reputations, finances and careers were shredded, they stood strong under the weight of an unimaginable burden and prevailed.

The only difference with the latter dismissal by TEA was that, this time, the El Paso media, Eliot Shapleigh and the host of early accusers was nowhere to be found. Bob Moore, Zahira Torres, Estela Casas and Rick Cabrera had all moved on to what can be assumed are greener pastures within the borderland community. Those that remained at The *El Paso Times*, KVIA and the other local news outlets had, understandably, all fallen silent on the subject of the EPISD "cheating scandal" months before. The feeding frenzy of the perp walks a little over four years earlier that gave credibility to the accusations and coverage behind the alleged cheating scandal had evidently now fizzled to a story that was no longer considered newsworthy. So shines a good deed in a weary world...

It ends as it began

The prologue of this book provided an analysis of how El Paso is run by an oligarchy consisting of a few prominent white families in a city that is 85% Hispanic. The saga of the fabricated cheating scandal emphasizes the truism "the more things change, the more they remain the same."

To some extent, the so-called scandal appeared to be about race. The main accusers were Anglo, and the primary victims were also white. Though the educators were accused of discriminating against Hispanic students, truth and an analysis of the defendants' backgrounds nullifies this preposterous allegation, and most of the members of the communities they served saw that. But inciting the appearance of racial bias was a methodology used to sway the jury of public opinion. Thankfully, in the end, it didn't work.

In fact, hundreds of Hispanic voices supported the defendants. They were heard at rallies at Austin High School and at school board meetings. These were the voices not allowed to be aired on the TV stations or quoted in the *Times*. In the fashion of paternalism that is often associated with oligarchies, those voices were considered unworthy of consideration.

It might seem ironic that in a "scandal" that was marketed as targeting Hispanic students, the only two convictions in this entire fiasco were against Hispanics. Myrna Gamboa was a victim who had succumbed to the power and terrorism of the FBI and DOJ by admitting guilt so that she would not have to live numerous years in prison for crimes she didn't commit. Lorenzo Garcia was pressured into pleading guilty for cheating that didn't occur in order to avoid a hefty prison term for a crime he did commit (steering a no-bid contract to his former lover). But knowing the power structure of El Paso, there's nothing ironic about it. Gamboa and Garcia both came from humble beginnings, pulled themselves up by their bootstraps and were living the American Dream until they were told it wasn't for them.

In many ways, El Paso hasn't changed a bit over its 400-year history.

EPILOGUE:
An open letter to El Paso

Are you listening, El Paso? Have you ever really listened? Have you ever been the least bit critical of what you heard? Did you ever truly pay attention? If you haven't, you need to be listening now, because the silence is deafening. The narrative once nurtured so enthusiastically by Bob Moore, former editor of the *El Paso Times*, and embraced by his cohorts at KVIA, KDBC, KTSM and KFOX, has finally given up the ghost.

The narrative, whose lungs Moore made sure were perpetually replenished with hot air from the FBI/DOJ of the Western District of Texas, Eliot Shapleigh, Susie Byrd, Beto O'Rourke, Dee Margo, Veronica Escobar, the Cabrera brothers, Dori Fenenbock, Vern Butler, Judy Castleberry, Michael Williams, Adam Jones to the Texas Education Agency, suffered a myocardial-infarction of a mistrial in June 2017. Moore stepped down from his job as editor of the *Times* a little over two months later, stating that he wanted to save newsroom jobs. Moore likely saw the writing on the wall and decided to begin disassociating himself as much as possible from his own creation.

The story received a bit of life support a year later when an evidentiary hearing was granted and Debra Kanof, the lead prosecuting attorney, danced for five hours giving an incoherent explanation regarding the retaliation charge she garnered from the Grand Jury while withholding key exculpatory evidence to the contrary. The evidence that she dumped on the defense almost three weeks into the trial, torpedoed what would have been an almost certain acquittal. By this time, Zahira Torres, the reporter who crafted The *El Paso Times*' scandal articles April through December of 2012 to coincide with the lead-up to the Weaver Report and the removal of the EPISD Board of Trustees, had taken over the job as editor of the *Times* trying to keep the narrative alive and a dying newspaper relevant.

The last glimmer of life manifested itself in February 2019 when it appeared that the U.S. Attorney's office and the FBI were going to take one more shot at the only two remaining defendants, James Anderson and John Tanner, as Judge David Briones set their retrial date for August 19, 2019. Zahira Torres, Estela Casas, Shelton Dodson, Robert Holguin and the gang cracked open its chest and massaged its heart one more time in the hopes of squeezing the last drop of blood out of a story that was more and more taking on the appearance of a turnip.

The press reported that Mark Tegmeyer and Nancy Love "took pretrial diversion (PTD) to avoid trial," though that was not the reason. The press explained that "it's similar to probation," but it's not. In PTD, all charges are dismissed against the defendant. And in this case, the prosecution did not ask for any type of admission of guilt which is unprecedented in the Western District of Texas. But the government, with the media as its mouthpiece, attempted to make the public believe that said defendants had actually copped to something.

But the narrative finally flat lined. On July 1, 2019, every media outlet discovered that the United States Attorney for the Western District of Texas filed motions with the court that James Anderson and John Tanner were offered PTDs and that the three individuals who pled guilty in the case (Damon Murphy, Maria Flores and Vanessa Foreman) were all allowed to withdraw their pleas in exchange for deferred adjudication and ultimate dismissal of charges, putting a metaphorical "Do Not Resuscitate" order on the final seal and death certificate. In a statement to the media, US Attorney John Bash remarked, "The pre-trial diversion and deferred prosecution agreements entered into in this case were accepted by all parties—the defendants and our office—as a just and appropriate resolution to the matter."

So the fanfare of the narrative had reached its crescendo the week that six people—now exonerated—were perp walked through downtown El Paso in handcuffs, shackles and county jail jump suits in April 2016 by the FBI and the US Attorney's office, as every one of the local media outlets salivated at the possible ratings bonanza, has gone gently into that good night. Bob Moore's seven-page reverse-print white-on-black exposé the following day and Eliot Shapleigh's crowing on every local news station that very night, have faded into conspicuous silence as time of death had been called. The tale they once championed, they now ignore and, it appears, that none of them nor their offspring will step up as next of kin and claim the body.

How is it that the citizens of El Paso have not heard one critical word about the El Paso Independent School District Cheating Scheme story going down in flames? Were they unaware that those who once promoted it vehemently, who patted themselves on the back for awards won and accolades bestowed as the initial geniuses who gave life to the creature, have now abandoned it to an archival refrigerator drawer with a

Jane Doe toe tag? Here lies the deafening silence to which El Pasoans need to be paying close attention.

The hollowness of an unsubstantiated narrative prepared, half-baked and served up to support the interests of the few and the wealthy instead of the masses of average, everyday El Pasoans. The untold number of meaningless clichés in empty reports. Those reports accompanied by images that had been reheated so many times, they were afraid that you would finally become aware, El Paso, that there wasn't a satisfying nutrient of fact to be found. Finally, the media fell silent as the narrative gasped its last breath.

The media was equally aware that Debra Kanof, Eliot Shapleigh and Bob Moore were snake oil salesmen. They were aware and complicit with the fact that these individuals had an amazing lack of morals and ethics which gave them the chutzpa to completely humiliate and crush the reputations of innocent people in order to give credence to their narrative. They were aware that these three had enough social and political capital in this state and city to make it happen. Joseph McCarthy would be proud. But how can it be that the reporting, the crowing and the spinning of this narrative suddenly stopped the moment its falsehood became glaringly apparent?

Because reporting it would only create problems for every person and entity who pushed this narrative from the beginning. Reporting the truth would expose the reporting for what it was—lazy, incompetent, biased and unethical. They were in so deep with these local and state politicians and the federal law enforcement that reporting looked like a carbon copy of the AUSA's press releases or an Eliot Shapleigh press conference. They would rather rely on letting it fade into the background because they believe they can count on the complacency of the people of El Paso. They wagered on a zombie-like apathy of their viewers, readers and loyal followers not to hold them accountable.

None of them really want the people of El Paso to ask why Bob or Zahira or Rick or Estela never once questioned the government's actions or mistakes even though it is their journalistic responsibility to do so, upheld in the first amendment. They must have been betting that El Pasoans would believe that these "good people" who smile and talk to us so pseudo-intelligently every night could never portray innocent people as criminals if it weren't true. They were counting on El Paso to willfully ignore the fact that, despite the mounting evidence of false accusations by the very law enforcement agency their stories relied on, their viewers and readers would never believe they dropped the story just to protect their own reputation and the narrative they nurtured and spun so methodically. Surprise! They would and they did.

The total lack of media coverage on these recent developments in this narrative alone should be proof enough, but there is more to it than that. Objectivity, fairness and truthfulness are the highest priority in journalism; therefore, it is the duty of these news outlets to report a high-profile story they have covered for years to its very end. The sudden lack of reporting on these developments demonstrates an incredible void of journalistic integrity of every editor, producer, anchor and reporter involved in this scam of a scandal.

The *El Paso Times*, which has taken the lead on this from the beginning, is particularly egregious. Zahira Torres and Bob Moore published an article on these events every time there was so much as a cough coming out of the US Attorney's Office. Mark Tegmeyer's PTD was written up in the *Times* the day it was filed with the court back in November 2018 and the television media reported the *Times* article that same day. The same can be said of the date the retrial was set for James Anderson and John Tanner. A *Times* reporter was obviously present for the status hearing in Judge Briones courtroom because, not only did they report the new date for trial, but it was there that they found out about the PTD agreement for Nancy Love. Once again, the local television media jumped all over the story that same day.

To have overlooked the implications of the latest developments is beyond the realm of possibility for responsible and ethical journalists. Bob Moore, Zahira Torres, Kevin Lovell, Estela Casas and all their colleagues purposely ignored it.

There are many questions to be answered, and Bob Moore, Zahira Torres and the *Times* are front and center on that list. Zahira Torres, like her predecessor and teacher Bob Moore, moved on some two weeks before the July 1 announcement that tolled the death of the narrative she helped create. This begs the obvious question. Did she even consider revisiting and acknowledging that the narrative that had made her career was now collapsing in a heap at the doorstep of the new federal courthouse or did she decide to follow the lead of her mentor and exit quietly under the guise of moral superiority and pray no one would notice the hypocrisy?

While all the television media in El Paso is guilty of the same, KVIA is the most powerful. Interestingly enough, it is the one with the closest connections to the narrative. For instance, why wasn't KVIA more upfront about Rick and Juan Cabrera's connection to Dee Margo and ALEC? While changes were brewing in state law to allow managerial experience to equal that of education experience for positions in education administration, Margo magically pulled Juan's name out of thin air for the EPISD job after rejecting two applicants who were far more qualified. About a year and a half ago, Rick Cabrera faded out of KVIA and into Margo's investment firm. Why didn't the local media look into and report on any of this?

Finally, on the night the mistrial was declared, instead of questioning the reasons behind such a huge debacle in a high profile case, Estela Casas and Rick Cabrera went over the cheating scheme timeline once more for good measure as if to buoy support for the government's case.

The other television stations followed suit, and not one dared question the case, the narrative or the US attorneys and the FBI. Should they be given an out? Do we let them off, excusing their inaction, protesting that perhaps they were afraid to do otherwise? If they were afraid, they can be assured from the experience of the five remaining educators that they had every right to be. They would have gone up against a branch of government against which there is no recourse.

One hoped, however, that they would have been more afraid of losing their integrity, which should be considered the central concern of any journalist's reporting. At some point there needs to be an understanding that the ratings of a station only indicate its popularity or that of an anchor or reporter. In no way are these a true measure or indication of integrity. Often, it means just the opposite, if truth be told.

And what of the Justice Department? Are El Pasoans not allowed to question the motivations of Debra Kanof, Robert Almonte, Rifian Newaz, Tom Murray and James Griego when they perp walked the defendants before an unquestioning local media? Was their purpose to frighten the accused into a plea bargain? Or was it, at the very least, to influence the potential jury pool because they knew they really had no case?

How is it possible that these infallible sleuths "missed" pivotal pieces of evidence that exonerated all five of the defendants from the retaliation and fraud charges that were the cornerstone of their accusations when they sought and received those indictments from the grand jury? Was this information held in the government's back pocket to dump on the defense and torpedo the trial in case it went badly? How many other "mistakes" like this have they made over the course of their careers? How many have never been discovered because the defendants simply decided to buckle to the pressure and plead? Yet after what these five have been put through, shouldn't the citizens of El Paso take the time to reflect on why the local media reporting was so biased and why they have apparently dropped the story all together?

It is hard to lay this all at the feet of the media, though their role is a prominent one. Is it possible for the people of this city to hold to account the politicians and wealthy business people who created the condition for the possibility of this injustice? Can El Paso forget Bob Moore's emails showing he worked behind the scenes with city officials helping them to implement their plans and making sure they came out in the best possible light?[1]

Will the people ever accept the facts about Beto O'Rourke's connection as the son-in-law of Bill Sanders, the architect of the REIT that created the "need" for the scandal? Will El Pasoans recognize Sander's connection to the PDNG, the Borderplex Alliance and the connection to other El Paso politicians and business people simply through him and his son-in-law? El Paso's leadership falls into a very small and very exclusive community. Do you think the silence by all these self-proclaimed champions of the poor—Shapleigh, Escobar, Byrd, O'Rourke, Rodriguez—as Duranguito fights for its life, is simply an oversight on their part?

Shapleigh had hours of interview time with The *El Paso Times* and the local television stations where he pontificated from the cheap seats with no shred of evidence to back his claims and the media never pressured him to produce anything concrete. If his claims had any validity, why didn't he stand up, take the reins and physically escort the harmed students back to be re-enrolled at the offending campus as was their constitutional right, a la Martin Luther King, Jr.? Is it because the "untold" number of students denied a proper education was an illusion and that Shapleigh was more akin to the Wizard of Oz than one of our greatest civil rights leaders?

El Paso needs to open its eyes as well as its ears. Or are these powerful manipulators correct in their assessment of the apathy of the average citizen? Maybe the average El Pasoan has just been beaten into complacency. Maybe that is at the heart of the power of the wealthy and well-connected. Perhaps a perk to their power is the ability to bend a narrative to their will at the expense of the innocent bystander and have the masses believe the sleight of hand.

Read the over 700 articles on the subject published by the *Times* and the transcripts of the reports done by each television news team before, during and after the trial, and you will see that it is completely and unequivocally one-sided. Fear of reporting the truth is no excuse. If anyone knew fear, it was the five educators. In the beginning, the FBI hinted at the hell the government would put them through, but they were innocent, and they knew it. Their minds would not let them believe how far individuals with complete immunity from accountability would go to try to get them to succumb to the government's contrived narrative. They each suffered three or more years of unemployment, accrued thousands of dollars of debt and several emptied retirement and savings accounts. The five innocents know the lengths to which absolute power will go to save face.

But this much is certain. The people should be afraid. This is not an anomaly. A good teacher always tries to get through to his or her students and pushes them to think critically and question authority, advising the student to even question the teacher. Journalists should know this better than anyone, but in this case, they failed.

Government agencies, parties, politicians and news organizations are made up of human beings and human beings make mistakes. Pride, greed and ambition can affect even the most moral minded who go unaware until the damage is done. Sometimes they refuse to face what they've done. This is most evident in the power of the US Attorney's office and the FBI and the immunity they have to withstand any form of litigation and the protection they afford those who did their bidding.

Today, the haggard five have little recourse. Their reputations will forever be strewn across the internet as non-convicted convicts sacrificed to public scrutiny as instigators of a cheating scandal that never existed. They have all had to start over and that isn't easy. They were stripped of the professions that they loved, where they did indeed help students greatly, for the greater good of the bank accounts of El Paso's wealthy who continue to hide behind a feigned concern for the poor and marginalized of the city.

As of May 2020, the Texas Education Agency has dismissed the case against the remaining four, leaving no doubt whatsoever about their innocence. Those who shouted guilt from the mountain tops have fallen silent at the defendants' ultimate victory. But calling this a victory for the five innocents would be a misrepresentation of the pain and suffering they endured and which they continue to process to their very core on a daily basis. TEA presented a farce of the decision to dismiss, claiming it was based on the COVID-19 pandemic. Despite the unrelenting pressure of powerful individuals and entities who needed them to fall, they survived. No other word captures their reality at this moment more clearly. They survived.

That silence that rings in the air of the city today is the sound of these powerful people and entities who are fearful that the people of El Paso will awaken and discover what has been done to their city and to their children out of ignorance and greed. It is the silence of the truth about the Texas Education Agency's cowardice and complicity through the actions of their lawyers working hand in hand with the FBI, the Safi group, the EPISD Board of Managers and current superintendent. It is Adam Jones, Judy Castleberry, Michael Williams and Vern Butler serving up the final nail in the coffin of public education and paving the road for re-segregation of the American educational system by charter school selection.

It is the silence of every individual within every entity who knew the truth and failed to speak out. But the truth has been spoken. As Christ repeated time and again, "Whoever has ears, let them hear." May the citizens of El Paso take the time to read thoughtfully, to think critically, and to listen carefully to that deafening ringing silence.

This was a book about defying the odds.

It was about being a .2 percenter. It was about turning the tables when 99.8 percent of cases in the Western District of Texas in 2017 ended in conviction.

This was, and still is, a story about underdogs.
This story shared an extraordinary account about winning with a losing hand.

The authors hoped to provide a detailed account that exposes serious questions about the methods and motivations of the FBI, the Texas Education Agency,
the oligarchy of El Paso and the El Paso media.

This was a real-life David and Goliath story.

Now all sides have spoken
and the record has been set straight.

References

Prologue
1. World Population Review. "Ciudad Juarez Population."
worldpopulationreview.com. https://worldpopulationreview.com/world-cities/ciudad-juarez-population/ (Accessed April 3, 2020).
2. Vacation Idea. "El Paso Elevation – Places to Visit."
Vacationidea.com. https://vacationidea.com/texas/el-paso-elevation.html (Accessed April 3, 2020).
3. Columbia Broadcast System. "America's 11 Poorest Cities." cbs.com. https://www.cbsnews.com/media/americas-11-poorest-cities/ (Accessed April 3, 2020).
4. United Press International. "Across Mexico Border from Safe El Paso, Violence Surges in Juárez." upi.com.
https://www.upi.com/Top_News/World-News/2019/01/23/Across-Mexico-border-from-safe-El-Paso-violence-surges-in-Jurez/2961548187558/ (Accessed April 3, 2020).
5. Best Places. "Religion in El Paso, Texas." bestplaces.net.
https://www.bestplaces.net/religion/city/texas/el_paso
6. Wikipedia. "Roman Catholic Diocese of Ciudad Juárez." wikipedia.com.
https://en.wikipedia.org/wiki/Roman_Catholic_Diocese_of_Ciudad_Ju%C3%A1rez 7.Wikipedia. "Fort Bliss." wikipedia.com.
https://en.wikipedia.org/wiki/Fort_Bliss 8. Wikipedia. "List of Mayors of El Paso, Texas." wikipedia.com.
https://en.wikipedia.org/wiki/List_of_mayors_of_El_Paso,_Texas

Chapter 1
 No References

Chapter 2
1. Roberts, Chris. "Shapleigh: Austin Pulls Scam." *El Paso Times*, June 26, 2016. Accessed April 3, 2020.
https://www.elpasotimes.com/story/archives/2016/04/27/archives-shapleigh-austin-high-pulled-scam/83601568/

Chapter 3
1. Wikipedia. "Eliot Shapleigh." wikipedia.com.
https://en.wikipedia.org/wiki/Eliot_Shapleigh (Accessed April 3, 2020).

2. Wikipedia. "Eliot Shapleigh." wikipedia.com.
https://en.wikipedia.org/wiki/Eliot_Shapleigh (Accessed April 3, 2020).
3. "Paul, I'll ask Beverly and Mr. Parker to process the invoice so that we can make the payment as soon as possible." Garcia, Lorenzo, "September Invoice," email to Eliot Shapleigh Assistant Paul Colbert regarding payment for services of Dr. Colby Stover, 2008.
4. Shapleigh, Eliot. "*Equipo* Bowie – Excellence Con Ganas." pdf Memorandum of Understanding between *Equipo* Bowie and the El Paso Independent School district, September 23, 2008.
5. Shapleigh, Eliot. "*Equipo* Bowie – Excellence Con Ganas." pdf Memorandum of Understanding between *Equipo* Bowie and the El Paso Independent School district, September 23, 2008.
6. Shapleigh, Eliot. "*Equipo* Bowie – Excellence Con Ganas." pdf Memorandum of Understanding between *Equipo* Bowie and the El Paso Independent School district, September 23, 2008.
7. WBEZ 91.5 Chicago. "Which Comes First? Closed Schools or Blighted Neighborhoods?" wbez.org. https://www.wbez.org/shows/wbez-news/which-comes-first-closed-schools-or-blighted-neighborhoods/50662c2f-4b12-4b6a-a58c-da3a043822f1 (Accessed April 4, 2020).
8. Shapleigh, Eliot, "*Equipo* Bowie MOU – Sept. 23, 2008," YouTube Video, 2:58, September 24, 2008.
https://www.youtube.com/watch?v=zIowl6tndi0 (Accessed April 4, 2020).

Chapter 4

1. Houston Press. "Former Spring Branch Administrators Face Investigations, Prison Time After Cheating Scandal in El Paso Area School Districts." HoustonPress.com.
https://www.houstonpress.com/news/former-spring-branch-administrators-face-investigations-prison-time-after-cheating-scandal-in-el-paso-area-school-districts-6718949 (Accessed April 4, 2020).
2. Houston Press. "Former Spring Branch Administrators Face Investigations, Prison Time After Cheating Scandal in El Paso Area School Districts." HoustonPress.com.
https://www.houstonpress.com/news/former-spring-branch-administrators-face-investigations-prison-time-after-cheating-scandal-in-el-paso-area-school-districts-6718949 (Accessed April 4, 2020).
3. "having the Coordinating Board collect and analyze the data is simply non-negotiable for us," Subject: "*Equipo* Bowie/Loose Ends," Edmondson, David, email to EPISD Chief of Staff Tomas Gabaldon, September 18,

2008. Chapter 5 1. Wikipedia. "Paso Del Norte Group." wikipedia.com. https://en.wikipedia.org/wiki/Paso_Del_Norte_Group (Accessed April 4, 2020). 2. Wikipedia. "Paso Del Norte Group." wikipedia.com. https://en.wikipedia.org/wiki/Paso_Del_Norte_Group (Accessed April 4, 2020). 3. Burnett, John. "A Toxic Century: Mining Giant Must Clean Up Mess." NPR.org. February 4, 2010. https://www.npr.org/templates/story/story.php?storyId=122779177 (Accessed April 4, 2020).

4. Flores, Aileen B. "City Proposes Site for $180 Million Downtown Arena." *El Paso Times*, October 13, 2016.

5a. USA Today. "Beto O'Rourke's Record on El Paso Real Estate Deal has some Latinos Troubled." usatoday.com. https://www.usatoday.com/story/news/politics/elections/2019/09/14/beto-orourke-el-paso-primary-city-council-plan/2307914001/ (Accessed April 4, 2020). 5b. Who Rules El Paso? Community First Coalition. Kindle Direct Publishing. 2020. 6. Columbia Broadcast System. "America's 11 Poorest Cities." cbs.com. https://www.cbsnews.com/media/americas-11-poorest-cities/ (Accessed April 3, 2020).

7. The Balance. "The Best and Worst Property Taxes by State." thebalance.com. https://www.thebalance.com/best-and-worst-states-for-property-taxes-3193328 (Accessed April 4, 2020).

8. "The Barrio Speaks Out: 'A Lack of Respect.'" YouTube Video, 6:39, October 15, 2007. https://www.youtube.com/watch?v=Wgv_aDrsOcg (Accessed April 4, 2020). 9. Henry C. Trost Historical Organization. "Henry C. Trost." henrytrost.org. https://www.henrytrost.org/family-history/henry-c-trost/ (Accessed April 4. 2020).

10. Housing and Community Development Network of New Jersey. "Spot Blight Eminent Domain." hcdnnj.org. https://www.hcdnnj.org/index.php?option=com_content&view=article&catid=19:site-content&id=623:spot-blight-eminent-domain (Accessed April 4, 2020).

Chapter 6

1. Editorial Projects in Education Research Center. (2011, July 18). Adequate Yearly Progress. Education Week. Retrieved Month Day, Year from http://www.edweek.org/ew/issues/adequate-yearly-progress/ (Accessed April 4, 2020).

2a. "As you know, our office has spearheaded "*Equipo* Bowie" an innovative, multi-agency, education pipeline' project aimed at systemic reform to improve student readiness in a key EPISD feeder pattern,"

Subject: "*Equipo* Bowie/Analysis of 9th grade and 10th grade population/test data," Shapleigh, Eliot, email to Robert Scott (Texas Commissioner of Education), August 12, 2009.
2b. Moore, Bob. "Former TEA Commissioner Talks about Cheating Scandal." *El Paso Times*. September 22, 2012. https://www.elpasotimes.com/story/news/politics/blogs/tx-capital-report/2012/09/22/former-tea-commisioner-talks-about-cheating-scandal/31501781/ (Accessed April 4, 2020).
3. "I know that your intention is not to move forward without the District's leadership and expertise. We all want to work for the success of Bowie as a collaborative effort." Subject: "Re: New Principal Takes Reins of Ailing Bowie High School (EP TIMES 5.5.08)." Garcia, Lorenzo, email response to State Senator Eliot Shapleigh, May 6, 2008.

Chapter 7
1. Allensworth, Elaine. "Why is Ninth Grade a Critical Time for Students? A Researcher Explains." Bill and Melinda Gates Foundation. K12education/gatesfoundation.org. https://k12education.gatesfoundation.org/blog/why-ninth-grade-critical-time-students/ (Accessed April 4, 2020).
2. Klein, Alyson. "No Child Left Behind: An Overview." Education Week. April 10, 2015.
3. Allensworth, Elaine. "Why is Ninth Grade a Critical Time for Students? A Researcher Explains." Bill and Melinda Gates Foundation. K12education/gatesfoundation.org. https://k12education.gatesfoundation.org/blog/why-ninth-grade-critical-time-students/ (Accessed April 4, 2020).
4. Campioni, Azzurra. "Dropouts and the Ninth Grade Bulge." Center for Mental Health in Schools at UCLA. smhp.psych.ucla.edu. http://smhp.psych.ucla.edu/pdfdocs/9thgrade.pdf (Accessed April 4, 2020).
5. Texas Education Agency. "PEIMS – PID: Personal Identification Data Base." tea.texas.gov. https://tea.texas.gov/reports-and-data/data-submission/peims/peims-pid-person-identification-database/peims-pid-person-identification-database (Accessed April 4, 2020).
6. Klein, Alyson. "No Child Left Behind: An Overview." Education Week. April 10, 2015.
7. "EPISD Cheating Scheme Timeline." *El Paso Times*. June 28, 2017. https://www.elpasotimes.com/story/news/education/2017/06/28/episd-cheating-scheme-timeline/437296001/ (Accessed April 4, 2020).

8. "Editorial: Shapleigh and EPISD." *El Paso Times*, April 24, 2016. elpasotimes.com. https://www.elpasotimes.com/story/opinion/editorials/2016/04/25/editorial -shapleigh-honored-episd-tenacity/83476302/ (Accessed April 4, 2020).
9. "Editorial: Shapleigh and EPISD." *El Paso Times*, April 24, 2016. elpasotimes.com. https://www.elpasotimes.com/story/opinion/editorials/2016/04/25/editorial -shapleigh-honored-episd-tenacity/83476302/ (Accessed April 4, 2020).
10. Casas, Estela. "Shapleigh Requested President Obama's Help Blowing Whistle on 'Bowie Plan.'" PDF file, April 27, 2016. KVIA.com.
11. U.S. Department of Education. "The Federal Role in Education." www2.ed.gov. https://www2.ed.gov/about/overview/fed/role.html (Accessed April 4, 2020).
12. MOTION FOR LEAVE TO FILE UNDER SEAL. NO. EP-14-MC-397-ATB. November 2014.
13. MOTION FOR LEAVE TO FILE UNDER SEAL. NO. EP-14-MC-397-ATB. November 2014.
14. Office of Inspector General. "El Paso Independent School District's Compliance with Accountability and Academic Assessment Requirements of the Elementary and Secondary Education Act of 1965." www2.ed.gov. June, 2013. https://www2.ed.gov/about/offices/list/oig/auditreports/fy2013/a06l0001.p df (Accessed April 10, 2020).

Chapter 8

1. KVIA ABC-7. "Ex EPISD superintendent Lorenzo Garcia sentenced to 3 ½ years in prison." October 9, 2012. Available at: https://kvia.com/news/2012/10/09/ex-episd-superintendent-lorenzo-garcia-sentenced-to-3-1-2-years-in-prison/
2. Connelly, Richard. "Lorenzo Garcia: El Paso ISD Chief with Local Ties Indicted Over Houston Contract." Houston Press. Aug. 2, 2011. Available at: https://www.houstonpress.com/news/lorenzo-garcia-el-paso-isd-chief-with-local-ties-indicted-over-houston-contract-6742879
3. FBI TEXT Messages Received as Discovery in Case No. EP-16-CR-0693.
4. FBI TEXT Messages Received as Discovery in Case No. EP-16-CR-0693.
5. Chavez, Adrianna. "Lorenzo Garcia Pleads Guilty." *El Paso Times*. June 14, 2012. Found at:

https://www.elpasotimes.com/story/archives/2016/05/03/2012-lorenzo-garc-pleads-   guilty/83875688/
6. Letter to the EPISD Board Members. (PDF), June 19, 2012. Chapter 9 1. Shapleigh, Eliot. "Why a Monitor Will Not Work." Reform EPISD.org. Found at: https://myemail.constantcontact.com/Why-a-Monitor-Will-Not-Work-.html?soid=1110593985569&aid=JqXiB5LyE3U&fbclid=IwAR3mGvyUO4Q8pmd1VT9GP3-NqWBoT_yWsP4afjocsjJgGmD41hUr5i6ovQk 2. Borunda, D. & Martinez, A. "EPISD cheating scheme charges dropped by U.S. Attorney's office." *El Paso Times*. July 1, 2019. Available at: https://www.elpasotimes.com/story/news/education/episd/2019/07/01/episd-cheating-scheme-charges-dropped-u-s-attorneys-office/1624664001/ 3. KVIA ABC-7. "Newspaper Calls For EPISD Board Members To Resign." June 17, 2012. Available at: https://kvia.com/news/2012/06/17/newspaper-calls-for-episd-board-members-to-resign/ 4. Dejo, Ben. "Kids First Reform EPISD PAC: What's Wrong and What's White." Deep Inside El Paso. May 1, 2013. Available at http://deepinsideelpaso.blogspot.com/2013/05/kids-first-reform-episd-now-pac-whats.html 5. EPISD Board Minutes Aug 2012. Available at https://www.episd.org/domain/211 6. EPISD Board Minutes Oct 2012. Available at https://www.episd.org/domain/211 7. Now defunct website. http://shapleigh.org 8. EPISD Board Minutes. Oct 2012. Available at **https://www.episd.org/domain/211**
9. TEA Organization Chart 2008, 2009. Available at https://l.facebook.com/l.php?u=http%3A%2F%2Fmansfield.tea.state.tx.us%2FTEA.AskTED.TSD%2FTSDfiles%2Ftsd2009%2Fnot_tagged%2Ftea_hierarchy_org_charts.pdf%3Ffbclid%3DIwAR1C73TbfRhlZZwWiAUsvMh2YgyN_awzOUDqgZW3Hm9c9UQoK-5NWmvtjqc&h=AT03iEB8BxfCfCVBHAjy38mCUeltOvHd6s3Oi_tDiBU3p_BN07ArgvWsruAqt5DEfkKPWyQ-jP92jtfDV-dSdpZAWCM1fVEF0-fDnjtDCDoqFgPZa1puVzsNhxBo-SMHKZfmLo-EHdblwXt122LHeQ
10. Johnson, Emi. TEA Internal Memorandum. January 2, 2012
11. Biography of Dee Margo. Available at https://d3dkdvqff0zqx.cloudfront.net/groups/epcc/attachments/mr_%20dee%20margo%20bio.pdf
12. Jones, Adam. Memorandum of phone interview with Judy Castleberry. October 25, 2012.
13. Safi Notebook. Received as Discovery in Case No. EP-16-CR-0693
14. Weaver Report. Available at https://l.facebook.com/l.php?u=http%3A%2F%2Fwww.sao.texas.gov%2Fr

eports%2Fmain%2F13-
047.pdf%3Ffbclid%3DIwAR0hkTNkSsDDNtOJv27KNK5sUwXf8mr0_Y
DJPssSrA_1KROWathvprUQ3hM&h=AT03iEB8BxfCfCVBHAjy38mCU
eltOvHd6s3Oi_tDiBU3p_BN07ArgvWsruAqt5DEfkKPWyQ-jP92jtfDV-
dSdpZAWCM1fVEF0-fDnjtDCDoqFgPZa1puVzsNhxBo-SMHKZfmLo-
EHdblwXt122LHeQ
15. Ibid
16. Ibid and TEA TEC 25.094
17. EPISD Board minutes April 2012. Found at
https://www.episd.org/domain/211 18. Parker, Kenneth. Letter responding
to the Weaver Report. April 1, 2013. Found at
https://holtthink.tumblr.com/post/46990431505/former-episd-cfo-ken-
parkers-letter-to-board
19. Adam Jones Email 8-16-2012. Weaver Group internal emails
20. Adam Jones Email 8-16-2012. Weaver Group internal emails 21. Safi
Notebook. Received as Discovery in Case No. EP-16-CR-0693 22.
October 25, 2012. Adam Jones emails. Received as Discovery in Case
No. EP-16-CR-0693

Chapter 10
None

Chapter 11
1. EPISD Discovery. Ruben Cordero Documents Incident. November 2,
2009.
2. EPISD Discovery. Student Statement against Ruben Cordero.
September 22, 2011 3. EPISD Discovery. Findings of EPISD Investigator
Chere Williams Regarding Incident with Ruben Cordero. June, 2012.
4. State Board of Educator Certification. Available at
https://l.facebook.com/l.php?u=https%3A%2F%2Ftea.texas.gov%2Ftexas-
educators%2Finvestigations%2Feducator-discipline-
faqs%3Ffbclid%3DIwAR3EN4cDnRYOYxrfQZSDvZq8SDWjbrSsuI_RT
kCavDdINCqRQE4F_KSSoZ4&h=AT0NuBSaqeP4djQ5rfkaiLNP8isQoE
hlb1G1DOuH2amnOearjPfe5u1kN9i0y_-
STtSHFj5rquriCHDM8mmyRbNJMAvPB-
PCrSiFFPzl8vRaUHMLYLajOgmlpZIZnHDQo9Mo06gCYpihemV0iPSJ
Vg
5. EPISD Discovery. "This means that all of your comparatives will be off
between five to eight teacher FTE's and additional cuts may be
necessary." Subject, "Re: Important Calculation Error on Needs

Assessment Comparative for Regular High Schools." Email, Theresa Thompson to Diane Thomas, March 11, 2013.

6. EPISD Discovery. Grievance of Ruben Cordero against John Tanner. May 15, 2013.

7. KVIA ABC-7. "TEA Commissioner Appoints New Board of Managers to Oversee EPID School Board; Board President Reacts. January 14, 2013. Available at https://kvia.com/news/2014/01/14/tea-commissioner-appoints-new-board-of-managers-to-oversee-episd-school-board-president-reacts/

8a. Raw video: Education Commissioner Michael Williams appoints EPISD monitor. May 18, 2015. Available at https://www.youtube.com/watch?v=VXfvxIbIoUY

8b. Letter to the EPISD Board Members. (PDF), June 19, 2012.

9. Montes, Aaron. El Paso Dee Margo possibly in violation of state financial disclosure requirements. *El Paso Times*. June 12, 2019. Available at https://www.elpasotimes.com/story/news/2019/06/12/el-paso-mayor-dee-margo-possibly-violation-state-financial-disclosure-requirements-ethics-complaint/1437456001/

10. EPISD Board Minutes. December 2013. Available at https://www.episd.org/domain/211 11. Stuart Baggish emails to FBI. Received as Discovery in Case No. EP-16-CR-0693

Chapter 12

1. The Center for Media and Democracy. "Privatizing public education, higher ed policy and teachers." October 13, 2017. Available at https://www.alecexposed.org/wiki/Privatizing_Public_Education,_Higher_Ed_Policy,_and_Teachers

2. Esquivel, Erika. "El Paso City Council replaced man who opposes their development plans. July 24, 2018. Available at https://kfoxtv.com/news/local/el-paso-city-council-replaced-man-who-opposes-their-development-plans

3. Sanchez, Sara. "EPISD cheating scheme victim graduates EPCC." *El Paso Times*. May 15, 2017. https://www.elpasotimes.com/story/news/education/2017/05/15/episd-cheating-scheme-victim-graduates-epcc/101597616/

4. Lopez, Meghan. "EPISD reaches out to students affected by its cheating scheme." KFOX-TV. April 29, 2016. Found at https://kfoxtv.com/news/local/episd-reaches-out-to-students-affected-by-its-cheating-scheme

5. Tony Conners Confidential Informant Memo. September 2013. Received as Discovery in Case No. EP-16-CR-0693

6. Ibid. Received as Discovery in Case No. EP-16-CR-0693. Available at https://l.facebook.com/l.php?u=https%3A%2F%2Fwww.youtube.com%2Fwatch%3Fv%3DJPzpOtn6onA%26fbclid%3DIwAR1gMa6RY4nghiyggVZxK68sXaVK3xZq03pkHv0Ra06oLXgEmoqm6OwKFpQ&h=AT0NuBSaqeP4djQ5rfkaiLNP8isQoEhlb1G1DOuH2amnOearjPfe5u1kN9i0y_-STtSHFj5rquriCHDM8mmyRbNJMAvPB-PCrSiFFPzl8vRaUHMLYLajOgmlpZIZnHDQo9Mo06gCYpihemV0iPSJVg

7. Anderson, Lindsey. "State sanctions ex-EPISD administrator Gina Oaxaca." *El Paso Times.* June 9, 2017.

8. TEA attorney Stuart Baggish to FBI James Griego and Thomas Murray on getting removal of education certifications signed. Received as Discovery in Case No. EP-16-CR-0693

9. Palafox and Shapleigh. Evidence to indicate their civic relationship. https://www.ywcaelpaso.org/wp-content/uploads/sites/37/AnnualReport08-04.pdf;
https://epcf.org/system/document/document/1/EPCF_ReporttoCom2018_Web.pdf

10. EPISD Discovery. "This means that all of your comparatives will be off between five to eight teacher FTE's and additional cuts may be necessary." Subject, "Re: Important Calculation Error on Needs Assessment Comparative for Regular High Schools." Email, Theresa Thompson to Diane Thomas, March 11, 2013.

Chapter 13

1. Fernandez, Manny. "Sentence cut in Texas for school official jailed in test scandal." NY Times. December 13, 2013. Found at https://www.nytimes.com/2013/12/13/us/sentence-cut-in-texas-for-school-official-jailed-in-test-scandal.html

2. Email, TEA response to SAO requests for emails, phone call notes, documentation. May 22, 2013

3. "Thank you for discussing your investigation of El Paso ISD with me this morning." Subject, "El Paso ISD Data Request," email, TEA Ombuds Officer Emi Johns to FBI Special Agent James Griego, November 8, 2011. Discovery in Case No. EP-16-CR-0693

4. Email from Bill Brown to Don Sutherland, Weaver Group.

5. "Former EPISD administrator sentenced to five years, probation for role in cheating scheme." *El Paso Times.* January 29, 2015. 6. 194B-EP-39077.

Serial 1146. Document entry of 1A's. "10…(U) Copies of Gamboa's notebooks." Received as Discovery in Case No. EP-16-CR-0693 Chapter 14 1. FCC Fairness Doctrine. Found at https://en.wikipedia.org/wiki/FCC_fairness_doctrine 2. Ibid 3. El Paso Downtown Plan Scam Timeline. November 3, 2012. Available at https://eptstadiumscamtimeline.blogspot.com/2012/11/timeline-of-events-of-el-paso-downtown.html?fbclid=IwAR3DeGtMe5pvPM2f4cFdHia9-vt7EWnCAYpRmlAJLbnw4yZ3iWdfbji99S4 4. Ibid 5. Williams, Chere. Cordero Timeline produced for Patricia Cortez, EPISD. Received as Discovery in Case No. EP-16-CR-0693, June 20, 2017.
6. Torres, Zahira. "Unheeded Warnings." *El Paso Times*. Dec. 2, 2012
7. Jordan, Terri. Letter to TEA Commissioner Robert Scott referencing correspondence to TEA Ombud Emi Johnson for assistance, May 9, 2012
8. "EPISD was following common practice throughout Texas, evidently condoned by TEA to the extent of its instructions to districts on who should take which tests." Subject, "USDOE NCLB audit exit conference," email, Safi, Anthony, EPISD Attorney to Ron Ederer, Lorenzo Garcia, Terri Jordan, James Anderson, Kenneth Parker, Patty Hughes, June 10, 2011.
9. FBI Press Release. "Former EPISD Superintendent Garcia Sentenced to Federal Prison." October 5, 2012. Available at https://archives.fbi.gov/archives/elpaso/press-releases/2012/former-e.p.i.s.d.-superintendent-garcia-sentenced-to-federal-prison?fbclid=IwAR3Q6KVuCVwZFoGYS6zTx8vYlOQIHHgOtTGWE MX43dBwbYfqQqXxLbt1dz8 (Accessed April 8, 2020)
10. August 5, 2010. Eliot Shapleigh letter to TEA Commissioner Robert Scott alleging TEA complicit and request Department of Education and Office of Civil Rights investigate.pdf

Chapter 15
1. Scott, A. (2014). Found at https://prezi.com/06dmuwpjip7o/what-makes-someone-a-monster/
2. Beck, R. (2015). We Believe the Children: A moral panic in the 1980s. Public Affairs, NY. pp. 147-169
3. Ibid
4. Ibid
5. Ibid
6. Nathan, D. & Snedeker, M. (1995). Satan's Silence: Ritual abuse and the making of a modern American witch hunt. USA

7. Beck, R. (2015). We Believe the Children: A moral panic in the 1980s. Public Affairs, NY. pp. 147-169

8. Ibid

9. Ibid

10. Ibid

11. Ibid

12. Ibid

13. Ballinger, C. (2011). *El Paso Times*, "EPISD Superintendent arrested on mail fraud, conspiracy and theft charges." August 1, 2011.

14. Human Rights Alert. January 20, 2011 http://docshare04.docshare.tips/files/4724/47248633.pdf

15. Lee, Jane. "Can a child sexual offender be cured? The Age. June 16, 2017 https://www.theage.com.au/national/victoria/can-a-child-sexual-offender-be-cured-20170608-gwnmux.html

16. Floyd, John. "Justice denied to Ramos and Compean by a Fifth Circuit Court of Appeals ruling." John T Loyd Law Firm. August 2, 2008. https://www.johntfloyd.com/justice-denied-to-ramos-and-compean-by-a-fifth-circuit-court-of-appeals-ruling/

17. Arrillaga, Pauline. "What really happened in the border shooting." Fox News. February 16, 2007. **https://www.foxnews.com/printer_friendly_wires/2007Feb16/0,4675,BattleontheBorder,00.html**

18. Hearing to Examine the Prosecution of Ignacio Ramos and Jose Compean. Committee on the Judiciary United States Senate. July 17, 2007. https://www.govinfo.gov/content/pkg/CHRG-110shrg53357/html/CHRG-110shrg53357.htm

19a. Ibid

19b. Campbell, Bob. "Cornyn, Sutton has out Border Patrol sentences." MRT. July 26, 2007. https://www.mrt.com/news/amp/Cornyn-Sutton-hash-out-Border-Patrol-sentences-7627508.php

20. Department of Homeland Security. Office of Inspector General. November 21, 2006. https://books.google.com/books?id=ux_4kLuXNCYC&pg=PA810&lpg=PA810&dq=compean+and+ramos+innocent&source=bl&ots=pHlIUFlsoZ&sig=ACfU3U3gEPQ1HZaGxdDKEflBh8abs2f3zA&hl=en&sa=X&ved=2ahUKEwjJrsuvq6zoAhWGqp4KHRScCEc4ChDoATAFegQIChAB#v=onepage&q=compean%20and%20ramos%20innocent&f=false

21a. National Border Patrol Council. American Federation of Government Employees. January 31, 2007.

https://web.archive.org/web/20070204154146/http://rohrabacher.house.gov/uploadedfiles/nbpc%20rebuttal_to_sutton.pdf

21b. Hearing to Examine the Prosecution of Ignacio Ramos and Jose Compean. Committee on the Judiciary of the United States Senate. https://www.govinfo.gov/content/pkg/CHRG-110shrg53357/html/CHRG-110shrg53357.htm

22. Arrillaga, Pauline. What really happened in the border shooting. Fox News. February 16, 2007. https://www.foxnews.com/printer_friendly_wires/2007Feb16/0,4675,BattleontheBorder,00.html

23. Carter, Sara. "We have seen better days: Ignacio Ramos and Jose Compean: Immigration Heroes." Hecubus. October 18, 2006. https://hecubus.wordpress.com/2006/10/18/ignacio-ramos-and-jose-compean-illegal-immigration-heroes/

24. Levin, Mike. "Bush commutes sentences for two former border patrol agents." Fox News. January 19, 2009. https://www.foxnews.com/politics/bush-commutes-sentences-for-two-former-border-patrol-agents

25. Lehy, Patrick. Hearing to Examine the Prosecution of Ignacio Ramos and Jose Compean. Committee on the Judiciary of the United States Senate. July 17, 2007. https://books.google.com/books?id=wB4102oF8pYC&pg=PA73&lpg=PA73&dq=sutton+and+kanof+should+have+been+prosecuted&source=bl&ots=AHlb4l-Kda&sig=ACfU3U0DuXX0HnitlY9VzckDkWNFdh554Q&hl=en&sa=X&ved=2ahUKEwiomr_9uazoAhXhN30KHQz0DzUQ6AEwAHoECAoQAQ#v=onepage&q=sutton%20and%20kanof%20should%20have%20been%20prosecuted&f=false

26a. Moore, Robert. "Prosecutors reveal new details in Lorenzo Garcia corruption case." *El Paso Times*. September 14, 2017. https://www.elpasotimes.com/story/news/2017/09/14/prosecutors-reveal-new-details-lorenzo-garcia-corruption-case/666257001/

26b. KVIA ABC-7. "Ex district clerk's former right hand man testifies 'Sanches, Jones would joke about corrupt deals." April 7, 2011. **https://kvia.com/news/2011/04/07/ex-district-clerks-former-right-hand-man-testifies-sanchez-jones-would-joke-about-corrupt-deals/**

27a. Oral Deposition of Lorenzo Garcia. December 9, 2015. Kennedy Reporting Service, Inc. SOAH Docket No. 701-14-3692.

27b. Oral Deposition of Lorenzo Garcia. March 10, 2016. Kennedy Reporting Service, Inc. SOAH Docket No. 701-14-3692.

28. Office of Inspector General. "El Paso Independent School Districts Compliance with Accountability and Academic Assessment Requirements of Elementary and Secondary Education Act of 1965. Available at https://l.facebook.com/l.php?u=https%3A%2F%2Fwww2.ed.gov%2Fabout%2Foffices%2Flist%2Foig%2Fauditreports%2Ffy2013%2Fa06l0001.pdf%3Ffbclid%3DIwAR2bxpRGxYpSiz5B63HhUGDQ6tQAi3i227rpLaOgYqPyOCBAZzDDTX1Iwwk&h=AT2k6W5Wk6SDT6rR33jUAnPDEbOGuJud7SqIUQuVV0SqFriOwUCJBsR8X8Pyv9CxSIL8P7Gvz7Ct0XdnQs0AtkqGZFNp3hQnaBXV-aJCHirvtEYn5vSU4p-xy0s5o_pfOERsoZjp7xJf8vG2w2Bbrw
29. Oberheiden PC. "What do I do when FBI agents show up to my house to interview me." https://federal-lawyer.com/fbi-agents-show-house-interview/
30. United States Sentencing Commission. Statistical Information Packet. Western District of Texas. Fiscal Year 2017. Available at https://www.ussc.gov/sites/default/files/pdf/research-and-publications/federal-sentencing-statistics/state-district-circuit/2017/txw17.pdf
31. Tarlton, Polk PLLC. "Tell the truth…and nothing but the truth." July 11, 2019. https://tarltonpolk.com/blog/federal-perjury-and-lying-to-the-feds/
32. Felton, Eric. "Are unrecorded FBI interviews a G-man's license to lie?" Real Clear Investigations. October 28, 2019. https://www.realclearinvestigations.com/articles/2019/03/18/is_an_fbi_interview_a_g-mans_license_to_lie_later.html
33. Kropf Mosely PLLC. "What is an FBI 302? The problematic nature of FBI agents interview memos." Grand Jury Target. May 18, 2017. **https://grandjurytarget.com/2017/05/18/what-is-an-fbi-302-the-problematic-nature-of-fbi-agents-interview-memos/**

Chapter 16
None

Chapter 17
1. Cohen, Jason. "Did breast cancer make an El Paso judge break bad." Texas Monthly. January 21, 2013. https://www.texasmonthly.com/politics/did-breast-cancer-make-an-el-paso-judge-break-bad/
2. Department of Justice. "Longest federal prison term in El Paso corruption investigation handed down this morning to former Aliviane

CEO Cirilo 'Chilo' Lara Madrid." United States Attorneys Office, Western District of Texas. April 15, 2013. Available at https://www.justice.gov/usao-wdtx/pr/longest-federal-prison-term-el-paso-corruption-investigation-handed-down-morning-former
3. Schladen, Marty. "Ex-county Judge Dolores Briones facing minor penalty in corruption case." *El Paso Times*. August 13, 2012. Available at https://insurancenewsnet.com/oarticle/Ex-County-Judge-Dolores-Briones-facing-minor-penalty-in-corruption-case-%5BEl-Paso-a-353861#.XnjrqohKjIU

Chapter 18
1. Benton, Joshua. TEA: Agency officials got friends contracts: Neely's likely successor, foundation advisor are named. Dallas Morning News. June 28, 2007. (Accessed May 3, 2020).
2. Tony Conners Confidential Informant Memo. September 2013. Received as Discovery in Case No. EP-16-CR-0693 Epilogue 1. City Council of El Paso released personal emails involving city business. https://www.facebook.com/Chucoleaks.org, (PDF), (Accessed May 24, 2014).

TIMELINE

2002
January
- NCLB becomes law

2003
- Adam Jones becomes Deputy Commissioner at TEA
- Lorenzo Garcia designated as Principal of the Year for state of Texas while a principal in Houston
- Sanders "completes the capitalization" of the Verde Group, begins to purchase border real estate (The beginnings of the Borderplex REIT)

2004
- PDNG meets to discuss possible future of El Paso
- PDNG discusses eminent domain to secure land for a new downtown

May
- Bowie and Austin enter Stage I of NCLB
- Over 20 EPISD schools are in sanctions either with state accountability, federal accountability or both

August
- Tanner becomes principal in EPISD of Ross Middle School

2005
February
- Lorenzo Garcia hired as superintendent of EPISD
- City Council forms partnership with PDNG who seeks to redevelop south EL Paso involving EPISD properties, including Bowie High School

May
- Bowie and Austin enter Stage 2 of NCLB (AYP)
- Shapleigh makes no public comment about the education challenges of EPISD

2006

February

- El Paso City Council approves the downtown redevelopment plan of the PDNG

March

- Official downtown plan unveiled

May

- Bowie and Austin enter Stage 3 of NCLB (AYP)
- Shapleigh makes no public comment about the education challenges of EPISD

July

- Glass Beach presentation of Old El Paso and New El Paso

2007

May

- Bowie and Austin enter Stage 4 of NCLB (AYP)
- Shapleigh makes no comments about the education challenges of EPISD
- Texas Observer publishes "Eminent Disaster: A Cabal of Politicians and Profiteers Target an El Paso Barrio"

2008

February

- Jesus Chavez hired as new principal of Bowie High School

May

- Bowie and Austin enter into Stage 5 of NCLB (AYP): Put on notice that schools will be closed if scores don't improve
- Shapleigh makes no comments about the education challenges of EPISD

August

- John Tanner hired as principal of Austin High School

September

- Eliot Shapleigh initiates *Equipo* Bowie. Shapleigh now wants to "help" Bowie High School by taking control of it

Oct

- Mark Mendoza implements plan to take pictures of students crossing the Mexico border and going to Bowie

2009

- EPISD sells Roosevelt Elementary in downtown El Paso to La Fe Charter School (run by Beto O'Rourke's wife, Amy) for pennies on the dollar ($1.36 million for buildings and land).

May

- Bowie and Austin meet all testing standards for both federal and state accountability They have to do it again next year to get out of trouble
- Shapleigh makes comments skeptical of Bowie's progress

2010

January

- Perry refuses federal money for Race to the Top
- Arne Duncan opines that Texas is lagging behind in education due to refusal to comply with Race to the Top.

April

- Dee Margo reveals he has over 10,000 shares of the Borderplex REIT for the first time

May

- Bowie and Austin are completely out of academic trouble
- Shapleigh writes a letter to Garcia with an ultimatum to follow the guidelines set for *Equipo Bowie*
- Garcia refuses to comply with Shapleigh's mandates regarding *Equipo Bowie*
- Shapleigh declares that Bowie and EPISD cheated on the state exams
- Garcia requests TEA to perform an audit regarding Shapleigh's allegations
- Shapleigh writes to Arne Duncan complaining that Perry won't comply with Federal plan for education—Race to the Top

June

- Garcia holds press conference at Coronado High School and has Tanner speak out in defense of the district in response to Shapleigh's accusations
- Anderson calls Emi Johnson at TEA to request audit of the district regarding Shapleigh's allegations. Johnson later claimed she never

received a phone call from Anderson, but phone records proved otherwise. Johnson denied Anderson's request.
- Shapleigh writes to USDE regarding his concerns with EPISD
- Shapleigh holds press conference at his office where he accuses Austin of cheating. Tanner publicly challenges Shapleigh
- TEA begins investigation of Shapleigh's allegations

July

- Shapleigh requests TEA to investigate EPISD regarding disappearing students. Shapleigh writes to the state agency after he has taken his "concern" to the federal level.

October

- TEA, under leadership of Adam Jones, clears EPISD of Shapleigh's allegations. No disappearing students.
- Shapleigh demands for TEA to investigate a second time. TEA complies. No disappearing students.
- TEA, under the leadership of Adam Jones, for the second time, clears EPISD of Shapleigh's allegations
- Shapleigh seeks advice from Richard Jewkes and conferences with FBI agents Griego and Murray. Also conferences with Debra Kanof

November

- Shapleigh writes to Obama asking for an FBI investigation
- FBI agrees to investigate EPISD

December

- FBI begins investigation of EPISD
- Mark Mendoza becomes clandestine insider for the FBI
- USDE investigates EPISD separate from the FBI

2011

April

- USDE finds no crime at EPISD. Offered improvements and was ready to develop final report
- Dee Margo reveals again he has over 10,000 shares of the Borderplex REIT

May

- FBI uncovers that Garcia pushed a no bid contract to his former lover
- FBI uses this to keep the "cheating scandal" investigation ongoing

June

- USDE decides to continue investigation considering Garcia accusation

August

- Lorenzo Garcia arrested by FBI at his EPISD office after a principals' meeting
- Garcia resigns from EPISD. Terri Jordan takes over as Interim Superintendent
- Shapleigh alleges that EPISD still has "cancers" that need to be removed

September

- Cordero attempts to run over student at Austin High School
- Cordero removed from Austin High School and reassigned to Pupil Services
- Mark Mendoza becomes Cordero's supervisor

December

- Dolores Briones (sister of Judge David Briones) pleads guilty to embezzlement of federal funds

2012

April

- Terri Jordan holds press conference. Places Jesus Chavez on administrative leave
- Zahira Torres, Bob Moore and the *El Paso Times* begin bimonthly Sunday articles promoting the idea of a cheating scandal

May

- Adam Jones resigns from TEA and begins to work for the Weaver Group

June

- Tanner given official evidence that Cordero committed what he was accused to commit Cordero recommended for termination
- Garcia pleads guilty
- Garcia's plead empowers the FBI, Shapleigh and the media to now define the alleged cheating scandal as "the" cheating scandal
- Media officially calls it the EPISD Cheating Scandal

- PDNG members letter to EPISD Board pushing for majority vote election over the plurality system a week after Garcia pleads. Will push for "state legislative action" if board doesn't act
- Baseball Park approved by City Council
- City Council votes to tear down City Hall for the Baseball Park

July

- Terri Jordan resigns as EPISD interim superintendent. Remains as Chief of Staff
- Ken George replaces Jordan, refuses to implement hit list and is removed within three weeks
- Shapleigh cites that there are other "cancers" in the district that must be removed

August

- 21: Under supervision of Mendoza, Cordero claims retaliation for being an FBI informant
- 29: Cordero speaks to FBI for the first time (7 days after lying that he was an informant)
- Susie Byrd speaks at EPISD school board meeting's open forum making a claim that Austin and El Paso High need to be investigated
- Debra Kanof does not indict Dolores Briones in an unrelated federal corruption case though Kanof associates Briones' actions with those of convicted Illinois Governor Rod Blagojevich

September

- Vernon Butler hired as interim superintendent

October

- Weaver Group tells its investigators that they have the EPISD contract two weeks before the EPISD Board publicly votes for the contract
- Byrd and Veronica Escobar address EPISD Board members during open forum and demand that they hire the Weaver Group for the purpose of investigating Austin and El Paso High
- EPISD Board votes to hire the Weaver Group
- Garcia begins his prison sentence

November

- Weaver Group begins its investigation
- Vern Butler's involvement with Weaver audit leads to contractual work after he completes his assignment at EPISD

- Jesus Chavez resigns from EPISD
- El Paso voters approve a "Quality of Life" measure of $500 million

December

- Board notified of its removal by TEA
- Terri Jordan resigns from district
- Anderson asked to resign
- Weaver continues its investigation as it works with the FBI
- Weaver begins to interview EPISD employees
- Anderson's efforts to ensure the district is ethical leads to an Office of Inspector General (OIG) investigation that is not wanted by the Weaver Group, the FBI, or Shapleigh

2013

January

- Dozens of EPISD administrators are interviewed by the Weaver investigators

February

- James Anderson resigns from the district
- All district leadership removed and replaced by interims and substitutes. In essence, two FBI agents and Kanof are running the district
- Liz Saucedo reports Diane Thomas to central office

March

- Needs assessment determines Halliday is a continuing teacher at Austin
- Needs assessment agrees to automotive shop class being discontinued at Austin
- 8 administrators placed on administrative leave due to the Weaver Report
- Protests and demonstrations at Austin in support of Tanner
- Dolores Briones sentenced to thirty months in federal prison for embezzlement

April

- 1: Weaver report released to press, but not to those cited in it
- 2: School board meeting that reinstated 7 of 8 administrators
- Focus of cheating scandal switched to retaliation

- Saucedo, allegedly at the direction of the FBI, tells Halliday that she is a victim of retaliation

May

- Cordero grievance against Tanner
- Tanner and Thomas recorded by Saucedo
- Board is removed and replaced by unelected Board of Managers

June

- Thomas interrogated by FBI
- Thomas refuses to sign false confession created by FBI
- Thomas reassigned to central office

August

- Tanner and Thomas placed on administrative leave allegedly for retaliation
- Cheating scandal back in the media
- Media does not report that OIG determined that EPISD followed the guidelines of TEA

September

- Protests and rallies in support of Tanner and Thomas
- Only news story that revealed the incident regarding Cordero is destroyed. Reporter claims that she doesn't remember it
- Tegmeyer submits grievance against EPISD
- Margo single-handedly hires unqualified superintendent who is charter school friendly

October

- FBI contacts Tegmeyer
- Tegmeyer leaves EPISD
- Love reassigned from Austin to Jefferson High School
- Love subpoenaed to speak to Grand Jury
- Margo informs Austin community that they won't get Tanner back
- El Paso City Council accused of using personal email accounts for city business

November

- Kanof tries to indict for the first time. Belief was that she was going to indict Tanner, Chavez, Gamboa, Jordan, and Murphy.

December

- Unelected Board of Managers vote to terminate Tanner and Thomas

- Garcia receives a deal to have his sentenced reduced.
- Beto O'Rourke makes a public statement that is printed by the *New York Times* urging for Garcia's sentence to not be reduced

2014
March
- Thomas loses hearing with TEA
- Thomas forced to resign from the district
- Anderson has successful real estate career
- Tegmeyer still in education
- Love still in education in EPISD
May
- Tanner forced to resign from the district
June
- Tanner moves to Olympia, WA to become a nursing home administrator
September
- EPISD conducts attendance audit of "all" schools, but its only focus was Austin. Tanner not notified of audit as he wasn't with the district. Tanner not allowed to know accusations against him or allowed to answer to the accusations
November
- Kanof offers "blue light special" to several people she wants to indict
- Myrna Gamboa makes a plea deal
- Garcia released from prison (11 months earlier than expected)

2015
Spring
- Tanner and Tegmeyer's attorney's inform them that Kanof is seeking an indictment

2016
April
- Kanof indicts Anderson, Tanner, Tegmeyer, Love, Thomas and Murphy
- Kanof files motion to replace Kathleen Cardone with David Briones as Judge in the case

- Media spectacle for the arraignment of Anderson, Tanner, Tegmeyer, Love Thomas and Murphy
- Media spectacle for arraignment of Anderson

June

- Foreman and Flores make plea deals

2017

January

- Murphy makes a plea deal

March

- Frye hearings

May

- Margo elected as mayor. Media would not give coverage to his challenger

June

- 12: Trial begins
- 23: Mistrial declared due to misconduct

July

- Massive amounts of undisclosed and exculpatory evidence discovered with FBI
- Grievance submitted regarding Kanof's misconduct
- First property tax increase under Margo's watch. Margo, a Republican, campaigned with a promise of no tax increases

October

- 17: Margo sells his shares of the Borderplex REIT reportedly at 2 to 3 times of its value to the City of El Paso. Property tax paid for the purchase.
- 17: Duranguito site officially chosen by City Council for a Sports Arena

2018

February

- Rick Cabrera (superintendent's brother and former anchor of KVIA) begins to work for Margo as his handler for his personal finances

June

- Evidentiary hearing for misconduct

- Retaliation charge dropped with prejudice
- Thomas completely free

July

- Rick Cabrera assigned by Margo to be the lead of finance for the downtown redevelopment project

August

- Bowie becomes partial charter school. When full charter, students in the area will have to qualify to attend it.
- Tegmeyer and Love offered PTD with no admission of guilt

November

- Tegmeyer agrees to PTD offer

2019

January

- Love agrees to PTD offer

April

- Anderson and Tanner offered PTD with no admission of guilt
- Foreman, Flores, and Murphy invited by feds to withdraw their plea deals and enter PTD

July

- FBI agents officially stopped all investigation of EPISD (after nine years)
- Love and Tegmeyer complete PTD

August

- Kanof receives a private reprimand from Texas State Bar

2020

January

- Anderson and Tanner complete PTD

May

- The Texas Education Agency dismisses civil charges against the credentials of Anderson, Tanner, Love and Tegmeyer and clears their teacher and administrative certifications

Glossary of Names

Abraham, Sib: original attorney of Damon Murphy. He died with massive debt.

Aguilar, Yolanda: Child Protective Service representative for the Dove and Noble case. Close friend of Kanof.

ALEC: American Legislative Exchange Council. Goal to dismantle US public education.

Almanzan, Robert: Former Associate Superintendent of EPISD.

Almonte, Robert: Assistant United States attorney working with Kanof and Newaz.

Anderson, James: One of the innocent five defendants. Former Assistant Superintendent of EPISD

Archuleta, Ed: Appointed by Michael Williams to the Board of Managers for EPISD. Member of PDNG.

Arrieta-Candelaria, Carmen: Appointed by Michael Williams to the Board of Managers for EPISD. Member of PDNG.

Bash, John: US Attorney for Western District of Texas. Removed Kanof from the case.

Borrego, Alfredo: Elected EPISD board member who was removed by Michael Williams. Moved to let the public speak during Open Forum at the April 2, 2013 Board Meeting.

Briones, David: Federal judge in the case against the innocent five defendants. Brother to Dolores Briones.

Briones, Dolores: Former County Judge in El Paso. Sister of David Briones. Served time for accepting bribes. Was an unindicted co-conspirator in another case.

Bunn, Sherilyn: Attorney for Diane Thomas

Bush, George W.: President of the United States who championed NCLB.

Bustillos, Adrian: One of the seven administrators who was reinstated at the April 2, 2013 Board meeting.

Butler, Vernon: EPISD interim superintendent who placed Cordero back on campus (knowing his propensity for violence) and who went on to perform contract work with the Weaver Group.

Byrd, Susie: City Council member. Friend of Eliot Shapleigh. Friend of Bob Moore. Linked to Beto O'Rourke, Veronica Escobar, and the PDNG. Attended second rally for reinstatement of John Tanner when she was seeking election to the EPISD Board of Trustees which included Austin High School.

Cabrera, Juan: Superintendent of EPISD who replaced Lorenzo Garcia. Chosen by Dee Margo.

Cabrera, Rick: Brother of Juan Cabrera. Former newsman at KVIA. Hired by Margo to run finances for his business and for El Paso's Downtown Redevelopment Plan.

Callan, Sam: Judge for the Dove and Noble case.

Cardone, Kathleen: Judge for the Compean and Ramos case. Originally assigned to the innocent defendants' case, but agreed to transfer to Judge Briones at AUSA Kanof's request.

Casas, Estela: News anchor at KVIA. Recently hired as Executive Director of University Medical Center and Children's Hospital Foundations upon recommendation of PDNG members including former EPISD Board of Managers member Carmen Arrieta-Candelaria.

Castleberry, Judy: TEA monitor for EPISD.

Chavez, Jesus: Former principal at Bowie High School. Was the epicenter of the EPISD Cheating scandal. Became an informant and liaison for both the FBI and TEA.

Comey, James: Former director of the FBI.

Compean, Jose: Border Patrol agent unjustly prosecuted. Sentence commuted by W. Bush.

Conners, Tony: Education attorney in Austin, Texas.

Cordero, Ruben: Auto shop teacher who falsely claimed retaliation because he was an FBI informant when he wasn't an FBI informant. Purposely tried to run down a student on school property with a car.

Cornyn, John: Republican U.S. House Representative from Texas. Called for a pardon for Compean and Ramos.

Cortez, Patricia: Executive Director of Employee Services at EPISD.

Crea, Jackie: Former reporter for KTSM who filed only report that hinted at the defense's case.

Darnell, Jim: Tanner's original attorney for the federal charges.

Davila, Osvaldo: Drug dealer protected by Kanof during the Compean and Ramos trial.

Dodge, David: Elected EPISD board member who made the motion to reinstate seven administrators at the April 2, 2013 Board meeting.

Dodson, Shelton: News anchor for a local El Paso TV station.

Dove, Michelle: Exonerated defendant and victim of Debra Kanof.

Duron, Juan: Reinstated administrator at the April 2, 2013 Board meeting.

Escobar, Veronica: Former El Paso County Commissioner and County Judge. Current US Congresswoman who took Beto O'Rourke's seat.

Closely associated with O'Rourke, Susie Byrd, Eliot Shapleigh and the PDNG.

EPISD: El Paso Independent School District.

Feinstein, Dianne: Democrat Senator of the United States who called for a pardon for Compean and Ramos.

Felder, Cheryl: a former principal of Austin High School who was removed when she had no schedules for students.

Fenenbock, Dori: EPISD Board president under Juan Cabrera. Close ties to J. Cabrera, Dee Margo, and PDNG.

Ferrett, Kristine: Reinstated administrator at the April 2, 2013 Board meeting.

Flores, Maria: Innocent victim of FBI/DOJ. Allowed to withdraw her plea.

Foreman, Vanessa: Innocent victim of FBI/DOJ. Allowed to withdraw her plea.

Gamboa, Myrna: Succumbed to pressure of FBI/DOJ and made a plea. Was convicted and served probation. Has since renounced her confession to the FBI.

Garcia, Lorenzo: Former EPISD superintendent who plead guilty to steering a no bid contract and for cheating. Served federal prison time.

Garcia, Ruben "Sonny": Associate of Dolores Briones who was convicted and served time.

George, Ken: Interim EPISD superintendent who was removed for refusing to terminate 14 EPISD employees without cause.

Griego, James: FBI special agent assigned to the EPISD case.

Halliday, Jeannette: speech teacher at Austin High School who claimed retaliation. That charge was dropped with prejudice.

Hanner, Tiger: Tanner's original TEA attorney.

Holguin, Robert: TV news reporter in El Paso.

Islas, Luis: Attorney for Mark Tegmeyer

Jewkes, Richard: Attorney assigned to Anderson. Wrote sealed motion to remove himself as Anderson's attorney. Was retained by Shapleigh for $1.

Johnson, Emi: Director at TEA who was secretly working with the FBI while she lied about Anderson's correspondence with her.

Jones, Adam: TEA official who oversaw EPISD cleared twice of impropriety. Then went to work for Weaver Group and landed the contract to audit EPISD for the purpose of finding impropriety.

Jordan, Terri: Former interim superintendent and chief of staff for EPISD. Resigned from the district and surrendered her certification to avoid indictment.

Kanof, Debra: Disgraced Assistant United States Attorney who was removed from the case because of her extreme prosecutorial misconduct. Was also the prosecutor in the Dove/Noble and Compean/Ramos cases.

Koehler, Bruce: Legal counsel for EPISD. Prevented Tanner and Thomas from receiving exculpatory evidence that cleared them of their charges.

Lara-Madrid, Cirilo: associate of Dolores Briones who served time in federal prison.

Love, Nancy: Innocent defendant in this case. Former assistant principal at Austin high school.

Loya, Luis: Administrator recommended for termination at the EPISD Board meeting of April 2, 2013.

Lucero, Guadalupe: Assistant attendance clerk at Austin high school who refused to give false information to the FBI that they were trying to mandate.

Margo, Dee: Republican Board of Managers President. Member of PDNG. Former member of ALEC. Mayor of El Paso. Hired Juan Cabrera. Raised El Paso taxes three consecutive years after he sold his Borderplex REIT shares to the City of El Paso.

Martinez, Carlos: Expert witness for the prosecution who established that the federal government probably did not have jurisdiction in the case.

Mills, Tom: Co-Counsel with Liz Rogers for Tanner.

Montelongo, Guadalupe: Lead attendance clerk at Austin High School who was named as an unindicted co-conspirator of the EPISD Cheating Scandal.

Moore, Bob: Editor-in-chief of the *El Paso Times* who omitted any story in favor of the defense. Close friends with Susie Byrd and Eliot Shapleigh. Close working relationship with FBI/DOJ.

Mueller, Robert: head of the FBI who authorized an investigation into EPISD.

Murphy, Damon: Former Associate Superintendent of EPISD. Former Superintendent of Canutillo Independent School District. Indicted and became a government witness against the innocence. Amazingly, allowed to withdraw his plea after he testified against the defendants when the government's case imploded.

Murray, Thomas: special FBI agent assigned to the EPISD case.

Newaz, Rifian: Assistant United States Attorney. Co-counsel with Kanof and Almonte.

Noble, Gayle: innocent and exonerated victim of Debra Kanof.

Oligarchy: a small group of people having control of a country, organization, or institution.

Late 15th century: from Greek oligarkhia, from oligoi 'few' and arkhein 'to rule'.

O'Rourke, Amy: wife of Beto O'Rourke. Daughter of Bill Sanders. Former member of PDNG. Runs a charter school in south El Paso near the area set for demolition.

O'Rourke, Beto: Former Democrat US Representative. Former El Paso Council member noted for his conflict of interest in the Downtown Redevelopment plan. Son-in-law of Bill Sanders. Closely associated with Eliot Shapleigh, Susie Byrd, and Veronica Escobar and Dee Margo. Publicly advocates for the poor of El Paso, but has not spoken against the destruction of south El Paso neighborhoods.

Palofox, Patricia: prominent El Paso attorney associated with Shapleigh regarding civic organizations. Served as TEA hearing officer for EPISD defendants. Sided with TEA 100% of the time.

Parker, Ken: Former CFO of EPISD. Wrote scathing letter criticizing the manner the Weaver Group was chosen to investigate EPISD.

Parra, Fernando: Connected to El Paso City and EPISD corruption. His compliance with Kanof help secure the indictment of Lorenzo Garcia.

Parsley, Rosario: Former counselor of Austin High School whose testimony helped secure a mistrial.

PDNG: Paso Del Norte Group. Known as El Paso's Illuminati that runs the city. Membership is secret. Founded and led by real estate mogul, Bill Sanders, father-in-law of Beto O'Rourke.

Perez, Robert: Attorney for James Anderson.

Perry, Rick: Former Governor of Texas.

Pine, Clyde: EPISD legal counsel who worked with the FBI/DOJ.

Ramos, Ignacio: Border Patrol agent unjustly prosecuted. Sentence commuted by W. Bush.

Rogers, Liz: Lead attorney for Tanner

Runkels, Grace: EPISD administrator reinstated at the Board meeting on April 2, 2013

Safi, Tony: Lead counsel for EPISD. Wrote many documents to DOJ indicating EPISD was innocent of all allegations. As case evolved, he complied with the contrived narrative of the FBI/DOJ.

Salcido, Michael: assistant principal at Austin who investigated the initial allegations against Cordero and found them to be true.

Sanders, Bill: Founder of the PDNG. Purported billionaire real estate mogul who initiated Downtown Redevelopment Plan. Father of Amy O'Rourke. Father-in-law of Beto O'Rourke.

Saucedo, David: Ran against Dee Margo for mayor. *El Paso Times* provided little to no coverage for his campaign.

Saucedo, Elizabeth: Head counselor at Austin. Informant for the FBI. Close friendship with James Griego.

Shapleigh, Eliot: Former Texas Senator. Fabricated the "cheating scandal." Attempted to take over downtown high school with *Equipo Bowie.* His primary allegation against EPISD was disproven numerous times although the El Paso media would not renounce it. Close ties to Susie Byrd, Beto O'Rourke, Veronica Escobar and the PDNG.

Southerland, Don: A primary investigator for the Weaver Group. Admitted during court testimony that he was not completely familiar with education law in Texas.

Stillinger, Mary: Attorney for Nancy Love

Stoever, Colby: Statistician hired by Shapleigh, but paid for by EPISD.

Student X: student victim who was almost run over by Cordero. Was likely threatened by the FBI with indictment if he told the truth.

Sutton, Johnny: Former US Attorney for Western District of Texas. Co-counsel with Kanof for the Compean-Ramos trial.

Tanner, Jai: spouse of John Tanner

Tanner, John: One of the innocent five defendants. Former principal of Austin High School.

Tapia, Dolores: Parent of students at Austin High School.

TEA: Texas Education Agency

Tegmeyer, Mark: One of the innocent five defendants. Former assistant principal of Austin High School.

Thomas, Diane: One of the innocent five defendants. Former assistant principal of Austin High School.

Thompson, Teresa: CFO of EPISD who replaced Ken Parker. Wrote instructive email to Diane Thomas that proved retaliation did not happen against Cordero or Halliday.

Torres, Miguel: Judge during the arraignment of the innocents.

Torres, Zahira: Pseudo-investigative reporter with the *El Paso Times.* Her one-sided reporting defined the false narrative of the fake cheating scandal.

USDE: United States Department of Education

Valle, Stephanie: El Paso news anchor.

Warmack, Michael: Assistant principal in EPISD who was known to be communicative with the FBI agents.

Williams, Chere: EPISD investigator who determined Cordero violated the rights and safety of Student X. After the FBI's involvement, Williams no longer possessed the evidence of her investigation and blamed it on Austin High School.

Williams, Michael: Former commissioner of TEA who removed the elected EPISD school board and appointed a Board of Managers per the recommendations of the El Paso business community. Three of his five appointees were members of the PDNG. He was a former Federal Prosecutor in Midland, Texas. He claimed to have mandated an audit on EPISD. That audit has never been made available to any defendant.

Wilson, Joyce: former City Manager of El Paso.

Winkelman, Eric: Director of Career Center of Technical Education (CCTE) in EPISD.

Woods, Randall: administrator reinstated at the April 2, 2013 EPISD Board meeting.